MASTERING LEADERSHIP FUNDAMENTALS:

MASTERING LEADERSHIP FUNDAMENTALS:

A Self-Directed Journey

PETER J. DEAN, Ph.D.

Library of Congress Control Number: 2022917697

ISBN:	Hardcover	978-1-6698-2959-1
	Softcover	978-1-6698-2958-4
	eBook	978-1-6698-2957-7

Copy Editor: Monica Warner Dimpfl

Print information available on the last page.

Rev. date: 10/07/2022

To order additional copies of this book, contact:
Xlibris
844-714-8691
www.Xlibris.com
Orders@Xlibris.com
842737

Contents

PREFACE

I was inspired to write this book because of my passion for sharing leadership knowledge, insights, and models, all in the hopes of encouraging collaborative and diverse leadership in present-day organizations. I believe that reviewing different styles and examining leaders from the past can more adequately prepare present and future leaders. In the chapters of this book, we will explore classic models and methods. Leadership behaviors of historical figures are seen in the appendix in order to develop a path forward to an evolved, twenty-first-century way of leading others. Critical aspects of this analysis will include the role of men and women and the construct of power that both play into the conventional thinking around what good leadership looks like.

As I set up the context for this book, the below-paraphrased quote from author (and former chairman of HSBC) Stephen Green struck me as an interesting and direct way to introduce the fundamental situation for men and women leaders at work:

The overwhelming fact is that for most of history the vast majority of women have played a marginal role in society, have been denied education or any serious chance to achieve their potential, and have lived in a domestic subjection that gave them few rights . . . one of the most striking glories of globalization is that the processes of urbanization, education, and communication are gradually righting this huge wrong. When women are empowered, the world discovers that women can lead commercially, professionally, and politically in any of the realms of activity that men through history have seen fit to arrogate for themselves . . . the potential for human social interactions take on a new and better quality through the free and full involvement of male and female perspectives."

Good Value; Reflections on Money, Morality and an Uncertain World, pages 225–230

Obtaining optimal organizational leadership requires the equal involvement of men and women, and requires the shedding of historical and societal norms, as Green so articulately states above. It starts with the reality that both men and women have the human personality and potential to learn and practice leadership if given a chance. This book will address how they can practice leadership in all work environments, especially male-dominated ones.

In these male-dominated work environments, affiliative, or partnership behavior—that uses shared power to get things done—is often perceived as inferior leadership. Instead, taking control or dominating others is seen as effective leadership. But in this type of work structure, power over others does not enable growth. As a result, people are not able to be creative and fully engaged in the decisions that have a consequence on their work, and the skills of listening, empathy, respect, civility, and openness are missing. Renowned author Riane Eisler agrees. In her book entitled *The Chalice and the Blade,* she suggests two views of human relations in work environments: the "dominator" role that is mostly male, and the "partnership" role that is mostly female.

Eisler further suggests that the difference in these views is not necessarily equated with inferiority or superiority, but rather the handling of power. The dominator role uses "**position power-over**," a view that ranks only those with position power *over* the other to make decisions for them, whereas the role of "**personal power-with,"** a view where social relations are primarily based on the principle of *linking* with others, rather than *ranking.* Assuming a humble approach includes both forms of power to be used with proper judgment, patience, empathy, and easing off ego surges.

Partnership encompasses personal power-with, which is traditionally associated with feminine qualities of empathy, compassion, truth-telling, and justice, and the position power-over view is associated with traits of command, control, and the crush of hierarchy. These two views can be used as fundamental principles of organization in examining the relations between the two sexes of any human system at work. The ultimate goal is to have a balance of power-over and power-with in an overall effort to generate "**partner-power."**

Power-Over Others	Power-With Others
• Relies on position power	• Leads by collaboration and personal power
• Holds power to control workplace	• Shares power to empower workplace
• Encourages others to listen	• Encourages others to talk
• Shares information with a chosen few	• Schedules time to share/gather information
• Controls their emotions	• Empathizes with the emotions of others

Eisler then further suggests that we have seen these views expressed throughout history. Most of the time they are male-dominant, power-over examples, yet there have been stories of the partnership view of power-with. For example, in the Elizabethan age when Queen Elizabeth I was sitting on the throne, feminine values were ascendant through a love for learning, scholarship, funding colleges, and pushing for more poetry, drama, painting, architecture, and music. A modern-day example might be Angela Merkel. In her book entitled *The Chancellor*, Kati Marton writes that no other modern leader has so ably confronted authoritarian aggression, enacted daring policies, and calmly unified an entire continent in an era when countries are becoming divided.

As it applies to the workplace, we can acquire one of two human systems of thought from which we perform in our sphere of influence. Whatever we accept as our social system manifests in our behavior. If you believe in a position power-over social system as necessary because that appears to be the reality of things, then you are likely to accept the notion to take by force and use fear to establish hierarchy and authoritarianism within your place of work. If you believe in a personal power-with social system that is more peaceful with less hierarchy and authoritarianism, that acceptance will manifest in more giving and nurturing behavior and an overall work environment. Men have a strong tendency, given early scripts in their life, to choose the dominator behavior. Women, based on early scripts and brain science tendencies, prefer peaceful partnerships that involve understanding emotions. The goal of this book is to transcend the conventional polarization where one is a usurper over the other, but rather encompasses both conscientiously for more collaborative, enlightened leadership. Holding to both views of power requires trust, talent, and seeing the big picture for men and women working together. It requires a fundamental shift in our ability to adapt.

PROLOGUE

Molly D. Shepard, MSM, MS

I was delighted to be asked to write the prologue for this incredibly insightful and important book for practitioners of leadership development as well as all leaders, *Mastering Leadership Fundamentals: A Self-Directed Journey.* I have been a leadership development consultant for over thirty years, primarily focused on helping professional women advance their careers in their organizations. To have a resource like this book to help me understand where the leadership theories and research began—and how they evolved over time—is enlightening, and to understand more clearly how the traditional male model as leader was instilled through literature and the mindset of the times as the paragon of "good leadership" over hundreds of years made today's challenges for women all the more real. As an example, to see where the Great Man Theory—one of the early models—fits into our studies of leadership helps to explain where women leaders are today. As Dr. Peter Dean notes, the Great Man Theory was probably the first one to emerge in the field of leadership study, and its sexist view of what makes a great leader were qualities mostly seen in men. Trait Leadership Theory evolved from the Great Man Theory and continued to underscore the importance of certain leadership traits, which were, again, seen mostly in men. Although these leadership theories did not prove to be successful, they set the stage for how "strong" leadership would be described and emulated for decades. Any woman who held a leadership position since the mid-1800s has been seen as an anomaly and not the norm. This perception of women not possessing leadership qualities has continued in today's modern workplace.

My work has been primarily focused on women and their challenges in achieving equal footing with their male counterparts in their corporations. There are many reasons why women have not advanced as quickly as we hoped. Given that women represent almost 50 percent of the workforce, many people like myself feel that change is long overdue.

A recent study by Catalyst shows that less than 6 percent of our largest companies are led by women and only 26 percent of women have made it to senior-level executive roles in these organizations. One might presume that women's socialization and even voices and physiques have made it impossible for us to lead large organizations. One has only to look at leaders like Angela Merkel, Christine Lazard, Oprah Winfrey, and Madeleine Albright to see how those very characteristics deemed too feminine to lead have actually served these strong women well, especially in times of peril and conflict. Nevertheless, it has been difficult to get our voices heard at leadership tables primarily dominated by men.

Research shows that approximately 75 percent of people who quit their jobs do so because of their direct line managers. Bad leaders are the primary cause of voluntary turnover worldwide, and according to professor of business psychology Tomas Chamorro-Premuzic in his book *Why Do So Many Incompetent Men Become Leaders*, he suggests that leaders, inept or otherwise, are usually male. The S&P reports confirm this assertion, citing that the number of women in these index companies decreases at the senior levels so this then begs the question: "Would the prevalence of bad leadership decrease if fewer men, and more women, were in charge?" The short answer is "yes." In this book, Peter J. Dean goes one step further than Chamorro-Premuzic by saying the goal is for men and women to work together as leaders, not to have more women over the number of men. It is this challenging concept of how men and women can lead together that is the future of the workplace.

In this book, Dr. Dean will share some of the challenges that women face when leading with men, then offer some practices that will help better the partnership between the sexes to include models, methods, and measures to help both sexes.

So what ***is*** holding women back from the top spot in organizations? Major issues for women in the workplace, as cited in my book *Breaking into the Boys' Club*, include:

- Communicating effectively
- Networking strategically

- Being politically savvy
- Promoting their strengths
- Making the most of their sponsors
- Balancing work and life
- Developing style and presence
- Taking control of their careers

Women also face double binds that can affect professional reputation and growth within an organization:

Positive Traits of Women	Perceived by Others
• Good listeners	• Passive
• Politely let others speak first	• Not real participants
• Serious about work	• No sense of humor
• Solicit opinions and feedback	• Indecisive
• Relationship developers	• Waste of time
• Demonstrate empathy	• Soft and emotional
• Give detailed reports	• Rambling

Women are willing and able to step up to the challenges of the workplace, and it is clear from the current workforce numbers that women are major contributors and population in the workplace. It is also clear that they encounter numerous obstacles, from historical norms and societal expectations to innate behaviors and their misinterpretations. So what practices can professionals and leaders apply to alleviate these long-standing, pervasive issues?

A model that would help men and women interact in the workplace for optimal productivity and leadership comes from Dr. Dean's earlier book, *Leadership for Everyone*, and includes the mastery of the following interaction skills:

- Listen to learn
- Empathize the emotions of others
- Attend to others' aspirations
- Diagnose, detail, decide
- Engage ethically
- Respond with respect
- Speak with specificity and clarity

In my opinion, women have innate leadership capabilities. We are naturally inclined to be more strategic in our thinking. We see the whole picture when analyzing a problem and the short- and long-term implications of a decision. We lean toward collaboration, inclusiveness, and building trust. We are very good at leading others, and there has been a proven direct correlation between gender diversity on a team and positive bottom-line results. The core challenges that make it difficult for women to break into the C-suite have to change, and in that shift, companies will benefit and women will fulfill their legitimate desires to sit at the leadership table.

This book will explore the fundamentals of leadership and their practices and further offer guidance on their practical application in the workplace. In reviewing the evolution of leadership, understanding power dynamics in the workplace and being open-minded, readers can develop a new way of leading with inclusivity and collaboration and usher in a new generation of leadership practices by men and women together. Special attention should be paid to the building blocks of leadership theorists from the past, including the 10 Commitments for Leaders presented by Kouzes and Posner in chapter 1. If every professional committed to these aspirational goals in their day-to-day leadership, what a better and healthier culture they would establish in their companies!

INTRODUCTION

Arguably, the most important need in society today is to develop individuals with positive and progressive intentions and solid fundamentals who will become future leaders in companies, organizations, governments, and institutions. Additionally, there is an ever-increasing societal interest in knowing and understanding more about positive leadership. There have been numerous publications, both theoretical and practical, that attempt to explain the concept of leadership and how to lead others. Additionally, there has been an increasing number of university centers, programs, or even entire departments dedicated to the study of leadership.

One unintended consequence of this increased attention has been an acceptance that leadership exchanges should only occur with the people who hold *positions* of leadership. But in actuality, leadership must be present at all levels in a work system for maximum performance. The overarching theme throughout this book is this: there is an opportunity to practice leadership with every interaction, therefore anyone can be a leader, whether or not he or she has a position of power in their organization or place of work.

So if every interaction is an opportunity to demonstrate leadership, the question becomes, "Can one learn how to lead?" And the answer is yes! So then the "how" of it comes into play. The basis of this is to start small and begin to develop your leadership abilities where you are now in your life. From the preface, we know that there exists two approaches to workplace partnership leadership—position power-over others and personal power-with others. Often position power dominates personal power. In this book, I will recommend a vantage point of partnership where both power-over and power-with are available as and when needed.

Why You Should Read This Book:

With this notion in mind, it is imperative that individuals know the context and evolution of leadership as a field of study. Also, they should know how to integrate the basic elements of leadership—or the fundamentals. There is no commonly accepted process for developing leadership skills, yet much can be learned from leadership models, theories, and practices of those that have come before us. The belief that everyone possesses a sphere of influence within which they can lead and develop their own leadership abilities is a central theme throughout.

Who Should Read This Book:

The target audience for this book includes anyone who wants to learn the fundamental practices of leadership and how to partner with others and lead collaboratively. This book is designed for those seeking to master the partnership skills of a leader. In particular, I reveal the essential practices for men and women engaging together in strategic practices that increase the power of partnership and how it produces successful leadership. Direct benefits from reading the book will be a clear understanding of how to use the essential elements of leadership to motivate and inspire others in their sphere of influence.

Historical Look at Leaders

Why must we speak so specifically about including women as co-equals with men in leadership? Because it rarely happens! In the appendix, there is a truncated list of historical leaders down through the centuries. We see men dominating as the common theme. In almost all cases, the male leader invaded, conquered, and then set up social systems to serve the needs of their kingdom. Would a more partnership approach have given the same result without invasion? There is a long list of mostly men dominating with aggression punctuated by some rulers or periods of history where partnership was the way to expand a social system.

The idea that only a few can lead and the rest must follow will be challenged. This book will reveal the powerful impact of individuals acting responsibly and taking action to lead, which then fosters development at all levels of the organization. Moreover, the most important lesson for leaders—the value of learning while leading—will be explored. Ultimately, leadership can be learned, and so this book is a guide on a journey of self-development. Looking at the dynamics of power and strengthening partnerships will help us improve the practice of positive, inclusive leadership.

CHAPTER 1

Fundamental One: Research in "Leadership"

Learning Objectives

1-1. Recognize and distinguish among great person leadership, trait leadership, transformational leadership, transaction leadership, and fusion leadership
1-2. Become familiar with a number of studies of leaders' behaviors, including the Ohio State model and the Managerial Grid
1-3. Become familiar with studies of leadership functions and be able to distinguish the scientific management approach from the human relations approach
1-4. Distinguish task achievement and group maintenance and what is meant by the task leader, the socio-emotional leader, concern for production, concern for people, task behavior, and relationship behavior
1-5. Know what is meant by Fiedler's Contingency Model and how it suggests different leadership styles may be appropriate in different situations
1-6. Appreciate the differences among House's Path Goal Theory of Leadership; Vroom and Yetton's Decision Making Model; Reddin's theory and eight leadership styles; Hersey and Blanchard's Life Cycle Theory of Leadership and the four styles of situational leadership they defined; and the relationship between leadership styles and follower maturity
1-7. See how good leaders often act as stewards of their vision and how they may place the needs of stakeholders above their own needs
1-8. Know what is meant by Jim Collins' Level 5 research and be able to describe the characteristics of great leadership he uncovered
1-9. Recognize Kouzes and Pozner's five practices of exemplary leadership and their ten leadership commitments

CHAPTER OUTLINE

Overview of Leadership Studies
Great Person Leadership
Trait Leadership
Studies of Leaders' Behavioral Styles
Studies of Leadership Functions
Tasks and People
Studies of the Situational Aspects of Leadership
Transformational Leadership
Fusion Leadership
Stewardship as Leadership
Good to Great Leadership

Overview of Leadership Studies

The extensive literature on leadership attests to the substantial interest researchers have shown in the subject. Numerous classification systems have been designed to describe leadership, and various theories have been offered to explain leadership dynamics.[1] This chapter presents studies of leadership under the following general headings:

1. great person theories
2. studies of leaders' traits
3. studies of leaders' behavioral style
4. studies of leadership functions
5. task and people
6. studies of the situational aspect of leadership
7. transformational leadership
8. fusion leadership
9. steward leadership
10. good-to-great leadership

Great Man Leadership

The Great Man Theory of leadership, probably the first theory of leadership, discusses leaders as individuals with special qualities that enable them to capture the favor of the masses.

Research

These special qualities were explained in the research as a result of inheritance from previous generations and as a result of the intelligence, energy, or moral force of the leader.[2] Other early theorists suggested that a person was considered great not because of inheritance or biological energy, but as the result of time, place, and circumstance. That is, a leader does not inject leadership when a situation requires a certain type of action; rather, the leader is the instrumental factor through which a resolution to the situation problem is achieved. The limited success of the *Great Man* Theory was probably due to its sexist overtones and its insistence on only the hero view of leadership. The limited success of the environmental theory was probably due to its relativistic nature where leadership was simply due to circumstances.[3]

Trait Leadership

Even though the Great Man Theory of leadership had only limited success in explaining leadership, it did leave researchers with the question, "If a leader is endowed with special qualities that separate him or her from followers, is it possible to identify these qualities?" This question resulted in the most common approach to the study of leadership traits.

Research

The studies were conducted under the assumption that leaders possess a trait or a combination of traits that distinguish them from other people. Traits studies focused on physical characteristics, age, intelligence, insight, judgment, originality, adaptability, dominance, initiative, persistence, introversion-extroversion, ambition, responsibility, integrity, conviction, self-confidence, emotional control, social skills, popularity, cooperation, masculinity, sensitivity, conservativeness, and other traits. These physical, intellectual, and personality traits were researched in hopes of finding the most essential traits of effective leadership and of using that information to select people for leadership positions.

Stogdill[4] made an extensive examination of the research relevant to leadership traits and found a few traits were common in fifteen or more of the studies surveyed. These traits were intelligence, scholarship, dependability, activity, social participation, and socioeconomic status. If traits that were common in ten or more of the studies surveyed were considered, Stogdill's list increased to include sociability, initiative, persistence, knowing how to get things done, self-confidence, alertness to and insight into situations, cooperativeness, popularity, adaptability, and verbal facility. In spite of these findings, Stogdill[5] concluded: A person does not become a leader by virtue of some combination of traits, but the patterns of the personal characteristics of a leader must bear some relationship to the characteristics, activities, and goals of the followers.

Do Leadership Traits Explain Leadership?

In general, research focusing on leadership traits alone has not had lasting value in explaining leadership. Hemphill,[6] after reviewing many nonsignificant empirical studies using the trait approach, suggested that leadership is a dynamic process, varying from situation to situation, with changes in leaders, followers, and situations. Jennings[7] summed up a review of trait theory research in the following way: Fifty years of study have failed to produce one personality trait or set of qualities that can be used to discriminate between leaders and nonleaders.

Ghiselli[8] did find a significant correlation between leadership effectiveness and traits of intelligence, supervisory ability, initiative, self-assurance, and the way performance of work was carried out. However, these correlations were not impressive enough to redirect research interest in the traits above. One of the reasons for this lack of inspiration might have been the failure of many other studies to show a significant correlation between traits and instances or incidents of leadership. Also, such studies failed to show that leaders are the only people possessing so-called leadership traits. In spite of the lack of results in trait theory research, the evidence did continue to show that a key variable for a selection of a leader was the social situation. This indicated that certain traits of leaders in one situation were different from leader traits in other situations. Stogdill[9] reported this point as follows: It is not especially difficult to find persons who are leaders. It is quite another matter to place these persons in different situations where they will be able to function as leaders. It becomes clear that an adequate analysis of leadership involves not only study of leaders but also of situations. The findings suggest that leadership is not a matter of passive status or the mere possession of some combination of traits. It appears rather to be a working relationship among members of a group, in which the leader acquires status through active participation and demonstration of his or her capacity for carrying cooperation tasks through to completion.

Sleeth[10] reported that the combined analysis of leadership research by Bird,[11] Jenkins,[12] and Stogdill[13] suggested four conclusions:

1. Selection of leaders on the basis of traits was largely unsuccessful.
2. Leaders and followers might differ on many traits.
3. Traits necessary in a successful leader differed with the situation.
4. The interaction between leader and followers could not be ignored.

Studies of Leaders' Behavioral Style

As trait theory research continually failed to produce definitive results during the 1940s, the study of leadership shifted to the behavior of the leader but still in the frame of the leader as hero. Researchers began to focus on the set of behaviors or the observed style that characterizes the leader's performance. The style, or set of behaviors, of the leader was not investigated in hopes of finding a reflection of the personality attributes in the area of leadership styles.

Research

The three best-known researchers in the area of leadership styles were Kurt Lewin, Ronald Lippitt, and Ralph White. While Lewin and Lippitt[14] initially researched leadership styles using the polar functions of democratic and autocratic, Lewin, Lippitt, and White[15] described three leadership styles: democratic, laissez-faire, and authoritarian. In their studies, democratic leadership produced group cohesiveness, the greatest originality in output, and motivation to perform in the absence of the leader. Laissez-faire leadership led to poor performance, low morale, and a lack of group unity. Authoritarian leadership manifested more time on task but greater hostility, especially when the leader was absent.

The effects of these different styles of leadership behavior on groups of young people were investigated at the University of Iowa in 1938 to 1940. Study participants responded best in the democratic leadership situation. However, research subsequent to these studies has indicated that it is incorrect to stereotype a leader as being democratic, autocratic, or laissez-faire because leaders tend to vary their behavior according to the situation.[16]

A popular theory for explaining styles of leader behavior is the model developed by the staff of the Bureau of Business Research at Ohio State University.[17] The Ohio State model is based on the two dimensions of initiating structure and consideration, which refer to task behavior and relationship behavior. Initiating structure is described as the extent to which an individual is likely to define and structure her or his role and those of subordinates toward goal attainment.[18] Consideration is the extent to which an individual is likely to have job relationships with subordinates and share mutual trust, respect for their ideas, sensitivity to their feelings, and a show of warmth.[19] These two dimensions are scaled from low to high and plotted on horizontal and vertical axes to define four leadership styles, as depicted by the quadrants in figure 1-1.

FIGURE 1-1
Leadership Styles According to the Ohio State Model

Consideration	(Low) Initiating structure	(High)
(High)	High consideration and low structure	High structure and high consideration
(Low)	Low structure and low consideration	High structure and low consideration

Source: *Ralph M. Stogdill and Alvin E. Coons, eds., Leader Behavior: Its Description and Measurement, Research Monograph No. 88 (Columbus: Bureau of Business Research, the Ohio State University, 1957). Used with permission.*

Korman[20] reviewed the research with the Ohio State Model and concluded: "Despite the fact that *consideration* and *initiating structure* have become almost bywords in American industrial psychology, it seems apparent that very little is now known as to how these variables may predict work group performance and the conditions which affect such predictions. At the current time, we cannot even say whether they have any predictive significance at all . . . There is as yet almost no evidence on the predictive validity of *consideration* and *initiating structure* nor on the kinds of situational moderators which might affect such validity."

No Consistent Trend Favoring One Style Over Another

The Ohio State studies were summarized by Porter, Lawler, and Hackman.[21] Reviews (for example, Korman,[22] Sales)[23] fail to reveal any substantial consistent effects associated with given behavioral styles of leaders or any consistent trend for one or another style to be particularly effective in terms of individual or group performance, although there seem to be some tendencies for employee morale to be positively associated with a considerate, employee-oriented style.

Ivancevich et al.[24] considered the major criticism of the initiating structure-consideration approach to leadership theory to be "the fact that situational factors and the influence of these factors on leadership effectiveness model were not considered."

The Ohio State studies were further popularized by Robert R. Blake and Jane S. Mouton in *The Managerial Grid*,[25] which has been used extensively in management development programs. In the Grid, the concepts of concern for production and concern for people are the basis for five types of leadership behavior, described as follows:

1. *Impoverished*: exertion of minimum effort to get required work done is appropriate to sustain organizational membership.
2. *Country Club*: thoughtful attention to needs of people for satisfying relationships leads to a comfortable, friendly organization atmosphere and work temperament.
3. *Task*: efficiency in operations results from arranging conditions of work in such a way that human elements interfere to a minimum degree.
4. *Middle-of-the-Road*: adequate organization performance is possible through balancing the necessity to complete work while maintaining the morale of people at a satisfactory level.
5. *Team*: work is accomplished by committed people, and interdependence through a common stake in organization purposes leads to relationships of trust and respect.

FIGURE 1-2
Managerial Grid Models of Leadership Styles

	1, 9 (Country Club)	(Team) 9,9
(High)	5.5	(Middle Road)
Concern for People (Low)	1,1 (Impoverished)	(Task), 9, 1
	(Low) Concern for Production (High)	

Source: *Robert R. Blake and Jane S. Mouton, The Managerial Grid CR. Houston: Gulf Publishing Co., 1978. Used with permission.*

These styles are plotted on a scale from one to nine and divided into four quadrants as shown in figure 1-2.

The Managerial Grid and the four quadrants of the Ohio State studies may be superimposed as shown in figure 1-3:

FIGURE 1-3
Merging of the Ohio State and the Managerial Grid Theories

	1, 9 (Country Club)	(Team) 9,9
(High) Concern for People	High consideration and low structure	High structure and high consideration
	Low structure and low consideration	High structure and low consideration
(Low)	1,1 (Impoverished)	(Task) 9, 1
	(Low) Concern for Production	(High)

It should be noted that a significant difference exists between the two frameworks. "Concern for people," used in the Managerial Grid, is an attitude toward production and people, while the Ohio State model tends to describe the observable behavior of a leader.

Beck[26] summarized the Ohio State studies by stating that leaders should use task-oriented and relationship-oriented styles of leadership. However, it is not clear if a leader should use Style 2 (high, high), Style 1 (high task), Style 3 (high relationship), or all three. Also, there is no indication of when a leader should use each type of behavior.

Clothier[27] states that the Ohio State Model and the instruments which were developed along with it—Leader Behavior Description Questionnaire (LBDQ), Leader Opinion Questionnaire (LOQ), and Organizational Climate Description (OCDQA)—are the most frequently used models and instruments in leadership research. He further states that this line of research has indicated positive correlations between a high Initiating Structure style and increased worker productivity and between a high Consideration style and increased worker satisfaction. Yet in spite of these findings, no single style for leader as hero has been identified as the best style for all circumstances.

Studies of Leadership Functions

This research dealt with the observable functions of the leader, that is, what the leader does and what the leader should do to be effective.

Research

Weinholtz[28] looked at the numerous studies done on leadership during the 1940s and 1950s and discerned that while many researchers focused on leadership styles,[29] many other researchers[30] examined leadership functions.

Studies of the observable functions of leaders appear to have roots in the scientific management movement founded by Frederick R. Taylor[31] and the human relations movement generally associated with Elton Mayo.[32]

Researchers using the scientific management approach, not appreciating all of Taylor's concepts, were concerned with discovering the key variable in an organized and efficient environment. Human relations researchers attempted to discover the extent to which interpersonal relationships related to work. The human relations approach to leadership investigation grew from the failure of those using the scientific management approach to attend to interpersonal variables. Leavitt[33] reported a comparison of the scientific management approach and the human relations approach (see table 1-1).

Hersey and Blanchard[34] summarized the essence of these two approaches to leadership as follows: "In essence, then, the scientific management movement emphasized a concern for task (output), while the human relations movement stressed a concern for relationship (people). The recognition of these two concerns has characterized the writings on leadership ever since the conflict between the scientific management and the human relations schools of thought became apparent."

TABLE 1-1
Comparison of Approaches Between Scientific Management School and Human Relation School

Dimensions of Approaches	Scientific Management	Human Relations
1. Management's goal for worker	Productivity by satisfying his economic needs	Productivity by satisfying his social needs.
2. Theoretical orientation	If material rewards are closely related to the employees' work efforts, they will respond with maximum performance according to their capability.	If work and organizational structure were related to social needs of employees, they would be happy; organization therefore would obtain full cooperation and effort and thus increase its efficiency.
3. Regard for the worker	Individual compared to a machine	Individual considered with desires, emotions, feelings and attitudes.
4. Consideration of the work process	Standardized worker is dependent on the organization, hence no conflict between work and organization.	Flexible worker is independent hence conflict is inevitable; in a sense, conflict is considered desirable.
5. Organizational structure	Firm and rigid supervision is a necessity; centralized	Information and not much need for supervision; decentralized
6. Nature of authority	Autocratic; the top management decides	Democratic; anyone is allowed to take part
7. Participation in decision-making	Top manager's responsibility	Views and concerns of employees included
8. Communication	One-way direction from top to bottom; almost nil among peers	Very permissive between and among horizontal and vertical levels of management
9. Management focus	On the task itself more than on the worker	On the worker as he relates to his work and social surroundings

This conflict between the scientific management movement and the human relations movement might have caused the disparity in the studies of leader functions.

Hemphill[35] reported five functions common to a wide variety of leaders:

1. advancement of group members
2. administration
3. inspiring group activity and setting the group pace
4. lending a feeling of security to individual members
5. acting without regard to their own self-interest

This list seems to offer a balance between the two approaches to leadership functions. However, Kretch and Cruthfield[36] offer a list of fourteen functions that seem to favor mostly the scientific management school. They include: "executive, planner, policy-maker, expert, external group representative, controller of internal relationships, surveyor of rewards and punishments, arbitrator, exemplar, group symbol, surrogate for individual responsibility, ideologist, father figure, and scapegoat."

Stogdill[37] identified leader functions as follows:

1. Defining objectives and maintaining goal direction
2. Providing means for goal attainment
3. Providing and maintaining group structure
4. Facilitating group action and interaction
5. Maintaining group cohesiveness and member satisfaction
6. Facilitating group task performance

Tasks and People

All of the above-listed functions of a leader as a hero can easily be broken down into two main concerns: Leaders must be concerned with the function of (1) task achievement (output) and (2) group maintenance (people). Many researchers have found these two categories to exist.

Research

Bales[38] discussed the task leader and the socio-emotional leader. In their factor-analysis study, Fleishman, Harris, and Burtt[39] found the factors of task achievement and group maintenance accounted for 83 percent of the explainable leader behavior. Tannenbaum and Schmidt[40] perceived leadership behavior as existing on a continuum ranging from bosscenter (or authoritarian leadership) to subordinate-center (or democratic leadership). Cartwright and Zander[41] describe leadership behavior in terms of the two functions of goal achievement and group maintenance. McGregor[42] offers his *Theory X,* where the goals of the organization are emphasized, and *Theory Y,* a balanced view of the worker in the context of the organization. Likert[43] describes the functions of leader behavior as *job-centered,* as having concern for the production of the organization, and *employee-centered,* a concern for the people in the organization.

Katz et al.,[44] after conducting survey research to identify indicators of effectiveness at the University of Michigan, found two concepts that were labeled *production orientation,* emphasizing production and technical aspects of the job, and *employee orientation,* which emphasizes the human relationship aspects of the job. Fiedler[45] described two major functions of leadership: they are *task orientation,* which satisfies the leader's need to gain satisfaction by performing a task, and *relationship orientation,* which emphasizes attaining a position of prominence and achieving good interpersonal relations. Blake and Mouton[46] proposed a managerial grid that has two orthogonal dimensions:

1. *Concern for Production*, which includes the kinds of policies that are established and the methods to maintain organizational growth and development.
2. *Concern for People*, which includes good working conditions and a commitment to one's job, and self-esteem and trust for the organization.

Relationship Orientation

Vroom and Yetton[47] described autocratic and democratic modes of leader behavior. Reddin[48] perceived leadership behavior as a function of task and relationship. Citing research conducted at Harvard, the University of Michigan, and Ohio State University, Reddin[49] described the function of *task orientation* as the direction of the manager for his or her own efforts and for the efforts of his or her subordinates. This direction could be carried out by organizing or initiating. The function of *relationship orientation* centers on the leader's personal job relationships that are characterized by listening, trusting, and encouraging. According to Reddin, both of these functions are independent of each other. Hersey and Blanchard[50] use the terms *task* and *relationship* to describe the functions of a leader, much the same as Reddin,[51] but the former descriptions are more specific.

Task behavior is the extent to which leaders are likely to organize and define the roles of the members of their group (followers); to explain what activities each is to do and when, where, and how tasks are to be accomplished; and to establish well-defined patterns of organization, channels of communication, and ways of getting jobs accomplished.

Relationship behavior is the extent to which leaders are likely to maintain personal relationships between themselves and members of their group (followers) by opening up channels of communication, providing socio emotional support, *psychological strokes,* and facilitating behaviors.

From whatever research one cites, the breakdown of leadership functions of the hero leader into the two broad categories of task and maintenance, or the breakdown of leadership styles into the two dimensions of initiating and consideration as mentioned above, it all attempts to integrate leadership theory and provides categories for further study without specifically looking at the interpersonal conversations in the dynamics of leadership as if that kind of research was too difficult. In support of that notion, Carter et al.[52] report that both leadership styles and leadership functions have been shown to be related to the situations in the studies. Again, the frame of reference is the leader as hero.

Studies of the Situational Aspect of Leadership

As the limitations of the *best style* or *best function* approach to leadership became apparent, there was increasing evidence of leadership's situational nature. Many studies showed that if leaders varied their behavioral style or function to a variety of situations, they were more successful. Again, the mental frame of reference was the leader as hero.

Research

In his 1948 review of the literature, Stogdill analyzed 124 studies, which indicated that patterns of leadership traits differed as the situation was changed. As an example, Stogdill used Terman's 1940 study where it was found that children who are leaders in one situation may not be the group leader when placed with different children in other settings.

Weinholtz[53] cited the following studies indicating the situational nature of leadership. Hemphill[54] demonstrated that leaders can be created by unequal distribution of power, prestige, and skill, or by providing a task that requires a division of labor. Leavitt[55] showed that central figures in communications networks tend to become leaders. Ruding[56] and Katzel et al.[57] found that authoritarian, centralized leadership is more effective for simple tasks, while Torrance,[58] Korten[59] and others found it preferable when stress is high. Several researchers[60] found that group member satisfaction is improved when leadership style is consistent with member expectations.

These studies provided the evidence necessary for a new group of theories about leadership to evolve. The theories or lines of research that subsequently emerged were all founded on the premise that leader behavior must vary to fit a variety of situations.

Contingency Model of Leadership Effectiveness

Fiedler[61] offered the first major research on situational leadership with his *contingency model of leadership effectiveness*. In 1971[62] he postulated, "The performance of interacting groups is contingent upon the interaction of leadership style and situational favorableness." His model specified that *socalled task-oriented* leaders perform more effectively in very favorable and very unfavorable situations, while relationship-oriented leaders perform more effectively in situations intermediate in favorableness. Fiedler operationalized leadership style through a measure of leaders' attitudes concerning their *least preferred co-workers* (LPCs). He theorized that autocratic leaders would view LPCs less favorably than would democratic leaders. His instrument measured esteem for the leader's least preferred coworker to score general leadership style. A low LPC score indicated a tendency for a leader to be task-oriented, and a high LPC score indicated a tendency toward relationship-orientation.[63]

Situational favorableness was operationalized through ratings of leadermember relationship, task structure, and position power. Fiedler and Chemers[64] define these as follows:

1. *Leader-Member Relations* is the acceptance of the leader by workers, the climate of their relationship, communication, and trust existing between them, and the worker's feelings toward the leader.
2. *Task Structure* is the clarity of the task that the work group is to perform, how easily and carefully it can be measured, the completeness and simplicity of directions given, and the degree to which job assignments are proceduralized.
3. *Positive Power* is the amount of power the organization invests in the leader to affect workers' standards, rewards, and evaluation.

The theory predicts which of the two leadership styles is most effective in each of eight situations defined by various combinations of the three contingency factors. Fiedler's 1964 studies correlated the leader's LPC scores with group performance in each of the various octants. The results of his research and the predicted most effective leadership style are summarized in table 1-2. It lends support to the premise that different leadership styles are appropriate in different situations.

TABLE 1-2
Most Appropriate Leadership Styles for Maximizing Group Performance, According to Fiedler's Contingency Model

	Leader-Member Relations	Task Structure	Position Power	Favorable Leadership Style
Octant I	Good	Structured	Strong	Task oriented
Octant II	Good	Structured	Weak	Task oriented
Octant III	Good	Unstructured	Strong	Task oriented
Octant IV	Good	Unstructured	Weak	Relationship oriented
Octant V	Poor	Structured	Strong	Relationship oriented
Octant VI	Poor	Structured	Weak	Relationship oriented
Octant VII	Poor	Unstructured	Strong	Relationship oriented
Octant VIII	Poor	Unstructured	Weak	Task oriented

Source: Fred E. Fiedler, A Theory of Leadership Effectiveness. New York: McGraw-Hill, 1967, p. 142. Used with permission.

Weed, Mitchell, and Moffitt[66] found a significant three-way interaction among leadership style, subordinates' personality, and the type of task, supporting the assumption of effective leadership as situationally determined. Weed et al.[67] concluded that the supervisor who is considerate of people may be liked best but may not necessarily be the most effective unless leadership style, subordinate personality, and task type are well matched.

Weinholtz[68] points out the validity of Fiedler's theory as follows: "Although the validity of the LPC measures has been questioned,[69] Fiedler's model has proven to be quite resilient. A review of 25 investigations[70] revealed the model's high predictive performance for task groups in field situations, while demonstrating its difficulties regarding individually oriented laboratory groups."

Path-Goal Theory of Leadership

Another situational theory of leadership is commonly known as *House's Path-Goal Theory of Leadership.* This theory deals with the effects of leader behavior on the motivation of subordinates as it explains the effects of four types of leader behavior on three attitudes or expectations of subordinates:

1. satisfaction
2. acceptance of the leader
3. expectations that effort will result in effective performance, and that effective performance is the path to rewards

Two classes of situational variables or contingency factors mediate the effects of the different leadership styles. These effects are:

1. personal characteristics of the subordinates, to include achievement motivation, self-perception of ability, locus of control, and degree of authority
2. environmental factors, to include group size, nature of authority system, and factors involved in the task such as repetitiveness, complexity, and ambiguity[71]

Clothier's four leadership styles[72] are summarized as follows:

- *Instrumental leadership* features the planning, organizing, controlling, and coordinating of subordinate activities. This directive style is characterized by giving specific guidance on what should be done and how to do it, clarifying roles in the group, scheduling work, maintaining standards, and enforcing rules. This style appears most appropriate in dealing with subordinates having high authoritarianism orientations who are working at ambiguous tasks.
- *Participative leadership* is characterized by the sharing of information, power, and influence between supervisors and subordinates. Participative leaders treat subordinates mostly as their equals and allow them to influence their actions and

decisions. This supportive style is characterized by showing concern for status, wellbeing, and needs of subordinates. Such leaders do little things to make work more pleasant, and they are approachable. This style will have its most positive effects when the work is dissatisfying, frustrating, or stressful to subordinates.

- *Supportive leadership* refers to behavior that includes giving consideration to the needs of subordinates, displaying concern for their well-being, status, and comfort, and creating a friendly and pleasant climate. This achievement-oriented style is characterized by setting challenging goals, seeking improvement in performance, and showing a high degree of confidence that subordinates will assume responsibility, put forth effort, and achieve challenging goals. This style is most effective when used with subordinates performing ambiguous, nonrepetitive tasks.
- *Achievement-oriented leadership* is characterized by leaders who set challenging goals, expect subordinates to perform at their highest level, continuously seek improvement in performance, and show a high degree of confidence that subordinates will assume responsibility, put forth effort, and accomplish challenging goals. This participative style is characterized by consultation with subordinates and taking subordinates' suggestions into consideration when making decisions. This style is related to satisfaction and productivity when tasks are nonrepetitive and ego-involving. When tasks are not of this nature, only low-authoritarian subordinates are influenced by participative leadership.

Beck[73] reports the results of path-goal studies as interesting but not illuminating. He goes on to report that three of the four styles are useful with ambiguous tasks. With clear tasks, some followers prefer to be directed, while others prefer to work without direction. Another result shows that when problems are pressing, people need support.

The value of House's Path-goal Theory is that it clearly shows that all of the leadership styles can be effective, depending upon the situation, which confirms the hypothesis that no one style is best.

Vroom and Yetton Decision-Making Model

The next situational theory is the *Vroom and Yetton Decision Making Model* that describes styles of decision-making rather than styles of leadership. Vroom and Yetton[74] describe four categories of leadership styles of decision-making: Autocratic (A), Consultative (C), Group (G), and Delegated (D), as depicted in table 1-3.

TABLE 1-3
Decision Methods for Group and Individual Problems According to the Vroom-Yetton Model

Group Problems	Individual Problems
A1. You solve the problem or make the decision yourself using information available to you at the time.	A1. You solve the problem or make the decision yourself using information available to you at the time.
A11. You obtain the necessary information from your subordinates, then decide the solution to the problem yourself. You may or may not tell your subordinates what the problem is in getting the information from them. The role played by your subordinates in making the decision is clearly one of providing the necessary information to you, rather than generating or evaluating alternative solutions.	A11. You obtain the necessary information from your subordinates, then decide the solution to the problem yourself. You may or may not tell your subordinates what the problem is in getting the information from them. The role played by your subordinates in making the decision is clearly one of providing the necessary information to you, rather than generating or evaluating alternative solutions.
C1. You share the problem with the relevant subordinates individually, getting their ideas and suggestions without bringing them together as a group. Then you make the decision, which may or may not reflect your subordinates' influence.	C1. You share the problem with the relevant subordinates individually, getting their ideas and suggestions without bringing them together as a group. Then you make the decision, which may or may not reflect your subordinates' influence.

C11. You share the problem with your subordinates as a group, obtaining their collective ideas and suggestions. Then you make the decision, which may or may not reflect your subordinates' influence	G1. You share the problem with your subordinates and together you analyze the problem and arrive at a mutually agreeable solution.
G11. You share the problem with your subordinates as a group. Together you generate and evaluate alternatives and attempt to reach agreement (consensus) on a solution. Your role is much like that of chairman. You do not try to influence the group to adopt your solution, and you are willing to accept and implement any solution which has the support of the entire group.	D1. You delegate the problem to your subordinate, providing him with any relevant information that you possess, but giving him responsibility for solving the problem by himself. You may or may not request him to tell you what solution he has reached.
Source: Victor H. Vroom and Philip W. Yetton, Leadership and Decision-Making. Pittsburgh; University of Pittsburgh Press, 1973, p. 13. Used with permission.	

Vroom and Yetton[75] define seven *problem attributes* that describe situational variables influencing the decision process:

- importance of quality
- leader information
- problem structure
- subordinate acceptance important to implementation
- subordinate acceptance expected if decision is made independently
- subordinate commitment to organization goals
- likelihood of conflict

This theory is normative in the sense that the attributes distinguish the problem situations, which in turn provides a way to determine which method is best for any given situation. This is accomplished by organizing the decision methods and problem attributes into a *flow chart* or *decision-making* tree, which guides a leader to examine any situation in terms of each attribute and thus find the style that will best meet the need of the specific situation.

Vroom's 1976 research indicates that leaders typically employ a range of styles in order to use the right style at the right time. Those that follow this *Model I Complex,* it is proposed, will be more effective than those who do not. This has not been tested in the field, but laboratory simulations determined that training improves a leader's ability to diagnose situations.

Reddin[76] proposed a third dimension of effectiveness to the earlier models. This fostered the idea that any of the four leadership styles in the four quadrants of the two-dimensional Ohio State Model (see figure 1-4) could be effective or ineffective depending on the situation.

FIGURE 1-4
Leadership Styles

(High) Relationship Orientation	Relationship	Integrated
(Low)	Separated	Task

Source: William J. Reddin, "The 3-D Management Style Theory," Training and Development Journal 21, April 1967, p.11.

Reddin[77] points out: "If any style may be less effective or more effective, depending on circumstances, then each style will have two behavioral counterparts, one less-effective and the other-more-effective." Reddin proposed that the essential difference between the less effective and more effective styles is determined by the extent to which a manager's style "fits the style demands of the situation he is in." He lists three elements composing the style demands:

1. the style demands of his [sic] job
2. the style demand of the superior
    a. the corporate philosophy
    b. the style of the superior
3. the style demand of the subordinates
    a. the expectations of subordinates
    b. the styles of subordinates

It is important to understand that the distinction between more-effective and less-effective styles of leadership does not lie in leader behavior expressed in terms of task and relationship only. Any amount of either or both does not guarantee effectiveness. Effectiveness, according to *3-D Theory*, leaves results from the style's appropriateness to the situation where it is used. Thus, the *separated* basis style, when appropriately used, is perceived as *bureaucrat*, and when inappropriately used is perceived as and called *deserter*.

Reddin's Eight Leader Styles

Reddin[78] defines the eight leader styles as follows:

1. *Autocrat:* a leader who is using high task orientation and a low relationship orientation in a situation where such behavior is inappropriate, and who is therefore less effective; perceived as having no confidence in others, as unpleasant, and as interested only in the immediate task.
2. *Benevolent autocrat:* a leader who is using a high task orientation and a low relationship orientation in a situation where such behavior is appropriate and who is, therefore, more effective; perceived as knowing what she or he wants and how to get it without creating resentment.
3. *Bureaucrat:* a leader who is using low task orientation and a low relationship orientation in a situation where such behavior is appropriate and who is, therefore, more effective; perceived as being primarily interested in rules and procedures for his/her own sake, as wanting to control the situation, and as conscientious.
4. *Compromiser:* a leader who is using a high task orientation and a high relationship orientation in a situation that requires high orientation to only one or neither, and who is, therefore, less effective; perceived as being a poor decision maker, as one who allows various pressures in the situation to influence him or her too much, and as avoiding minimizing immediate pressures and problems rather than maximizing long-term production.

5. *Deserter:* a leader who is using a low task orientation and a low relationship orientation in a situation where such behavior is inappropriate and who is, therefore, less effective; perceived as uninvolved and passive or negative.
6. *Developer:* a leader who is using a high relationship orientation and a low task orientation in a situation where such behavior is appropriate and who is, therefore, more effective; perceived as having implicit trust in people and as being primarily concerned with developing them as individuals.
7. *Executive:* a leader who is using a high task orientation and a high relationship orientation in a situation where such behavior is appropriate and who is, therefore, more effective; perceived as a good motivating force and a manager who sets high standards, treats everyone somewhat differently, and prefers team management.
8. *Missionary:* a leader who is using a high relationship orientation and a low task orientation in a situation where such behavior is inappropriate and who is, therefore, less effective; perceived as being primarily interested in harmony.

Reddin's theory is taken one step further in the *situational leadership theory* developed by Hersey and Blanchard.[79] This theory, first introduced as the *Life Cycle Theory of Leadership*,[80] adds a situation variable that can be used to determine appropriate leadership styles (see figure 1-5). The task and relationship behavior dimension in figure 1-5 corresponds to the *initiating structure* and *consideration* dimensions of the Ohio State model, and the style adaptability dimension of situational leadership theory corresponds to Reddin's *effectiveness* dimension.

Style Adaptability

According to Hersey and Blanchard,[81] *style adaptability* is the degree to which leaders are able to vary their style appropriately to the demands of a given situation according to Situational Leadership. People who have a narrow style range can be effective over a long period of time if they remain in situations in which their style has a high probability of success.

Conversely, people who have a wide range of styles may be ineffective if these behaviors are not consistent with the demands of the situation. Thus, style range is not as relevant to effectiveness as style adaptability; a wide style range will not guarantee effectiveness (see figure 1-5).

FIGURE 1-5
Leadership Behavior Style According to Situational Leadership Theory

(High)	High relationship and low task (S3)	High task and high relationship (S2)
Relationship Behavior (Low)	(S4) Low task and low relationship	(S1) High task and low relationship

Source: Paul Hersey and Kenneth H. Blanchard, Management of Organizational Behavior: Utilizing Human Resources, 4t h ed. Englewood Cliffs, NJ: Prentice-Hall, 1982, p. 200. Used with permission.

Reddin [82] and Hersey and Blanchard [83] use the third dimension, effectiveness and style adaptability, respectively, to stress that the flexibility of a storehouse of styles alone is not sufficient to ensure leadership effectiveness. Effectiveness comes with both a range of styles so that a leader is able to vary his or her leadership style and the appropriate match of style to the situation.

Hersey and Blanchard's additional variable, *task-relevant maturity,* helps this process. It is defined as a combination of *job maturity,* the ability and technical knowledge to do the task and *psychological maturity,* feelings of confidence and self-respect about oneself as an individual.[84] These terms refer to the ability and willingness of an individual to take responsibility for directing her or his own behavior. These variables of maturity are determined only in relation to a specific, observable task to be performed [85] and are referred to *task relevant maturity* as an all-inclusive term.

The two dimensions of task-relevant maturity are, like the other dimensions of the model, scaled from low to high, resulting in four levels:

- M1 is low in both ability and willingness. Individual followers or groups at this level lack both competence and confidence.
- M2 is low in ability but high in willingness. Followers or groups at this level are self-confident but lack needed skills to take responsibility.
- M3 is high in ability but low in willingness. The problem is often a lack of motivation rather than a sense of insecurity.
- M4 is high in both ability and willingness. Followers and groups at this level are both competent and confident to take responsibility.

Hersey and Blanchard[86] defined four styles of leader behavior (SI, S2, S3, and S4) and four levels of followers' task-relevant maturity (M1, M2, M3 and M4), which, in turn, define four categories of situations.

FIGURE 1-6
Relationships Between Leadership Styles and Follower Maturity

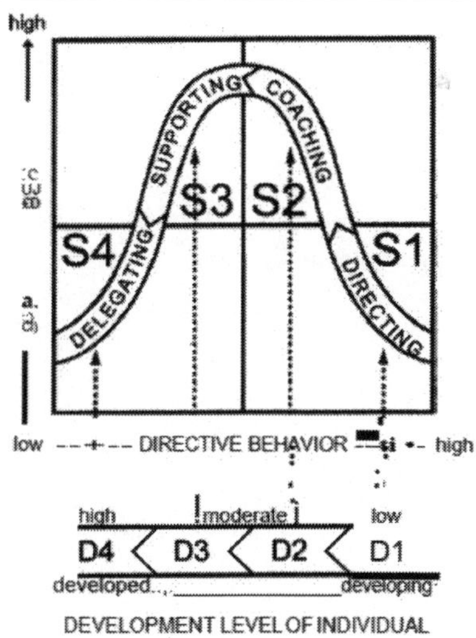

Source: Zigarmi, Blanchard, O'Connor and Edeburn, The Leader Within. Prentice Hall, 2005, p. 199. Used with permission.

According to Hersey and Blanchard,[87] as the level of maturity of the follower(s) continues to increase in terms of accomplishing a specific task, the leader should begin to reduce task behavior and increase relationship behavior. This should be the case until the individual or group reaches a moderate level of maturity. As the follower begins to move into an above average level of maturity, it becomes appropriate for the leader to decrease not only task behavior but relationship behavior as well. Now the follower is not only mature in terms of the performance of the task but also psychologically. Thus, situational leadership theory focuses on the appropriateness or effectiveness of leadership styles according to the task relevant maturity of the follower(s). This cycle is illustrated in figure 1-6 by a bell-shaped curve superimposed upon the four leadership quadrants. As the maturity level of one's followers develops along the maturity continuum from immature to mature, the appropriate style of leadership moves accordingly along the curvilinear function.

In determining what leadership style is appropriate to use in a given situation, one must first determine the maturity level of the follower in relation to a specific task that the leader is attempting to accomplish through the follower's efforts. Once identified, the appropriate leadership style can be determined by constructing a right angle (90 degrees) from the point where it intersects on the curvilinear function in the style of the leader portion of the model. The quadrant in which that intersection takes place suggests the appropriate style to be used by the leader in that situation with a follower of that maturity level, as shown in figure 1-6. Thus, the situational leadership theory contends that in working with people who are low in maturity (Ml), a high task/low relationship style (SI) has the highest probability of success. Similarly, low relationship/low task (S4) has the highest probability of success in working with people of high task-relevant maturity (M4).

Four Styles of Situational Leadership

Hersey and Blanchard[88] define the four styles of situational leadership theory as follows:

1. High task/low relationship (S1); referred to as *telling:* People who are unable and unwilling to take responsibility (M1) are not competent or confident. A directive *telling* style (SI) that provides clear, specific directions and supervision has the highest probability of being effective with individuals at this maturity level. It characterizes the leader's defining role in telling people what, who, when, and where to do various tasks. It emphasizes directive behavior.
2. High task/high relationship (S2); referred to as *selling:* People who are unable to but willing to take responsibility (M2) are confident but lack skills at this time. Thus, a *selling* style (S2) that provides directive behavior, because of their lack of ability, but also supportive behavior to reinforce their willingness and enthusiasm, appears to be most appropriate for individuals at this maturity level. Most of the direction is still provided by the leader; yet, through twoway communication and explanation, the leader tries to get the followers psychologically to *buy into* desired behaviors. Followers at this maturity level will usually go along with a decision if their leader also offers some help and direction.
3. High relationship/low task (S3); referred to as *participating:* People at this maturity level are able but unwilling to do what the leader wants (M3). Their reluctance to perform is more of a motivational problem. The leader needs to open the door (use two-way communication and active listening) to support the follower's effort to use the ability she or he already has. Thus, a supportive, nondirective *participating* style (S3) has the highest probability of being effective with individuals at this maturity level. The leader and the follower share in decision-making, with the main role of the leader being facilitating and communicating.

4. Low relationship/low task behavior (S4); referred to as *delegating:* people at this maturity level are both able and willing, or confident, to take responsibility. Thus, a low-profile *delegating* style (S4), which provides little direction or support, has the highest probability of being effective with individuals at this maturity level (M4). Even though the leader may still identify the problem, the responsibility for carrying out plans is given to these mature followers.

Situational leadership theory is prescriptive in that it indicates how a leader should act in various situations, and it is developmental in that it claims that as task-relevant maturity increases, leadership style should progress accordingly. Failure to manifest style adaptability can result from the inflexibility on the part of the leader or from failure to select the appropriate style for particular situations.

Clothier[89] reminds the leader to bear in mind that regardless of the past maturity level of an individual or group, a constant reassessment should occur. Maturity will change as the tasks change and maturity may change for a variety of reasons in relation to even familiar tasks. A successful leader must, therefore, move backward and forward along the prescriptive curve as his or her assessment of the present situation demands.

Transformational Leadership

The concept of leadership as it relates to the task-relevant maturity of the followers may have been better explained by James MacGregor Burns:[90] Leadership is the process that transforms individuals developmentally by constantly focusing on elevating their goals, not just focusing on the accomplishment of tasks.

Research

Bums' comprehensive study of leadership looked at the vast reservoir of data, analyses, and theories on leadership, as well as the expression of thoughtful experience of leaders. His quest was an intellectual breakthrough in the leadership process across cultures and across time, focusing on elevating the goals of individuals:

- Processes of leadership must be seen as part of the dynamics of conflict and power
- Leadership is nothing if not linked to collective purpose
- The effectiveness of leaders must be judged not by their press clippings but by actual social change measured by intent and by the satisfaction of human needs and expectations
- Political leadership depends on a long chain of biological and social processes, interaction with structures of political opportunity and closures, and the interplay between the calls of moral principles and the recognized necessities of power
- In placing these concepts of political leadership centrally into a theory of historical causation, we will reaffirm the possibilities of human volition of common standards of justice in the conduct of people's affairs

Transactional and Transformational Leadership

Burns [91] identified two basic types of leadership: transactional and transforming. *Transactional leadership* involves a joint effort of leaders and followers with the common aim of exchanging one thing for another, such as jobs for votes. These transactions, or "mutually rewarding exchanges" as Stogdill refers to them in his explanation of exchange theory, comprise the relations of most leaders and followers.

Transforming leaders initially recognizes and capitalizes on the existing need of potential followers, but eventually seeks to satisfy higher needs of the followers. This engagement of the full person of the follower converts followers into leaders and may convert the transforming leaders into moral agents.

The conversion of the transforming leader into the moral leader concerned Burns the most. His concept of moral leadership suggested leaders and those led have relationships not only of power but of mutual needs, aspirations, and values. In responding to leaders, followers have adequate knowledge of alternative leaders and programs, and the capacity to choose among those alternatives. Leaders take responsibility for their commitments. If they promise certain kinds of economic, social, and political change, they assume leadership in bringing about that change.

Burns[92] contends that moral leadership is not mere preaching or the uttering of pieties or the insistence on social conformity. Moral leadership emerges from, and always returns to, the fundamental wants and needs, aspirations, and values of the followers. This kind of leadership can produce social change that will satisfy followers' authentic needs—less the Ten Commandments than the Golden Rule. But even the Golden Rule is inadequate, for it measures the wants and needs of others simply by our own.

Burns's search for the moral foundations of leadership assisted him most in identifying patterns in people that account for leadership, and in isolating those acts of leaders that serve ultimately to help the leader release full human potential that is locked up in the ungratified needs and crushed expectations of followers.

Burns's 1978 description of leadership is an insightful and intellectual portrayal of the process a leader would traverse to become a great leader. Theoretically, it seems to describe leadership as beginning with the mutual openness of the leaders in power and the followers in the situation of needing leadership, and progressing to satisfy the fundamental wants and needs, aspirations and values of the followers. In a sense, it removes the stalemate of the Great Man Theory and the environmental theory by suggesting that for leadership to begin, the mutual exchange of power, openness and purpose is necessary. "Leadership over human beings is exercised when persons with certain motives and purposes mobilize, in competition or conflict with others, institutional, political, psychological and other resources so as to arouse, engage and satisfy the motives of followers."[93] Much like Stogdill,[94] Bums suggests that a person does not become a leader by virtue of some combination of traits, but the patterns of personal characteristics of the leader must bear some relationship to the characteristics, activities, and goals of the followers.

Relationship Between Leader and Follower

More recent opinions about leadership[95] support what Stogdill and Burns have reported on the importance of the relationship between leader and follower. The information that follows resulted from an investigation of recent literature and conversations with Anne and Jerry Gilley of Colorado State University.

Focusing on change in the workplace is the key in transformational leadership,[96] where leaders change things from what could be to what is. The results of this reality-based approach increase energy, innovation, acceptance of change, and dedication to a common vision. According to Tichy and Devanna,[97] leadership can be practiced by leaders if they "define the need for change, create new visions, mobilize commitment to those visions, and ultimately transform the organization." Tichy and Devanna developed a three-step model to illustrate transformational change efforts:

1. Recognize the need for change by capitalizing on catalysts or trigger events, such as changes in legislation, to help others feel the need for change
2. Create a new vision and focus the organization on the positive; mobilize commitment and make it happen
3. Institutionalize change by making it part of daily organization life

Fusion Leadership

Daft and Lengel's 1998 work on transformational leadership is called *fusion,* the opposite of fission. Fission creates negative energy by splitting atoms. Fusion creates the energy of a common vision by reducing the obstacles or barriers to change. Fusion creates partnerships and connections through conversations and taking joint responsibility for action across the silos of an organizational system. Fusion is about joining together for information sharing. Daft and Lengel suggest the following practices for fusion leadership:

1. mindfulness (use independent thinking and creativity)
2. vision (work for a higher purpose)
3. heart (be caring, compassionate, and positive in relationships)
4. communication (listen, discern, and influence others through respect to vision, values, and emotions)
5. courage (enable others to step outside the traditional boundary of doing work)
6. integrity (be honest and trustworthy)

Stewardship as Leadership

Stewards of leadership exercise responsible care when transforming the people and the organization in the workplace.[98] Good leaders possess a deep sense of purpose and intention, a compelling rationale for change, and act as stewards of their vision. Further, these leaders often gauge their own success by the response of those whom they serve.

Block's 1996 description of servant leaders is representative of stewardship as he suggests placing the needs of stakeholders above the leader's own needs. Stakeholders may be employees, customers, peers, or stockholders. For the purpose of the approach to leadership detailed in this book, stakeholders are all the people the leader interacts with within their territory or sphere of influence. Similarly, servant leaders, who are able and willing to help others, make certain that these people in their territory of influence are equipped with the tools (training, resources, information, technology, emotional and practical support, and so forth) needed to achieve their goals. These leaders serve their followers by treating them like partners, engaging their minds and hearts, recognizing their contributions, and celebrating achievements large and small.

The authors of transformational, fusion, servant leadership are often criticized for setting unreal expectations on the part of the leader and rarely do they provide evidence in the form of actual, live leaders who consistently model the behaviors described. Studies observing the practice of leadership and then deriving capabilities based on leadership practice follow.

Good-to-Great Leadership

Jim Collins[99] five-year study of companies deemed great yielded intriguing insight into leadership. First, companies considered great met tough standards—in part, the ability to sustain above-average cumulative stock returns for fifteen consecutive years.

Research

This research on leadership found in organizations that achieved greatness is called Level 5, which refers to the highest achievable level in a hierarchy of identified executive capabilities:

- *Level 5: Executive* - Builds enduring greatness via a blend of personal humility and professional will
- *Level 4: Effective Leader* - Catalyzes commitment to a vigorous pursuit of a clear and compelling vision, stimulating higher performance standards
- *Level 3: Competent Manager* - Organizes people and resources for the effective and efficient pursuit of goals and objectives
- *Level 2: Contributing Team Member* - Contributes individual capabilities toward the achievement of group objectives and works effectively with others in a group setting
- *Level 1: Highly Capable Individual* - Makes productive contributions through talent, knowledge, skills, and good work habits

Characteristics of Level 5 leaders are "a study in duality: modest and willful, humble and fearless."[100] These characteristics seem to work in the relationship between leader and follower as their personal ambition for the company is opposed to their own private ends. These results-driven leaders set high standards so the level of accomplishment trends upward. Yet, at the same time, these successful leaders recognize their own limitations and, as a result, proactively grow and develop their successors. Typically they are not the highest-paid leaders in their industry; instead, they are motivated by the desire to make the business a success, not collect a personal fortune.

Kouzes and Posner

James M. Kouzes and Barry Z. Posner contend in *The Leadership Challenge*[101] that the world is much faster paced now than ever before. Decisions need to be made quickly. Companies are global. Power has shifted to those with technology, skills, and relationships. No longer is society hierarchical, rather organizations are moving toward a more centered organization around empowered people, not empowered bosses. Their book discusses five general characteristics of leadership practices and is written for managers, not for the rank and file. The detailed interpersonal approach of the L.E.A.D.E.R.S. Method goes deeper into the interpersonal to include everyone in an organization.

The world has become fragmented; it is far from a community, say Kouzes and Posner. [102] Diversity and disparity are apparent in the country, our organizations, and our work. There is also a renewed sense for meaning. Most people are searching for a greater purpose in their lives. Values and virtues are discussed more openly. Family and friends are still our most trusted sources of information. Rapid change necessitates leaders up and down the organizational hierarchy.

Kouzes and Posner provide an extensive model—not method—for challenging ourselves to be leaders. Their 1995 work, based on research of 60,000 people at various levels in various public and private organizations, found a consistent set of characteristics that leaders of organizations exemplified. They identified five fundamental practices of exemplary leadership:

1. challenging the process
2. inspiring a shared vision
3. enabling others to act
4. modeling the way
5. encouraging the heart

When the leaders in their research were at their personal best, these characteristics emerged.

Challenging the Process

Leaders do not wait for opportunities to fall in their laps. Rather they go out and find them. Essentially, they want to find better ways of doing things.[103]

First Commitment: Find Challenging Opportunities

The first commitment for this practice is to search out challenging opportunities for change, growth, innovation, and improvement. Kouzes and Posner suggest treating every job like an adventure, treating every assignment as starting over, questioning the status quo, and assigning people opportunities as ways to practice this commitment. It is up to the leaders of an organization to let go of the reins and create these opportunities for those in the organization. Then the organization will be filled with leaders from all levels.

Second Commitment: Learn from Success and Failure

The second commitment is experimenting, taking risks, and learning from both successes and failures. This is a huge challenge for many; however, those who embrace this commitment shine as leaders. These leaders make it safe for others to experiment. Leaders tend to approach stress positively; they exhibit psychological hardiness. *Psychological hardiness* means considering change events as interesting, believing they can affect the outcome, and seeing such events as opportunities for development. Kouzes and Posner[104] encourage leaders to create a culture around such hardiness.

Inspiring a Shared Vision

Collins and Porras[105] identified companies that had superior long-term performance, which largely had to do with having a common vision and sticking with it. A strong vision is one that includes a core ideology and an envisioned future. The core ideology includes the core purpose and core values. The core purpose is the "reason why the organization is in business."

Core values are the "essential and enduring principles and tenets of an organization."[106] Successful companies do not change the core ideology as they change their practices and procedures for the changing world. Rather the core ideology is what keeps the character of the organization as it reacts to the changes in the markets.

Third Commitment: Envision an Ennobling Future

Kouzes and Posner[107] applied the concept of vision and made it a fundamental practice for leadership. The third commitment is included under this exemplary practice of envisioning an uplifting and ennobling future. This requires thinking about the past and then deciding what you want the organization's future to look like. It is critical for leaders to work with each other and understand their expectations to ensure that the envisioned future works for the organization.

Kouzes and Posner define vision as "an ideal and unique image of the future." Leaders are visionaries. Exemplary leaders are continuously looking toward the future and seeing what their ideal organization looks like. According to Kotter,[108] vision is the picture that explains the future and clarifies the direction that the organization needs to move. A vision is created in order to guide an organization through the many changes that are demanded from external factors and out of dissatisfaction with the current organization. Kouzes and Posner suggest that leaders desire to change themselves and others in order to achieve this vision.

Kotter identifies key principles to consider when creating the vision of an organization:

- First, the vision needs to be focused, simple, and direct. This will help with decision-making in the change process.
- Second, it needs to be imaginable, which means that the workforce understands it and believes that it can happen in their organization.

- Third, it needs to be desirable. All stakeholders need to understand the link of how the vision will affect their long-term interests.
- Fourth, the vision needs to be feasible for the organization. For a vision to be feasible, the leaders need to have a clear understanding of the organization, its markets, and competition. This should also enhance the credibility for change strategy.
- Fifth, it needs to be flexible. As the changes occur and strategies are refined, the vision needs to allow for individual initiative without compromising the goal of the vision.
- Finally, it needs to be communicable. The communication should be clear, widespread, consistent, and repeated often. The more the employees hear, read, and see the vision, the more they will believe in it.

Additionally, the communication should include two-way dialogue. This will provide the leaders with valuable input from employees about their thoughts on the process and how it impacts the vision and strategy.

Dialogue with the employees allows the executives and managers to explain the congruence of the vision and process based on the feedback they receive.

Accordingly, setting a strong vision during the planning phase is critical and just the beginning.

James Collins's book, *Good to Great,*[109] describes how eleven companies went from mediocre to great in an average time frame of twenty years. One of the key elements is the *hedgehog concept.* This simple concept includes three circles that intersect to help define the future:

- What are you deeply passionate about?
- What drives your economic engine?
- At what you can be the best in the world?

As simple as this concept may seem, many leaders and organizations have failed because they went outside those circles when envisioning their future. The hedgehog concept is a tool that leaders can use to test their assumptions. If they find they are falling outside the circles, they need to seriously consider whether or not they are staying true to their core ideology.

Fourth Commitment: Enlist Others to a Common Vision

The fourth commitment included in the practice of inspiring a shared vision is to enlist others to a common vision by appealing to their values, interest, hopes, and dreams.[110] This requires leaders to practice speaking positively from the heart about their vision. They need to listen to those around them to understand the concerns, the excitement, and the uncertainty. Then they need to listen again. An important aspect of this commitment is to make the vision tangible.

Notable leadership authors Warren Bennis and Burt Nanus explain this concept in *Leaders: Strategies for Taking Charge*. They explain that the leaders they interviewed found that when an organization's leaders have a clear sense of direction and purpose and can positively and clearly explain it to their employees, there is more energy surrounding the vision. This energy is maximized when the employees feel that their values align with the vision as well. Excitement and vigor surround the work that the employees perform because they feel that they are engaged in a new venture for the good of the organization. They can see it, feel it, and hear it. It is tangible.

Enabling Others to Act

This is the concept of Kouzes and Posner's third exemplary practice of enabling others to act: "Leadership is a team effort." It is critical to include the people who will make the vision a reality. Kouzes and Posner explain that the more information, authority, and discretion people have, the more likely that the organization will get extraordinary results. The following commitments will help leaders gain this edge.

Fifth Commitment: Promote Cooperative Goals

Kouzes and Posner's fifth commitment is fostering collaboration by promoting cooperative goals and building trust. This is the opposite of a competitive environment. Kouzes and Posner discuss research performed by Alfie Kohn and the team of David W. Johnson and Roger T. Johnson indicating that cooperative environments promote higher performance than those that are competitive or individual in nature. However, the more employees there are to collaborate with, the more differing views and conflicting interests will arise. Collaboration will work if leaders develop cooperative goals, seek integrative solutions, and build trusting relationships. Shared goals require people to work together as a team, resulting in more productivity. Leaders need to foster a community of reciprocity in order for people to cooperate and avoid being taken advantage of. Additionally, it is important for ongoing interaction to occur so that the cooperation is lasting and the consequences of acting outside of collaboration are memorable. This will ensure that people remember that teamwork will result in a more successful work environment. The most challenging part of promoting collaboration is explaining that the long-term payoff is greater than the short-term in order to get the necessary buy-in.[112]

Another important aspect of fostering collaboration is communication. Leaders must encourage dialogue among all levels of the organization and constantly say, "we." This communication will foster trust within the organization. People will feel that their opinions matter and that there is a genuine concern. Leaders should seek integrative solutions with all levels of the organization. They should listen to those actually doing the work to determine if there are alternatives to issues the organization is facing other than those determined by top-level management. By committing to include everyone, whether through problem-solving partnerships, holding regular meetings to keep people up to date or having group process consultations so that employees have the ability to voice their concerns, leaders are fostering an environment of trust, commitment, and ultimately, increased productivity. [113]

Sixth Commitment: Share Information and Power

The sixth commitment further promotes this practice by sharing power and information to strengthen people. This includes giving power away, providing choice, developing competence, assigning critical tasks, and offering visible support.[114] The importance of this commitment is that it furthers the commitment of everyone in the organization because they have the information and power to take initiative and make decisions. The leaders and the employees do not see the organization as "us" (employees) versus "them" (leaders). Kouzes and Posner's research reflects that the more perceived employee power exists, the more successful the organization. In order for this employee power to exist, it requires leaders to believe and trust in their employees. Leaders are promoting leadership at all levels of the organization.

James Collins, in *Good to Great*,[115] explains this concept when describing the Level 5 Leadership phenomenon: "Level 5 leaders channel their ego needs away from themselves and into the larger goal of building a great company." The characteristics of humility and professionalism will provide a solid foundation for the relationship between the leader and the employee. Level 5 leaders acknowledge their limitations and surround them with people who can help move the organization forward. He or she does not allow her or his ego to stand in the way of employees succeeding for the good of the organization. Most importantly, Level 5 leaders look for successors who can carry the organization into the future after the Level 5 leader departs. These leaders want the organization to be successful with the help of everyone, not just through his or her own power.

Kouzes and Posner[116] offer tips for leaders pursuing the sixth commitment:

- Decorate your office with mementos of family, friends, and interests instead of a large desk and expensive artwork. This will show that you are more approachable and more of a team player.
- Enlarge people's sphere of influence by giving them more authority to make decisions. This includes increasing amounts required for signatures of managers, removing unnecessary

approval steps, encouraging innovative solutions, assigning nonroutine jobs in order to expand knowledge and skills, and increasing job flexibility with respect to processes.

- Educate the teams, especially when asking them to do new jobs and utilize different competencies. Support new and innovative training and development solutions.
- Make sure the delegated tasks are relevant by increasing the individuals' influence over what is important for the organization. This includes having employees on all tasks forces for critical tasks and issues.
- Make heroes of other people by publicizing the work that the employees are doing, sending letters of appreciation to key supporters, and putting stories of team members in newsletters.

Modeling the Way

Leaders must behave consistently with the shared values of the organization. Jim Collins and Jerry Porras, in *Built to Last: Successful Habits of Visionary Companies,*[117] explain that core values of the organization are the "timeless guiding principles" that have "intrinsic value and importance to those inside the organization."

If that's true, what happens when the leaders are not embracing those values? We can all look at some of the failed organizations over the past three years: Enron's "values" were integrity, respect, and excellence. Arthur Andersen's values were quality service, quality people, meritocracy, one firm approach, integrity, innovation, and stewardship. Clearly, each company's demise suggests that the organization's leaders did not uphold all of those values. Accordingly, even if these companies do last, it will be difficult for the employees to believe in the values since leadership did not.

Seventh Commitment: Demonstrate Credibility

This leads us to the seventh commitment postulated by Kouzes and Posner,[118] setting the example and doing what you say you will do.

This commitment is important for emerging leaders to build credibility and also for leaders that need to reassess their leadership skills. This commitment is about taking a look in the mirror and auditing your actions. This is the commitment where you are the most vulnerable because you need to come face to face with whether or not you are truly modeling the way and being a role model for those around you. "Practicing what you preach," "walking the talk," "acting consistent with your words," and "putting your money where your mouth is" are all ways to demonstrate your credibility. The more credible the leader, the more likely the employees are to follow.

Unfortunately, there is more skepticism about the intentions and abilities of a new leader. Kouzes and Posner discuss in *The Leadership Challenge* tactics that Lillas Brown, director of Business and Leadership Programs at the University of Saskatchewan, used when she was new to the university system. Every night she would ask questions of herself such as: "What have I done today that demonstrated value of what is near and dear to me?" "What do I need to do to more fully express my values?" and "What have I done inadvertently to demonstrate this is not a value for me?" By clarifying these questions daily, she was able to strengthen her resolve to contribute, which helped her to accomplish more and develop into a more credible leader.[119]

Lillas Brown identified what was of value to her. Determining the congruence of personal and organizational values is an important element of this commitment. Leaders and employees should have a clear understanding of their own values and their organizations' values and use those values to guide their behavior. Those employees with the strongest value congruence have the greatest commitment to the organization and effectively advance toward the goals of the organization and their own personal goals, say Kouzes and Posner. They discussed the findings of John Kotter and John Heskett that organizations with a strong culture based on shared values outperformed other organizations in the areas of revenue growth, job creation, stock price, and profit performance. However, they concluded, each organization has a separate set of values, and the values that work for one organization may not work for another.

It is important for leaders to promote these values within the organization through hiring and socialization. Core values of an organization should be communicated during the hiring process, as research has indicated that individuals and organizations are attracted to each other when they have similar personalities, goals, and values.[120] Similarity is preferred because there will be reduced dissonance, improved communication, and increased predictability of social interactions.

Eighth Commitment: Demonstrate Progress

The eighth commitment is to achieve small wins: building commitment to action. By achieving small wins, Kouzes and Posner say leaders are able to demonstrate the progress that the organization is making. Additionally, they are celebrating the success of those around them, which is an important element of leadership. Employees will feel more committed when they see that the results of their work contribute to the greater good of the company.

Collins[122] also describes this idea in *Good to Great.* His concept is the flywheel, which needs a lot of momentum to get moving. It is a manual process that starts off hard, gets a little more manageable, and gets easier until finally the flywheel spins on its own. Collins suggests that many of us do not realize the pain, courage, effort, and exhilaration that good to great companies experienced before they sustained greatness. Often the public hears of the breakthrough moments when a company "hits the jackpot."

However, there are usually many years before that when the company was pushing the flywheel as hard as they could.[123] As the flywheel built momentum, the companies were achieving small wins through results visible internally to those in the organization. As these results could be seen within the organization, more people were energized by the work they had contributed, and the momentum continued until, eventually, the organization broke through. Typically, it wasn't until the breakthrough point that the public heard about it.

Building momentum by achieving small wins allows organizations to establish commitment for a change or project. According to Kouzes and Posner,[124] leaders do not expect to see the "grand" results immediately, but they expect to see fast results for those actions that are achievable and within the capabilities of the employees. Once the employees realized that they could complete one task, they were motivated and committed to succeed at the next task. The exemplary leader encourages constant movement through the tasks, which ultimately succeeds in accomplishing the larger change or project.

Kouzes and Posner[125] explain that although achieving small wins may sound easy, leaders must develop a plan, guided by the organization's vision and values, in order to understand the larger picture. This plan serves as a guide through the small steps and, hopefully, small wins. With each step and win momentum builds, which leads to empowerment and commitment. Changes will seem less threatening when the leaders break the process into manageable pieces.

Sustaining commitment usually occurs much faster when those involved have volunteered. It is much more difficult to demand change from people through some sort of coercion. Accordingly, providing choice (within reason) will make the employees feel much more accountable for their decisions, say Kouzes and Posner. Additionally, the decisions that the leaders and the employees make need to be visible. It is much harder to back out of a decision if everyone knows about it. Consequently, if decisions are made visible, so too should the progress, and eventually the small wins. Make recognition public. This is the best way to encourage continuous improvement.

Encouraging the Heart

If we take a moment to look back at some of the leaders in our lives, each of us probably has a story of someone who gave us their heart and constantly encouraged us. They got us through that difficult project when we were working through the night; they encouraged us to keep going even though we didn't get the promotion; they rewarded us with a raise after all the effort and success of the project. Of course, we each have not-so-great stories of those supposed leaders who did none of that. However, in our minds, the latter were not leaders.

Ninth Commitment: Link Rewards to Performance

The ninth commitment is recognizing contributions by linking rewards with performance.[126] Recognizing individual contributions is one of the highest skills noted in exemplary leaders. Research has discovered that the number one reason that people leave their jobs is limited praise and recognition." [127] Providing this recognition builds the employee's self-confidence. Leaders have found that the more self-confidence that exists, the more extraordinary work that can be done. It is up to the leaders to constantly encourage the employees through their influence to accomplish and exceed expectations.

Additionally, it is extremely important to set criteria for performance. Rewards need to be clearly linked to the expected performance set by the leaders. Research has proven that when linking performance to rewards, it is critical to ensure that people know what is expected of them, that feedback is given about their performance, and that only those who meet the standards are rewarded.[128] The performance should also be measurable. This allows it to be easily tracked and understandable by the employees. It also alleviates any subjectivity regarding the performance, which may cause unhealthy competition among employees.

Additionally, since everyone has different motivations, it is important to vary the types of rewards and recognition. It may be money, praise, a day off, more challenging work responsibilities, or a promotion.

Exemplary leaders are skilled at staying within the criteria they set for performance and often are creative with their rewards. By understanding what motivates people, the leaders have a better chance of rewarding performance more often when financial means is not always available. Many leaders do not rely solely on formal rewards such as bonuses and promotions but also on intrinsic rewards that are already built into the job.[129] Intrinsic rewards may include a sense of accomplishment (winning the proposal) or the thrill of creation (launching a new product) from which individuals feel immediate satisfaction. However, these events need to be recognized by leaders verbally in order to validate the success of the individual. Praise should also be in front of peers in order to model what is expected of everyone.

When the individual feels more empowered and the peers further understand expectations, it's a win-win situation.

When the motivations are understood through dialogue with the employees, it may also be appropriate to set the reward/recognition system participatively.[130] Shared understanding of the system would make individuals more willing to push the limits and exceed expectations. They will recognize how their efforts truly affect the overall good of the organization and will understand how that effort is rewarded. Additionally, exemplary leaders provide feedback along the way to provide an understanding of the successes and failures. If they are not performing as expected, that feedback should not come at the end. Leaders should be continuously coaching their employees to achieve optimal performance.

Tenth Commitment: Celebrate Accomplishments

Kouzes and Posner's tenth and final commitment is celebrating accomplishments. Commitment number nine is more about recognizing individual achievements, but, as all exemplary leaders know, it is the ultimate effort of the group that achieves success. Accordingly, celebrating the overall effort of the group is of utmost importance. Teamwork should be recognized as valued and victories celebrated.

As discussed in commitment number nine, it is critical to celebrate successes that are consistent with the values and vision of the organization. Leaders are often cheerleaders and they commend the efforts that are consistent with the organizational values.[131] The more celebration, the more motivated the groups within the organization will be to continue to model the values and achieve success. Leaders must stay consistent in celebrating the key values of the organization. They also cannot just celebrate in a grand fashion. They too must be consistent in the way they model their own behavior. Otherwise, the celebration will not appear authentic.[132]

As with individual contributions, celebrations should be public. They can range from a yearly party celebrating the anniversary of the company to an impromptu gathering cheering on the success of a winning proposal. The real success is in the public nature of the celebration. Everyone is rewarded and sharing in the success. This is especially important in breaking down barriers between departments, say Kouzes and Posner.[133] Often, departments are in silos and do not recognize the effect that the other departments have on the ultimate success of a project. By having a public ceremony, the departments are able to see all contributions and be supportive of each other in future endeavors.

Many leaders do not understand the concept of celebrations. They focus on achieving the big contracts, reorganizing companies, and reengineering accounting processes as key job aspects. However, as mentioned earlier, many people leave their jobs because of a lack of praise and recognition. It may be a part of their jobs to be innovative, creative, and cost conscious. However, efforts that exceed expectations on a regular basis should be recognized. Otherwise, morale will decrease and motivation will be lost. Exceeding expectations may quickly drop to just meeting or not meeting expectations.

"Leaders are always on the lookout for people who are doing the right things in the right way so that they can celebrate those victories."[134] Celebration sustains commitment and motivation of all those involved.

CHAPTER 1 REVIEW

Answers to the review questions and self-test questions are found in the back of the textbook.

Review Questions

1-1. What have studies shown about being able to correlate specific traits (popularity, verbal facility, initiative, etc.) and leadership effectiveness?

1-2. What do studies of behavioral styles show about their influence on effective leadership? What does the Ohio State model explain? What happens when the Ohio State model is superimposed on the managerial grid? What correlations did Clothier discover?

1-3. What is meant by leadership functions? Give two or three examples of comparing the scientific management school and human relation school when addressing specific approaches.
1-4. Distinguish McGregor's Theory X and Theory Y. Distinguish between task behavior and relationship behavior.
1-5. Fiedler's theory measured leadership effectiveness and aspects of group behavior. What is the principal value of Fiedler's theory?
1-6. Compare Clothier's four leadership styles to Reddin's eight leader styles.
1-7. What is meant by style adaptability? How do people with a narrow style range differ from those with a wide range of styles?
1-8. According to Hersey and Blanchard, how should a leader respond (in terms of task behavior and relationship behavior) as the level of maturity of a follower increases in terms of completing a specific task?
1-9. How does transactional leadership differ from transformational leadership? What is meant by fusion leadership?
1-10. Name and describe four or five of Kouzes and Posner's commitments and explain how each might operate in a real-life situation.

Self-Test Questions

T F 1-1. Trait theory of leadership focuses on social skills; popularity; sensitivity, etc.; behavioral theory focuses on style (e.g., democratic, authoritarian, concern for people, concern for production, etc.).

T F 1-2. In studies of leadership functions, specifically organizational structure, scientific management would favor decentralization; human relations would favor centralization.

T F 1-3. The Managerial Grid is used in management development and describes five types of leadership behavior including task, team, and middle-of-the-road.

T F 1-4. Situational leadership theory is prescriptive (indicating how a leader should act in various situations) and developmental (with an increase in task-relevant maturity, style should progress).

T F 1-5. According to Reddin, the benevolent autocrat style of leader is perceived as distant and passive (low task, high relationship) but interested in the task and therefore highly effective.

T F 1-6. Transformational leadership is called fusion (as opposed to fission) since it creates the energy needed to overcome obstacles to change.

T F 1-7. Kouzes and Posner identified five fundamental practices of exemplary leadership including encouraging the heart and enabling others to act.

CHAPTER 2

Fundamental Two: Identifying Human Systems and Power Differentials

Learning Objectives

2-1. Understand the concept of power differentials in the work environment and how it impacts individual behavior and organizational systems
2-2. Define and discuss the importance of the three types of system blindness: spatial, temporal, and relational
2-3. Identify the three role classifications people occupy in organizations
2-4. Analyze the role classifications, particularly in relation to Maslow's hierarchy of needs
2-5. Describe the importance of roles in organizational dynamics and success
2-6. Discuss common scenarios in role relationships
2-7. Identify obstacles to everyday leadership
2-8. Understand and discuss the concepts of structural and cultural inertia
2-9. Explain the concept of the paradox of culture

CHAPTER OUTLINE

Introduction

Power differentials, the inequities that exist within interpersonal relationships, can produce destructive behavior patterns in work systems. Barry Oshry[135] has conducted systems research at Boston University and is an expert on total system empowerment and building community in the face of differences. Oshry contends that powerful systems of hierarchy exist in organizations, the unseen effects of which can negatively affect both the individual's interpretation of and response to events and people. Many human beings are oblivious to the mechanics of these invisible systems within which they work, yet they know the frustration and stifled ambitions result in poor performance and a reduced capacity for contribution.

Oshry[136] provides a systems view and understanding of the unrecognized ways in which the structural scheme of these systems influences our behavior. However, influence does not bring about incentives to participate in everyday leadership unless we first understand the structural schemes. When we recognize these systems operating within our place of work, we can tailor everyday acts of leadership to achieve significant change. When the practice of leadership expands beyond those with positions of authority to the practice of leadership within one's sphere of influence throughout the organization, relationships become reciprocal and communication flourishes.

System Blindness

According to Oshry, system blindness is seeing individuals within the system without seeing the whole system—the team, the partnerships, the processes, and the overall environment. There are three types of system blindness: spatial, temporal, and relational.[137]

Spatial Blindness

Spatial blindness means seeing only *our* part of the system and is experienced by one who is familiar with his or her specific role but not knowledgeable about the workings of the rest of the organization. This lack of functional interconnection frequently results in the formation of unrealistic perspectives. This can prompt one to assign unwarranted praise or blame to oneself or others, or to misunderstand events witnessed in other aspects of the system. When such an individual must interact with others beyond his or her self-imposed specialization, he/she has wandered into unfamiliar territory.

While nothing is wrong with a strong commitment to one's own territory of influence, it is important not to be completely unaware of events in other areas of the organizational system. Developing a holistic understanding of the workings of the entire system gives one the ability to assess accurately his or her own sphere of influence. Oshry[138] suggests that much of the time we think we are dealing person-to-person, we are in fact dealing context-tocontext possibly resulting in uncertainty, ambiguity, unfounded perceptions, and rumors. Viewing the system in its entirety helps reduce misperceptions and fears, allows for the practice of everyday leadership skills, and leads ultimately to improved productivity.

Temporal Blindness

Temporal blindness is seeing only the present but not the past. All current events within the system have a history. Having temporal blindness results in viewing the present time as unrelated to or removed from the past. In reality, there is a coherent tale that has led to this particular point in time. Blindness to the history of the moment is a source of considerable misunderstanding and conflict internally and externally. This temporal provincialism makes the present appear devoid of meaning. Understanding the history of the place in time where you work lends a context and a wealth of meaning to the present. Seemingly scattered events become connected in a story alive with continuity and purpose.

Relational Blindness

Relational blindness is not seeing relationships or their impact. This will vary depending upon where one works in the organization.

Relations with others are a key factor determining our success regardless of the system in which we work. Thus, it is essential for everyday leaders to understand relationship blindness. Most people regard themselves as self-governing entities operating with independence. Gaining an understanding of the roles we play in systems, along with comprehension of the ramifications of these roles, enables one to achieve a higher level of performance and productivity. It also helps to set the context for everyday leadership.

Role Relationships

To understand the obstacles inherent to the roles people occupy, it is useful to classify roles into three categories. According to Oshry,[139] they can be labeled top, middle, or bottom.

Tops

The designation of the top is reserved for those individuals who occupy positions of great importance and power in a system. They are charged with responsibility for the entire system but usually divide those responsibilities among one another. This can result in reduced loyalty to the goals of the organization as a whole. Instead of relating to others in other sections of the organization, tops may overemphasize how the organization as a whole should be managed.

Tops are conscious of the prestige differentials associated with the different segments of the organization. Certain realms of the organization are considered more significant than others, so greater respect is afforded to tops, among whom power struggles abound and relationships may degenerate. Practicing everyday leadership will often help improve relationships and limit these struggles. With everyday leadership, leadership is practiced at all levels of the organization. Individuals act as leaders within their spheres of influence, and communication among tops, middles, and bottoms flows more freely and more productively.

Middles

Middles are a large group of members in any system that holds neither highranking nor low-ranking positions.[140] Individual middles often do not feel like they belong to any group at all. Middles can be highly competitive, harsh, and quick to judge one another based on superficial qualities such as physical appearance and manner of speech. Given this kind of atmosphere, it is hardly surprising that middles fail to reap the benefits of everyday leadership.

Bottoms

Bottoms are low-ranking members of any system. They share a feeling of vulnerability and have a tendency to band together to alleviate their insecurities. They cope with the threatening and unpredictable environment by joining together as one united group. Power in numbers is a philosophy of bottoms. Because as individuals they have trouble gaining the respect they believe they deserve from the middles and the tops, bottoms often command increased respect and power as a cohesive group. They enhance their unity by defining group boundaries, often pushing away the middles.

Bottoms' interpersonal pressure toward uniformity can stifle creative and potentially beneficial ideas. The herd mentality discourages people from developing everyday leadership. Bottoms need to differentiate themselves and value the potential of their individual contribution. The irony is that bottoms have the best grasp of the overall system and are most aware of their own sphere of influence.

Analyzing Group Behavior

The behavioral dynamics of the various categories of individuals within systems may be analyzed through the work of American psychologist Abraham Maslow, considered the father of humanism in psychology.[141] Maslow reported a hierarchy of needs that can explain much human behavior. The basic physiological needs within the hierarchy must be met as a prerequisite for higher level functioning. In other words, lower-level needs must be fulfilled before higher level needs will motivate an individual's behavior. Human needs can be broken down from lowest to highest:

FIGURE 2-1
Maslow's Hierarchy of Needs

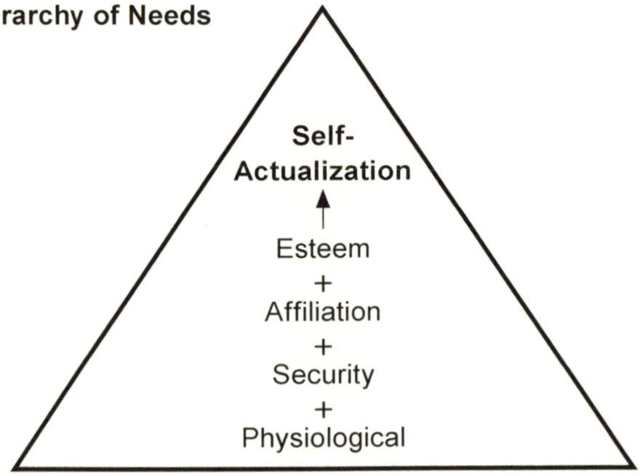

Physiological

Physiological needs are food, water, air, shelter, and clothing. People who want any of these things are first preoccupied with attaining them. Only after these basic needs are met can the individual consider satisfying higher-level needs.

Security

Security needs are for safety, stability, and the absence of pain or illness. Again, people with these needs become preoccupied with satisfying them.

Affiliation

Affiliation needs are for love, affection, and a feeling of friendship and belonging. When the physiological and security needs are satisfied, the social or affiliation needs arise to motivate individual behavior. These needs are most evident in a person's conduct as it relates to job satisfaction, work ethic, team participation, family ties, and general well-being.

Esteem

Esteem needs include personal feelings of self-worth, recognition, and respect from others. People with esteem needs want others to accept them for what they are and to view them as capable. The needs are fulfilled when the individual receives recognition and feedback from others regarding his or her competence and ability.

Self-Actualization

Self-actualization needs are the highest in Maslow's ranking. They are the needs for self-fulfillment and the realization of personal potential. People who are striving for self-actualization usually accept themselves and others, are superior at problem solving, are more detached, and have a desire for privacy. One irony is that people driven by ambition often willingly sacrifice everything to achieve their quest.

In the context of Oshry's role relationships, bottoms are concerned with safety, job security, and putting to rest their ever-present feelings of vulnerability. In contrast, tops have achieved a much higher status in the system, having taken care of their safety and belonging needs, so they are focused on self-esteem needs. Their desire for recognition and status is an outgrowth of their attempt to develop high self-worth. Many tops are motivated by their need for self-actualization in order to fulfill their potential as human beings and are not nearly as concerned by mundane everyday events. Regardless of whom they are working with, they should be concerned about moving in the direction of self-actualization one conversation at a time. The challenge for each individual—whether a top, bottom, or middle—is to recognize the role they play in the system, optimize each interaction with everyday leadership, and move forward with renewed clarity and power.

Predicting Behavior Patterns

Tops feel strained by the enormity and complexity of their responsibilities. They need to adapt continuously to new situations and changing circumstances while making quick decisions, often with incomplete information. Tops often sense that middles are not doing their jobs well.

Bottoms feel stifled by the system. Tops and middles have more authority to make a variety of decisions that will impact their lives, yet rarely solicit opinions from bottoms. As do the tops, bottoms feel the middles are ineffective and disorganized.

Middles are figuratively torn by their position between the tops and the bottoms. In some respects, the middle's role is the most difficult of all. Middles often share little emotional support with one another, and rarely do they receive praise for their hard work from anyone. They are usually spread so thin it is extremely difficult to do superior work.

Common Scenario: Top/Bottom Relationships

Within the top/bottom relationship, the bottom person is a member of a system in which the top has official authority. Frequently in this situation, whatever responsibility for the well-being and performance of the system the bottom initially possesses gradually dissipates while the top assumes more and more control. Both parties are responsible for the shift in responsibility. Tops have a tendency to take responsibility from those of lower rank, while bottoms are used to abdicating responsibility and control to those above them. As a result, tops are overwhelmed and bottoms become resentful.

Fortunately, something can be done about this if it is recognized. Tops can create ways for others to be responsible for the system. Bottoms can choose to stop viewing themselves as insignificant members of the system and choose instead to identify themselves as everyday leaders with much to contribute to the organization's well-being and their own leadership development.

Common Scenario: All Three Relationships

Another scenario finds middles torn between the competing demands of bottoms and tops (ends). Typically, ends become increasingly dependent on the middle to solve more and more of their problems. In turn, the middle acquiesces to the demands of the ends and attempts to take on the problemsolving role, accepting responsibility for far more than is realistically feasible for anyone. The inability of the middle to resolve all of the ends' problems should not be surprising, but it often leads individual middles to blame themselves for personal failure.

To end this cycle of accepting more responsibility, middles and ends need to practice everyday leadership. Middles need to become assertive to induce and support ends to solve their own problems. Ends need to realize they have the strength and the capabilities required to resolve their own problems. Tops, middles, and bottoms should practice more everyday leadership in their relationships with one another.

Inertia and the Paradox of Culture

Both structural and cultural inertia can result from success and block everyday leadership. Some companies with successful products or services assume that it is the current structure and culture that are the underpinnings for their success and they resist change. This stifles everyday leadership since everyday leadership requires an ongoing learning strategy, one that challenges the norm, adjusts values, and develops new habits of behavior.

Without everyday leadership, problems worsen as politics, social factors, and technology change and the organization does not respond.

Structural Inertia

Structural inertia is resistance to change rooted in the size, complexity, interdependence, and interlinking of an organization's structure, systems, procedures, and processes. An incremental approach to change will probably not work as well as using interventions that engage the whole system for rapid change. For example, an internet retailer might address making sure they have the ideal set of quality products available for distribution. Without addressing a cumbersome and untimely delivery system, the sales model may fail.

Cultural Inertia

Cultural inertia has its roots in age and success. Learning becomes embedded in shared expectations about how things are to be done. Norms, values, social networks, stories, and myths result. The more institutionalized these norms are, the greater the cultural inertia, with complacency and arrogance often setting in. When confronted with discontinuities, the very culture that helped an organization to be successful over time may now become a significant barrier to change.

Paradox of Culture

Culture is a critical factor in the performance of a business. The paradox is often that the culture associated with the earlier success of the company is the same culture that can lead to its downfall. Organizational culture is the key to both short-term success and, unless managed well, long-term failure. Culture can provide competitive advantage or an obstacle to innovation and change.

CHAPTER 2 REVIEW

Answers to the review questions and self-test questions are found in the back of the textbook.

Review Questions

2.1 Outline the intersection of Maslow's hierarchy of needs with the roles people occupy suggested by Oshry.

2.2 What is system blindness? In what ways does it negatively affect the interpretation and response to events?

2.3 Define the terms tops, bottoms, and middles as they apply to roles? How does one differ from the others?

2.4 Generally, which role (top, bottom, or middle) seems to have the best understanding of the system as a whole? Why is that?

2.5 Describe the outcome of a scenario when all three roles are in play.

2.6 What is the name for the situation which occurs when HOW things are done is institutionalized? Does this facilitate change?

2.7 In what way is structural inertia an obstacle to everyday leadership? Give an example of how this might manifest itself in an organization.

2.8 What are the "invisible systems" posited by Oshry? Are they constructive or destructive? Why is that?

2.9 As more responsibility is assumed, how can middles and ends practice everyday leadership to solve problems?

2.10 In what ways is the Paradox of Culture an obstacle to everyday leadership?

Self-Test Questions

T F 2-1. Middles occupy positions of great power in an organization, often keep responsibilities to themselves, and exclude others.

T F 2-2. Spatial blindness results in a confused perspective since it means a lack of an understanding of how an area of specialization fits in with other areas of specialization.

T F 2-3. Having a sense of the power in numbers is a characteristic of tops.

T F 2-4. Temporal blindness is the ability to forecast the future without seeing the present

T F 2-5. Everyday leadership will result in a needed change when one "sees" the systems at work within an organization.

T F 2-6. Most people regard themselves as self-governing entities; as such, when we understand the roles we play we can then become more productive.

T F 2-7. Everyday leadership applies to individual behavior and should not be used for analyzing group behavior.

T F 2-8. Power differentials help to equalize relationships and encourage innovation throughout the system.

T F 2-9. "Ends" are the roles occupied by those just entering or just exiting an organization.

T F 2-10. The very culture that encouraged organizational success in the past can become an obstacle in the future when the organization comes face to face with uncertainties.

CHAPTER 3

Fundamental Three: Developing Human Systems into Teams

Learning Objectives

3-1. Understand team dynamics and their importance in organizational development
3-2. Identify and describe the five major stages of team development
3-3. Define "action learning" and its relevance to the third stage of team development
3-4. Explain the impact of group diversity on the decision-making process and how it differs in crises situations and in times of rapid change
3-5. Understand the four multidepartmental team stages and their relevance in managing complex organization issues
3-6. Describe three features of the Team Learning System and their relevance in organizational dynamics
3-7. Discuss how the ability to learn enables organizations to deal with change
3-8. Identify the features of effective and ineffective teams

CHAPTER OUTLINE

Introduction
Stages of Team
Development
Value of Diversity
Diversity Problems
Understanding Change
Effective/Ineffective Teams
Chapter 5 Review

Introduction

Teams are an integral part of change. While they are a means and not an end, they are generally a very effective means. This chapter will explore teams and apply the team concept to processes of change.

Leaders must be concerned with team composition, roles, development, flexibility, and performance. The literature on teams is extensive but does not necessarily offer practical advice. The primary emphasis in many organizations is on individualism. Therefore, management must promote the use of teams and provide team members with basic and advanced training to make them effective. Facilitators must be available to help with the team process, even after training has been provided.

In highly compartmentalized organizations, teams can not only encourage people to talk and understand one another but also serve as agents of change.

Stages of Team Development

In 1998, twenty physicians with a wide range of skills, near completion of an executive MBA course at the University of Tennessee, identified the stages of team development. They reported their experience and observations after working together for ten months in one large team and smaller subteams. They identified five major stages of team development.

Novel-Polite

In the first stage, novel-polite, there were many concerns about interaction. Types of behavior found to support this stage included: tentative, reserved, measuring one another (as they searched for information about one another), learning about and from one another, confusion and frustration in communication, and experiencing self-doubt along with self-confidence. This stage of the team process was concerned more with self-orientation and less to do with teamwork. A group began to form only when feedback about performance (from one another and from university faculty) was introduced in the process.

Goal Clarity

During this stage, the attention of each member of the group shifted from a self-orientation to an external objective. Only with feedback that demonstrated the gap between the *observed* performance and the *expected* performance did they observe a change in the process. When the challenge of the MBA, including the criteria and degree of learning was clear, the group began to orient itself to the task at hand. Like the first stage, the second stage also involves orientation. The difference from the first stage, however, is that the group as a whole is motivated to succeed. Shortly after this group realization, the energy of the group crystallized, and a third stage, vying for voice, emerged.

Vying for Voice

With the energies of group members beginning to move in the same direction, vying for voice emerged. This is a period when there is potential for conflict. Team members will have different agendas and ways of doing things and there will be bids for power over the group and within the group. In this third stage, adversity and diversity in thought and action originating from different experiential vantage points emerged as often as did persuasion and provocation. There was also a sense among the physicians that the diversity of talent in the group was useful for better decision-making.

Perseverance through this stage is important if the group is ever to become a team. The third stage is the greatest challenge for the team-to-be as the convergence of individually based norms of behavior that are centered around self-interest is reconciled with the more universally accepted norms of behavior, which assure fairness and equal dignity to each human person.

While recognizing the dynamics of this third stage, the physicians also noticed that this stage never goes away completely as the team development process continues. Vying for voice is a subprocess within the overall process of team development and is key to the success of the team.

"Action learning" is a subprocess of team building.[142] It has been suggested that action learning is an ethical addition to the team process because each team member can voice his/her opinion. All members can present and can argue their opinions. Depending on the level of resolution of the conflict between self-interest and universal norms on different topics of their study program, the physicians reported that there were different outcomes. Better communication, greater respect, and sharing of information occurred when a greater number of members of the team reached a consensus on the direction of the action to be taken.

Constructive Communication

During constructive communication, members have the opportunity to exhibit true team behavior. Individual egos are still active but in greater awareness of a common mission. All can contribute and will be listened to, regardless of the intensity or diversity of their voices. Problems will be worked through until the majority reaches consensus. Working through the problem ensures optimal learning about the problem issue itself. As this stage continues, synergy within the group develops.

Synergistic Collaboration

In contrast to individual behaviors or a series of individual behaviors, synergistic collaboration occurs when the team's overall discipline, determination, and dedication work to make the best decisions that can be made. Synergistic collaboration may not be a stage at all since it surfaces and disappears seemingly on its own. The longevity or brevity is not dependent on individual behavior but on the synchronicity of a team's behavior. In fact, one physician remarked that working to maintain synergy often causes it to diminish.

Value of Diversity

The physicians in the previous section identified many of the variables that have been researched in the literature on teamwork. Ann and Bob Harper, in their 1998 book entitled *Skill-Building for Self-Directed Team Members,* suggest that successful teams have a shared goal, a climate of trust and openness, honest communication, diversity valued as an asset, members who are interdependent, and consensus decision-making where no one person dominates the team. The Harpers discuss turning conflict into opportunity and having adults participate in mature continuous learning. They identified that the value of diversity of the group can be useful for better decision-making. Diversity of opinions, ideas, and experiences is encouraged rather than practicing "group think," where differences are viewed as deviance from the norm.

In order to succeed, everyday leaders need to know that team learning requires a kind of "shadow" design to operate. The process in question may have suppliers in other units of the "regular" (formal) organization, and the customers of the process may be in yet a different set of units. Thus a team that comes together to work on a process that is causing trouble may be diverse or multidisciplinary (sometimes referred to as cross-functional vantage points) and be composed of individuals from a variety of formal organizational units or professional backgrounds. Indeed, the suppliers and/or the customers involved may even be outside the formal organizations. It is the transient nature of these teams that makes them work and prevents their interference with the ongoing activities of the formal organization. Berwick[143] suggests that teams must be created and trained with competent leadership to tackle complex processes that cross customary department boundaries.

Everyday leadership using the L.E.A.D.E.R.S. Methods Skills,[144] described in chapter 4 of this book, can make the road to team success much easier to travel. Professionals must come out of their individual departments and professional orientation to form multidisciplinary groups and collectively take responsibility for organizational processes. Members of multidisciplinary teams must develop common goals, engage in cooperative and coordinated activities, and take advantage of a mix of professional skills. These heterogeneous groups have the potential to provide a breadth of ideas and prevent the limited mindsets that inhibit creative problem solving.

Diversity Problems

Multidisciplinary groups, however, bring their own sets of problems and limitations. Bettenhausen[145] remarks, "Most studies have found that diversity hinders group and organizational performance, especially in times of crisis or rapid change." Malfunctions can arise from a complex of individual member characteristics and group dynamics such as territoriality (by department or profession), role confusion, or lack of experience/training in-group processes. Gaucher and Coffe[146] observe that multidepartmental teams go through the four stages described below: form, storm, norm, and perform.

Form

During this stage, members wait for their roles to be clarified before addressing the issue at hand. The focus is on the team leader and on domineering team members.

Storm

During the "storm" stage, there is an interchange of ideas, but they are oneway, critical, and conflictful. The leader becomes less of a focus.

Norm

In this stage, conflict is addressed and reduced as objectives are clarified, people become comfortable with the ground rules for group behavior, and trust and common interests are developed. At this point, the leadership must challenge the group to set and reach new goals and try new techniques and approaches to spur group development.

Perform

Team members contribute data, facts, and logic and are motivated by the results. Team members share leadership according to their knowledge and skills, and the task gets accomplished effectively and efficiently.

Understanding Change

Kochan and Useem[147] suggest that learning is essential for engaging in systemic, continuous change and going beyond the isolated shifts and periodic lurching observed in so many organizations. They also suggest that the organization that has learned how to learn will master the challenges of change. For this to happen, there must be members of the work system acting as everyday leaders. The Team Learning System, described in greater detail in chapter 3 of this book, puts team members in situations where they "learn how to learn" in a team, each participating as an everyday leader. There are three mutually reinforcing features of the Team Learning System: innovation, a learning culture, and diversity.

Innovation

Faster innovation and flexibility help to ensure that hierarchic authority, centralized control, and fixed boundaries give way to cooperative designs that rely upon work teams, decentralized decision-making, and informal networks crosscutting formal boundaries. This fosters reciprocal information-sharing, shared commitment to sustained cooperation, and a common set of values.

Learning Culture

The Team Learning System requires a learning culture that stresses learning about business basics as rendered, for example, an MBA program with all of the standard knowledge components and the relationships among them, such as how finance integrates with human resources and marketing with computer systems.

Diversity

Diversity is an integral part of the Team Learning System and is utilized thoroughly rather than being simply managed or valued. The organization will capture the innovative potential of all participants. They are allowed to discover and act and not be limited by a hierarchy. When everyone in the organization is prepared for change, then everyone is capable of learning and enabled to act on his or her new knowledge.

Teams are an integral part of learning. In fact, learning about everyday leadership happens faster in teams.

Effective and Ineffective Teams

Examples of outcomes of effective and ineffective teams, as they respond to certain characteristics/attributes, are shown in the following chart (table 3-1). For example, when the goals are leader-generated, the team often does not feel ownership or a motivation to achieve the goals; when goals are team generated, the group has "buy-in" and will work toward goal achievement.

TABLE 3-1
Effective and Ineffective Teams

	Effective	Ineffective
Goals	• Clearly understood • Team-generated • Good match of goal to individuals and group • Stress on cooperation	• May or may not be clear • Leader-generated
Communication	• Two-way • Respect for ideas and feelings stated	• One-way • Ideas stated • Feelings not usually
Leadership and participation	• All team members share effort to develop participant-achieve goals	• Leadership based on authority • Stress on obedience • Participation unequal
Decision-making	• Based on situation • Aim for consensus through discussion other than leader	• Based on authority • Little discussion or involvement of members
Attitudes toward conflict	• Conflict seen as normal and positive • Opportunity for growth	• Conflict avoided or denied
Cohesiveness	• Acceptance of group members by one another important, leading to trust • Individuals feel free to be themselves	• Members' tasks seem not as important; cohesion not taken into account • Power controls • Conformity stressed
Ability to solve problems	• High	• Low
How group performance is judged	• By members • Emphasis on growth and development	• By authority • Emphasis on maintaining status quo
Effective work groups have	• High group loyalty • Effective interaction skills • High performance goals	

CHAPTER 3 REVIEW

Answers to the review questions and self-test questions are found in the back of the textbook.

Review Questions

3-1. Describe the four stages of multidepartmental teams proposed by Gaucher and Coffey. What kinds of malfunctions arise when teams form?

3.2 What are the characteristics of successful teams described by the Harpers?

3.3 According to the University of Tennessee study, what was needed in the earliest stage for the team to gel? What makes that factor so important?

3.4 Describe synergistic collaboration. Why is it difficult to assess and evaluate?

3.5 What are the three features of the Team Learning System? What makes them mutually reinforcing? Does one carry more weight than the others? Use an example from teams you may have participated in in the past to assess each.

3.6 How do goal setting, decision making, and leadership/participation manifest themselves in an effective team environment? In an ineffective team environment? Describe two new team attributes, not shown in table 3-1, and describe the outcome for effective and ineffective teams.

3.7 What is "action learning" and how does this subprocess fit in to the overall team dynamic?

3.8 Which stage of the University of Tennessee study presents the greatest challenge to the formation of a viable team? In what way do individually based norms and universally accepted norms influence the outcome? In what ways does diversity hinder the performance of groups and organizations? Does this occur at any special time of change?

3.9 Define, compare, and contrast team "group think" with "diversity of opinions, ideas, and experience." In what situations of team dynamics will one produce a better outcome than the other?

Self-Test Questions

T F 3-1. Leader-generated (as opposed to team-generated) goals are generally more realistic and therefore pivotal to the success and effectiveness of teams.

T F 3-2. Form, storm, norm, and perform are the four stages of a multidisciplinary team.

T F 3-3. The University of Tennessee study found a diversity of talent contributed to better decision-making.

T F 3-4. Via the Team Learning System, team members "learn to learn" and participate as everyday leaders.

T F 3-5. Centralized control and fixed boundaries are counterproductive to effective work teams.

T F 3-6. For a team to be successful, it is essential that conflict be addressed outside the normal team working process.

T F 3-7. Vying for voice is one of five stages of team development and disappears once the team forms constructive communication.

T F 3-8. Learning about everyday leadership occurs more quickly in a team environment

T F 3-9. Focusing on the maintenance of team synergy ensures it will flourish.

T F 3-10. The University of Tennessee study found that when clear goals are articulated, the group as a whole becomes motivated to succeed.

CHAPTER 4

Fundamental Four: Leading Organizational Change at Work

Learning Objectives

4-1. Understand the nature of organizational change and, specifically, the differences between continuous and discontinuous change
4-2. Become familiar with the change matrix and its elements: tuning, adaptation, re-orientation, and re-creation
4-3. Learn the steps organizations need to take to respond to change
4-4. Know what is meant by an ambidextrous leader and an ambidextrous organization
4-5. Identify CEO constituencies in times of change and how executive management should respond to each
4-6. Become familiar with the L.E.A.D.E.R.S. Method and how it can enhance performance in times of change
4-7. Distinguish between structural and cultural inertia. Know what is meant by the paradox of culture
4-8. List factors that can facilitate change and ones that can be obstacles to change
4-9. Become familiar with the S-Curve and what it means to innovation, discontinuity, and re-design
4-10. Site industry and company examples of change and what can be learned from each

CHAPTER OUTLINE

Change Matrix
Responding to Change
Designing Corporate Architecture
Managing Multiple Cultures
Ambidextrous Managers and Leaders
Leadership Requirements in Times of Change
The Board
CEO Constituencies
CEO Executive Management Challenges
CEO/Executive Management Responsibilities to Enhance Performance
Other Factors in Times of Change
Elements That Facilitate Change/Provide Barriers to Change
Lessons from Industries and Companies in Times of Change

Introduction

The core competency for business leaders in the twenty-first century will be change management. Organizations are moving from an era dominated by incremental change to one of discontinuous change, thus altering the fundamentals of organizations. Discontinuous change transforms the core aspects of an organization including leadership capability, corporate identity, and organization architecture.

Almost all successful organizations go through periods of incremental change punctuated by discontinuous or radical change. This can be caused by a number of factors. First, deregulation such as in the financial and airline industries led to waves of mergers and failures as companies worked frantically to redesign themselves. Second, political change such as in Eastern Europe and South Africa has had a similar impact as firms reorient themselves to the radical pressures for change. Third, technological change such as in the microprocessor industry revolutionized the computer industry.

Change can require a redesign of the whole system, and executive management must be ready to adjust radically and even destroy the very alignment that has made their organizations successful in the past. Dealing with these shifts can create havoc for managers and workers, as managers realign their organizations to accomplish the new strategic objectives.

Organizational learning and continuous improvement can help companies address change and succeed. Companies can improve the process of change by using feedback from external markets and from internal systems to refine the organization to get closer to adaptation, alignment, and congruence throughout the organization.

This chapter addresses the types and forms of change; important ways for organizations to respond to change; leadership requirements in times of change; elements that facilitate change; elements that are barriers to change; and lessons from industries and companies in times of change.

Change is inevitable and must be embraced. According to Jack Welch, former GE Chairman: "(In the future) . . . heroes and winners, will be entire companies that have developed cultures that instead of fearing the pace of change, relish it."

Organizational Change

Excellent leadership in business requires responding effectively to two kinds of change: continuous or incremental change and discontinuous or whole system change.

Continuous/Incremental Change

Continuous or incremental change is marked by cost-containment, efficiency, and incremental innovation.

Long-term success is marked by increasing alignment among the strategy, structure, process, people, and culture through incremental or evolutionary change punctuated by discontinuous or whole system change that requires a radical, simultaneous shift in strategy.

Strategy: An organization strategy defines how the organization will respond with products and services to customers and prospects.

Structure: Structure is the division and coordination of tasks using specialization and integration, centralization and decentralization, and formal patterns of relationships between groups and individuals.

Processes: Processes are the defined and measured sequence of steps, activities, and methods to produce specific goals, results, consequences, or output for a particular internal or external customer or market.

Systems: All the procedures for budgeting, accounting, training, etc. that make the organization run and a particular set of procedures, rules, policies, guides, and practices designed to control processes in a predictable way.

Competence: The skills of both employees and managers and the way managers manage and the way employees are placed, oriented, developed, and rewarded.

Culture: The patterns of basic shared assumptions, beliefs, attitudes, expectations, and values as revealed in everyday work performance, practices, policies, processes, and procedures.

People: Bringing all this together requires energizing the people working, the suppliers of resources, and the quality and impact of products and services to produce satisfied customers.

Discontinuous/Whole System Change

Discontinuous or whole system change is almost always driven by organizational performance problems or technological, competitive shifts in the market, regulatory events, or political conditions. Speed, flexibility, and radical innovations are critical to adapt to crises.

Discontinuous change is more about improvisation than management. The organization needs to be agile and adjust to shifts as they unfold. Effective change leaders allow change to emerge and develop within a common set of values, norms, and operating principles.

Whole system change requires an appropriate combination of central, lateral, and local initiatives. The artistry of leading change is determining appropriate ownership for all initiatives and how they link together in an integrated whole. The "soft" part of discontinuous change is the most difficult since both the structure and the informal organization must change.

Discontinuous change has associated risks since it can demand action without complete information. Change leadership requires highly personal activity and behavior and informal time with employees to make sure they trust the change process. The key role of the leader is to sell the need for change.

Change Matrix

Change takes a number of forms that can be described as tuning, adaptation reorientation, and re-creation. This change matrix is shown in figure 4-1.

FIGURE 4-1
Change Matrix

	Incremental	**Discontinuous**
Anticipatory	1 Tuning	3 Re-orientation
Reactive	2 Adaption	4 Re-creation
	Source: Nadler and Tushman, 1990	

Tuning: In this case, there is no fundamental change. Incremental change may have been initiated internally in anticipation of environmental events or in the search for efficiency or effectiveness. There has been no real requirement to change and change consists of improving policies, methods, commitment, strategic fit, and other areas.

Adaptation: Adaptation is a result of an imperative to change, otherwise the company will face negative (not life-threatening) consequences. Incremental change results from external conditions in the environment. These require a response and a reaction to the reality of the environment in which the company operates. For example, when Citibank introduced automated teller machines, customers and prospects responded positively and other financial institutions had to follow. Following was at a high cost in terms of dollars and other resources.

Re-orientation: This consists of visionary insights into environmental shifts and involves a fundamental redefinition of the enterprise. The change allows time to redesign the identity, vision, strategy, and values and maintain the fit among the work, capabilities, and attitudes of the people, formal structures, processes, and the culture. For example, between 1988 and 1994, AT&T, went through a major redesign and created a brand-new culture.

Re-creation: In this case, there is a fast and simultaneous change of all basic elements of the organizational system. This usually requires drastic shifts in the core identity of the enterprise. Often re-creation requires the destruction of certain elements that often have been key to past successes. For example, in the 1970s, Chrysler's discontinuity meant the elimination of full-size cars, divestiture of foreign operations, and other actions.

Responding to Change

Discontinuous change requires recognition, strategic choice, and organization change management. But where does one start?

Versatile, skillful companies constantly innovating and taking steps to ensure long-term survival with a variety of business units that support different structures, competencies, and cultures are often referred to as being "ambidextrous." Consistently successful corporations use various resources, skills, and cultures in different parts of the firm to take advantage of technology cycles and to develop new products.

There is a commonality among ambidextrous organizations in the areas of designing corporate architecture, managing multiple cultures, and encouraging ambidextrous leaders.

Designing Corporate Architecture

The design of an organization must be able to respond to a need for a constant alignment of strategy, structure, and culture. To stay agile and responsive, units within the organization should be kept small, manageable, and autonomous. On an ongoing basis, companies need to be certain to stay close to the customer and understand the customer's needs and requirements.

In a quickly changing technological world, companies should also stay ahead of technological developments as they apply to their products and the competitive world impacting their products and customers.

By staying consistent, sharing information, ensuring individual accountability, and establishing financial controls, the organization is setting standards and establishing a clear rationale for inter-unit rules and requirements.

Managing Multiple Cultures

By encouraging a culture of openness, autonomy, and initiative, the ambidextrous company is establishing an environment that is fertile with ideas and problem resolutions. The culture needs to be a loose one, allowing individuals to express their openness, autonomy, and initiative in their own, often unique, way.

Norms and values should be communicated clearly throughout the organization, thus promoting predictability and trust. Multiple organizational cultures will then link together, and create an excellent environment from which new strategies will spring.

Ambidextrous Managers and Leaders

Versatile, ambidextrous managers and leaders facilitate finding solutions by making sure they involve the people who “own” the problem—those who know the context of the problem best. They continually reinforce core values of autonomy, teamwork, initiative, accountability, and innovation to make sure certain problems are addressed as thoroughly as possible.

Ambidextrous leaders involve the whole system guaranteeing nothing important is missed or unaddressed. They do not venerate the past and continually reinforce the core values of autonomy, teamwork, initiative, accountability, and innovation to meet the future, now. Finally, they make certain the organization does not become arrogant and that it remains willing to learn from competitors with humility and modesty.

Leadership Requirements in Times of Change

CEOs and other executives have a responsibility to present the board of directors and other constituencies with the longer-term plans and strategies that anticipate and prepare for change. Executive management should also be ensuring that key employees have the resources that provide a foundation for continuous and discontinuous change.

The Board

Ambidextrous CEOs and other executive managers need to build a board equipped to respond to change. Requirements are that the:

- *Majority of directors are outside directors:* Often inside directors are more beholden to executive management since they are closely involved with day-to-day operations. Outside directors are more likely to question decisions and can bring fresh perspectives from alternate operating environments and cultures.
- *Lead director or directors are elected rather than chosen:* By being subject to election rather than choice, a wider range of thoughts and experiences are brought to bear on the decision. The selection can then be based more on talent and contribution than on other attributes such as influence and popularity.
- *Board meets alone (without inside directors) regularly:* In this way, the board is able to interact without the influence of executive management and is able to arrive at decisions clear of company management influence, subtle or otherwise.
- *Board conducts in-depth review of CEO and other senior executives:* The board has the opportunity to assess the CEO and executive management to be certain goals are being met and the needs of the owners (e.g., individual stockholders, institutions, and others) are being addressed.
- *Board embraces long-term goals:* The board needs to have the tools to support the long-term plans and goals of the organizations and provide guidance for reaching the set objectives.

- *Board attends fully to the job of selecting the best CEO:* When the need arises, the CEO position needs to be carefully vetted by the board to make certain that the position is filled by an executive with the talent and experience to meet the challenges of the company, working environment, and culture.

CEO Constituencies

In a world of rapid change, the CEO has several constituent areas to address carefully:

- *Board:* Sarbanes-Oxley is only one of many reasons for increased board involvement becoming a fact of life. The CEO needs to ensure the board works cooperatively with the CEO. Checks and balances that provide the board with the opportunity to address problems quickly and directly are imperative.
- *Shareholders/Finance Committee:* Shareholders and members of the finance committee require candor, a realistic assessment of current and future situations and scenarios, and accurate information and accessibility.
- *Governmental/Regulatory:* CEOs must have a mix of cooperative and confrontational skills. (For example, full disclosure may or may not be the best strategy when aggressive SEC prosecuting attorneys see problems where none exists.) The need for diplomatic and negotiating skills will only increase over time as regulation requires more and more transparency.
- *Senior Management:* The CEO has to set clear and challenging priorities and be certain senior management is motivated to provide outstanding performance.
- *Customers and Suppliers:* Both need to be treated as if they were partners, with the respect associated with a partnership.
- *Employees:* Providing ongoing job enrichment, self-managing teams, and broader spans of control all serve to reinforce the importance of all employees.

CEO/Executive Management Challenges

Leading change is challenging and requires the CEO and other executive managers to tap their deepest values and aspirations. The CEO's every word and move are often noted and interpreted, and it is, therefore, important to think and act carefully and thoughtfully. The development of a skilled senior team that does not allow itself to become insulated from the rest of the organization is vital.

The CEO position often carries with it enormous power and responsibility. The CEO needs to recognize the line between having a healthy self-image and excessive narcissism. Seeking candid feedback from trusted associates or a trusted personal advisor, acknowledging weaknesses, and using facts to support recommendations are important elements for success.

CEO/Executive Management Responsibilities to Enhance Performance

In addition to responsibilities to the board, constituencies, and themselves, CEOs and executive managers have a responsibility to work with the organization and make certain the resources are in place to embrace change.

Peter Dean in his book, *Leadership for Everyone*, presents skills that, if applied, can help develop great motivators, influencers, and leaders and thus prepare managers to be change leaders. These seven skills are referred to in the L.E.A.D.E.R.S. Method and can serve as a template for companies as they introduce a culture of continuous and discontinuous change:

- *Listen to Learn:* Listening results in learning. In the workplace in times of change, listening takes on even greater importance than just gaining content knowledge. It allows managers to gain insight into other managers and colleagues. This insight and deeper understanding can focus efforts and make sure managers are performing at the highest possible levels.

- *Empathize with Emotions:* Radical change can tax the emotions of managers and other employees. Understanding the emotional base from which a person is speaking helps empathize with that person and offers the opportunity to grasp the content as well as the context of his or her message. With this understanding, it is easier respond to issues and act like a leader, reacting with patience, fortitude, selflessness, and fair play.
- *Attend to Aspirations:* The third step in Dean's Leaders Method is to inspire and assist individuals in developing their goals and meeting aspirations. Change often creates new opportunities for managers and employees and being sensitive to those aspiring to new challenges can ultimately create a powerful workforce.
- *Diagnose and Detail:* All individuals are made up of their particular past experiences and acquired skills. These factors affect attitude and behavior.

In a work environment at a time of change, individuals are affected by specific expectations directly communicated to them; reliable feedback measures; and nonpay incentives such as recognition and rewards. With this in mind, managers can be prepared to understand more fully a person's performance at work.

- *Engage for Good Ends:* After listening to learn, empathizing with emotions, attending to aspirations, and diagnosing and detailing the situation, the manager is prepared to engage for good ends.

It is important to consider intentions, projected rules and standards, and the desired results of actions and comments. Leaders are made up of a combination of skills, history, and the outside forces that affect performance. Engaging for good ends requires stepping back and evaluating these factors in order to benefit colleagues and the organization in change.

- *Respond with Respectfulness:* Leadership and personal initiative flourish when everyone on the change team, for example, feels respected, free to speak, and free to act without prejudgment. When responding to another person, leaders should be open to the possibilities and strengths that a person brings to the table and establish an atmosphere of respect. By supporting words with actions and genuine respect, an atmosphere of trust and respect is created.

- *Speak with Specificity:* Excellent leaders need to choose words carefully and be conscious of their voice, facial expressions, eye contact, and body language. These verbal, vocal, and visual components are essential elements of all interactions and communicate more than any words on a page.

When all elements of communication are aligned to express a point, listeners are better able to grasp content. This is especially important when the organization is in flux, and leaders should speak with specificity imparting a true understanding of the rationale for change.

Other skills that can be improved to enhance performance during times of change include team skills, interpersonal problem-solving skills, ethical decision-making, and presentation skills

Other Factors to Address in Times of Change

Inertia

Structural inertia is resistance to change rooted in the size, complexity, and interdependence and interlinking of the structure, systems, procedures, and processes. An incremental approach to change will probably not work as well as using interventions that engage the whole system for rapid change.

Cultural inertia results from age and success. Here, learning gets embedded in shared expectations about how things are to be done—norms, values, social networks, stories, and myths. The more institutionalized these norms are, the greater the cultural inertia; complacency and arrogance then follow. When confronted with discontinuities, the very culture that helped an organization be successful may now be a significant barrier to change.

Paradox of Culture

Culture is a critical factor in the performance of a business. The paradox is often that the culture associated with the earlier success of the company is the same culture that can lead to its downfall.

Organizational culture can be the key to both short-term success and, unless managed well, long-term failure. Culture can provide a competitive advantage and be an obstacle to innovation and change.

Elements That Facilitate Change and Elements That Provide Barriers to Change

To Facilitate Change:

- Involve employees in planning the change
- Provide accurate and complete information
- Give employees a chance to air their objections
- Always take group norms, values, beliefs, and habits into account as change moves along
- Make only essential changes
- Learn to use problem-solving techniques

Barriers to Change:

- Failing to be specific about a change
- Failing to show why a change is necessary
- Failing to allow those affected by the change to be involved in the planning and process
- Using a personal appeal to gain acceptance
- Disregarding a work group's habit patterns
- Failing to keep employees informed
- Failing to allay employee worries about failure
- Creating excessive work pressure
- Failing to deal with anxiety over job security

Lessons from Industries and Companies in Times of Change

Semiconductor Industry

In the mid-1950s, the vacuum tube industry was the leading state-of-the-art technology. In 1955, with the advent of the transistor, a technological discontinuity, a major change in leadership of the industry commenced. Between 1955 and 1995, there was a shift in the semiconductor industry leadership with Sylvania, RCA, and others dropping out of the product class. Four out of the five leading vacuum tube producers entered the transistor market, but withdrew, unable to compete.

Lesson: Many companies in the vacuum tube industry made serious strategic errors in their attempts to enter the chip market and respond to the changing product market. The common variants of error were:

- They chose not to invest in the new technology or did not invest sufficiently.
- They chose to invest but chose the wrong technology.
- They invested but the organizational culture did not respond in a positive way to the change.

Swiss Watch Industry

In 1955, there were 2,300 firms employing 70,000 persons making mostly mechanical Swiss watches. In the mid-1960s Hattori-Seiko Watch Business made a decision to transform itself into being both a quartz *and* a mechanical watch company.

By the 1980s, two of the largest Swiss watch firms went bankrupt; the number of firms in the Swiss watch industry was reduced to 600 from 2,300; and the number of employees in Swiss firms dropped from 70,000 to 32,000.

Lesson: The Swiss invented both quartz (the new technology) and tuning fork movements (the old technology) but chose to reinvest in mechanical movements and failed.

VCRs

With the innovation of the VCR, competition arose between two standards Beta (Sony) and VHS. As the VCR gained acceptance and demand increased, one kind of product became the standard preferred by customers (VHS). Once the standard emerged (the discontinuity in this case), the basis for competition shifted from the design of the product to the price and features of the product.

Lesson: In this case, companies succeeded (Philips over Sony, for example) by process innovation, driving costs down, and adding features. Competing through price and features continues until a major new product or service is created, at which time the whole technology cycle again commences.

Then, the competition shifts back to product or service variation. (CDs replacing audio tapes; DVDs replacing videotapes; MP3 and iPod replacing CDs; iTunes (and other online services) replacing bricks and mortar.

Apple Computer

Founded in 1976 by Steven Jobs and Steve Wozniak, Apple Computer consisted of a small group designing, producing, and selling the personal computer. The personal computer was a new product with extremely desirable features. The desirable features were not the only reason for success. Apple also had a congruent organization design (structure, systems of manufacturing, marketing, distribution, and accounting/payroll aligned with processes of critical tasks). They had people with assigned roles and a culture of shared values of innovation, commitment, and speed.

Apple's continued success depended on the organization learning what works and what doesn't work. Accordingly, Apple's strategy changed from single product for personal computer users with a focused strategy, to a broader range of products and with a market-wide emphasis on the user, educational institutions, and industrial markets.

In order to ensure congruence of critical tasks, organization design, people, and culture, Apple evolved its strategy based on changing markets and technology. Apple grew and change was required with a different design. More structure, systems, and processes were added for efficiency and control. The culture changed to reflect new challenges as new norms emerged to demonstrate new priorities.

Lesson: As a product type matures (see S-Curve in figure 4-2), the basis of competition changes. For Apple early on, competition was based on product variation. Later competition shifted to features, efficiency, and cost. For the Mac, IBM's OS/2 and Microsoft Windows, product variation spurred competition, until Windows became the industry standard in operating systems. Subsequently, competition shifted to cost, quality, and efficiency.

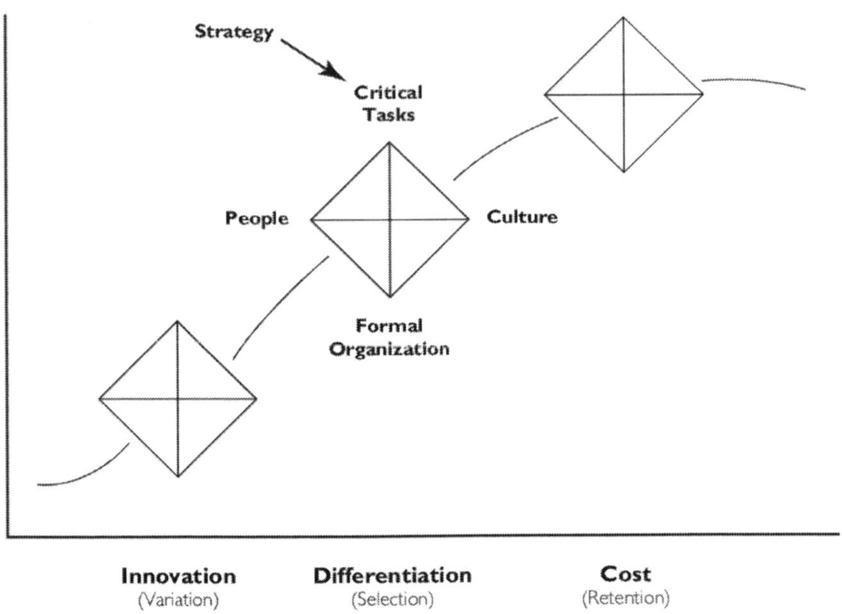

Source: Modified from Tushman & O'Reilly III,1996

Apple had to once again re-design the congruence among strategy, organizational design (the structure, systems and processes), the people, and the culture.

These different periods in Apple's history required radical changes in the design so new strategies would be congruent with structures, competencies, cultures, and leadership skills. Over this thirty-year period, Apple's incremental change was punctuated by discontinuous change and the company has responded, for example, most recently with the iPod, iTunes, and iPhone.

Xerox/Western Union

Xerox developed a graphic user interface (GUI) technology called PARC, but left it to Apple and Microsoft to exploit its paradigm and implement GUI's successfully. Western Union developed technology for telephony and allowed American Bell (AT&T) to capture the benefits.

Lesson: Xerox and Western Union recognized the difficulties in playing two different technological games, one of which had been successful and the other potentially successful, but were unable to resolve difficulties in dealing with this challenge of change.

British Airways

Since deregulation, the airline industry has faced serious cost, market, and competitive problems, with many hemorrhaging money or going out of business altogether.

Lesson: British Airways responded to change through a five-year, well-planned program. The program included a culture change program for its 37,000-person workforce and nearly all its 1,400 managers. The keys to success were that the program had magnitude, consistency, and support from the top.

Nordstrom

Growth in the retail industry requires expansion or acquisition. Nordstrom chose expansion and needed to anticipate a host of internal and external issues and problems.

Lesson: Nordstrom grew successfully from 36 stores and 9,000 employees to 76 stores and 35,000 employees by instilling norms and values and cultivating an improved culture.

IBM

Between 1990 and 1993, IBM lost a total of $14 billion in revenue; 200,000 employees lost jobs; and shareholders lost billions in dollar stock value.

Lesson: IBM's stumble has been a result of an arrogant culture bred by previous success, a sense of entitlement, and a preoccupation with internal procedures, rather than understanding the reality of a changing market.

Sears

Until 1991, Sears was the largest retailer in USA with 800 stores, 500,000 employees, and over 6,000 at headquarters in the Sears Tower in Chicago. Soon after, Sears lost 15 percent of its market share, and the stock price dropped by 40 percent. Chairman Ed Brennan failed to turn the company around and ultimately, in November 2004, Sears merged with Kmart.

Lesson: Like IBM, Sears was seen as having an arrogant culture rooted in a long tradition of dominating the retailing industry. Being prideful, inwardlooking, and resistant to change are obstacles for companies attempting to compete successfully in the twenty-first century.

HP/J&J

HP has gone from an instrument company to a minicomputer firm to a personal computer and network company. Johnson & Johnson (J&J) has moved successfully from consumer products to pharmaceuticals. The credo at J&J and "The HP Way" provide the shared norms and values that promote trust and predictability. Managers aren't second-guessed by headquarters, and strategy flows from the bottom up. In return for the autonomy managers are granted, there are strong expectations of performance.

Lesson: Hewlett-Packard and Johnson & Johnson have been able to compete in mature markets through incremental innovation and in emerging markets and technologies through discontinuous innovation. They have learned to keep units small and autonomous so that employees feel a sense of ownership and are responsible for their own results; flatten the hierarchy, yet retain the benefits of size and brand name in marketing and manufacturing; and keep decisions close to the customer.

CHAPTER 4 REVIEW

Answers to the review questions and self-test questions are found in the back of the textbook.

Review Questions

4.1 Describe the difference between continuous (incremental) change and discontinuous (whole system) change.

4.2 In order for a company to respond to change and succeed in the longer term, it needs to align its structure, people, processes, and what other four factors? Of all seven, which three would you say have the greatest impact and why?

4.3 List the elements of the change matrix. Describe why ones are considered incremental, anticipatory, reactive, or discontinuous.

4.4 What do we mean by "ambidextrous" when describing leaders or organizations? Why is it important in times of change?

4.5 How did the Paradox of Culture impact Apple, IBM, Johnson & Johnson, IBM, and Sears?

Self-Test Questions

T F 4-1. Whole system change refers, for example, to the systems that a purchasing manager is using to distinguish the calculation of sales tax for the whole country.

T F 4-2. In the change matrix, a good example of "tuning" is how other providers of cell phones have to respond/will be responding to Apple's introduction of the iPhone.

T F 4-3. In order to stay agile, and respond to change, units within an organization should be kept small, manageable, and autonomous.

T F 4-4. The development of a skilled senior team that stays above the fray of everyday operations is vital for ensuring the organization is not distracted from achieving goals.

T F 4-5. Ambidextrous companies are ones that are versatile and skillful, constantly innovating and taking steps to ensure long-term survival.

T F 4-6. Structural and cultural inertia both are essential elements of an organization's long-term success.

T F 4-7. Verbal, vocal, and visual components are essential elements of all interactions and communicate more than any words on a page. This is part of the "S" element of the L.E.A.D.E.R.S. Method.

T F 4-8. Among other things, the S-Curve demonstrates the need to reformulate the strategy, design, people, and culture of an organization on an ongoing basis.

T F 4-9. Had they invented the quartz technology, the Swiss watch industry would most likely be the leader in that category today.

T F 4-10. The VCR industry is a good demonstration that once a standard emerges, competition shifts from the design of the product to price and features until a major new product or service is created.

CHAPTER 5

Fundamental Five: Leading by Way of Feedback and Self-Disclosure

Learning Objectives

5-1. Appreciate the concept of spheres of influence and how they can help or hinder group interaction
5-2. Recognize how one person's sphere interacts with another's sphere and creates a meaningful experience
5-3. Identify important messages and use feedback effectively
5-4. See how the Johari Window enables individuals to improve the way they influence those around them
5.5 Appreciate that self-disclosure and soliciting feedback can increase group trust and group effectiveness
5.6 Recognize the need for both individual and environmental change when organizational change is required
5.7 See how leaders should not always be at the top of an organization; rather they should be everywhere in the system

CHAPTER OUTLINE

Introduction

Everyone in an organization has a *territory of influence* or *sphere of influence* irrespective of his or her position in the system. This influence can be defined as an ability to affect change in a given group or environment at a specific point in time. It can be used for better or worse, productive or nonproductive activity, or the individual can choose not to act but to simply observe. If the individual chooses to influence that sphere with an active and positive assertion of leadership, then the sphere benefits. This proactive, positive leadership can be practiced one conversation at a time in every interaction with one individual, a small group, or a larger group. Every conversation has the potential to influence and benefit the development of the individual and the growth of the group. Yet it is up to the individual to decide how he or she is going to use that sphere of influence.

Sphere of Influence - All Leaders Have One

Within their sphere of influence, everyday leaders can choose to affect behavior, motivation, cohesion, and the growth of others within the group. The individual decision to lead in one's own sphere increases the common knowledge of the individuals and reduces the misperceptions or blind spots people often have about one another. Also, it dismantles any unreal facades that can be created intentionally or unintentionally.

When an individual's sphere interacts with another's sphere, that whole, greater than the sum of the two parts, lends itself to a meaningful experience for the members and a productive vision of how work may proceed. For the purpose of doing work, collective cognitive ability becomes the basis for the vision of the organization as a whole. This occurs within the sphere of influence because each member has been allowed to act as a leader in concert toward a common goal. With individuals acting as leaders in their own sphere, all members accept that anyone can lead and relinquish the moment to the most promising or best idea in the discussion. This is a productive conversation.

In this environment of conversation, communication becomes better, change occurs faster, courage is taken, and people seem to care more for their work and the organization. The result is that better listening occurs, empathy is practiced, aspirations can be fulfilled, details of problems are worked out more easily, ethics emerge in conversations, respect abounds, and conversations have specific discernible directions. From the observation of others, leadership seems to float among members and not be held hostage by one or two individuals. All members develop as leaders, not just the boss.

Leading in Your Sphere of Influence

A leader's sphere of influence can expand through disclosure and feedback.

Disclosure

Listening and empathy allow us to build relationships. Discovering others' aspirations and revealing our own are pivotal goals for everyday leaders. Through these connections, leaders develop other crucial skills including diagnosing details, engaging with ethics, responding with respectfulness, and speaking with specificity.

Feedback

There are some things we know about ourselves and some things we don't know. There are some things that others know about us and some that they don't know. An everyday leader would attempt to expand the common knowledge of both parties in order to expand the potential for productivity, much like a transformational leader. We must be sure we receive *spherical feedback,* understand it, and can identify the most important messages so we can use the feedback effectively. If we see ourselves as others see us, we have the opportunity to develop and grow, and can then effectively attend to the aspirations of others.

The Johari Window

The Johari Window in figure 5-1 illustrates this point. Developed by psychologists Joseph Luft and Harry Ingram in the 1950s, it is a framework for understanding and analyzing human behavior and interaction.

Note that a change in one quadrant will affect all the other quadrants. Luft believed that enlarging the "know/know" Open Quadrant would be more rewarding and satisfying to the individual, and that this greater knowledge of oneself in relation to others would lead to greater self-esteem and self-acceptance. The Johari Window is a powerful tool for enabling individuals to see and improve the way they influence those around them.

FIGURE 5-1
Johari Window

	Known to self	**Not known to self**
Known to others	Arena *My common knowledge arena*	Blind Spot *My blind spots that no one has told me about*
Not known to others	Façade *My secrets that I haven't told anyone*	Unknown *The hidden potential that I never thought I could do*

Through the giving and receiving of feedback and building of trust, blind spots and secret areas become smaller and hidden potentials are explored for both individuals to attain their aspirations. As you develop this relationship with another person, the potential for leadership from both individuals increases. There are things about each of us that are not relevant to the leading relationship we have with others. As those things that are relevant are shared and are found to be helpful to the other person's aspirations, they can lead to a more trusting relationship.

Quadrant I or "Arena"

Quadrant I or "Arena" concerns pertinent information known both to ourselves and to others. The effectiveness or quality of an interpersonal relationship is often controlled by the information in this arena. The larger the arena, the more rewarding and effective will be the interactions within the relationship.

Quadrant II or "Blind Spot"

Quadrant II or "Blind Spot" concerns pertinent information unknown to ourselves and known to others. Since a party to an interpersonal relationship cannot act effectively on information he or she does not have, a large blind spot inhibits personal effectiveness and limits the size of the arena.

Quadrant III or "Facade"

Quadrant III or "Facade" contains pertinent information known to ourselves but unknown to others. This can be considered as a protective aspect of the relationship, in that the pertinent information is kept to oneself. As with the blind spot, this inhibits interpersonal effectiveness and limits the size of the arena.

Quadrant IV or "Unknown"

Quadrant IV or "Unknown" contains pertinent information that is unknown to ourselves and to others. This might include unknown potentials, learned idiosyncrasies, intuitive thinking patterns, or psychodynamic data. As interpersonal effectiveness is increased through feedback and self-disclosure, the size of the "unknown" should decrease.

Individuals differ in the degrees and effectiveness with which they disclose information and receive feedback. Individuals can determine the relative sizes and shapes of all four quadrants. Below are examples of various potential outcomes.

Analyzing each of the "windows" shows how sharing, responding, and receiving influence our spheres, where A=Arena; B=Blind Spot; F=Facade; and U=Unknown.

The Ideal Window - open in sharing information and responsive to receiving information from others. The size of the "arena" increases with the level of trust in the group, and norms are developed for giving and receiving feedback.

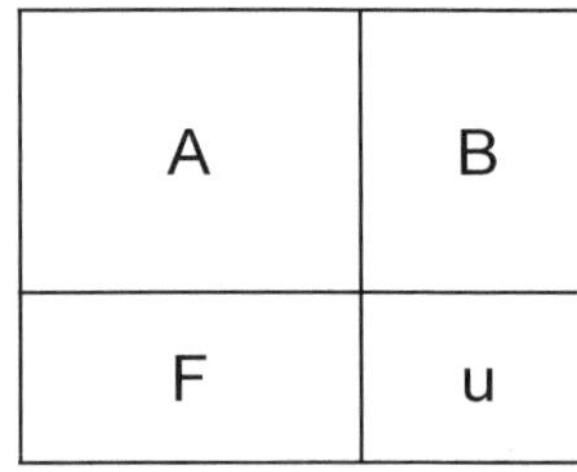

The Interviewer - overuses feedback while lacking self-disclosure, dominated by the "façade." Solicits information while rarely stating their own ideas or opinions. They want to know where other people stand before committing themselves to an issue. They appear to distrust others and may be seen as manipulative or superficial.

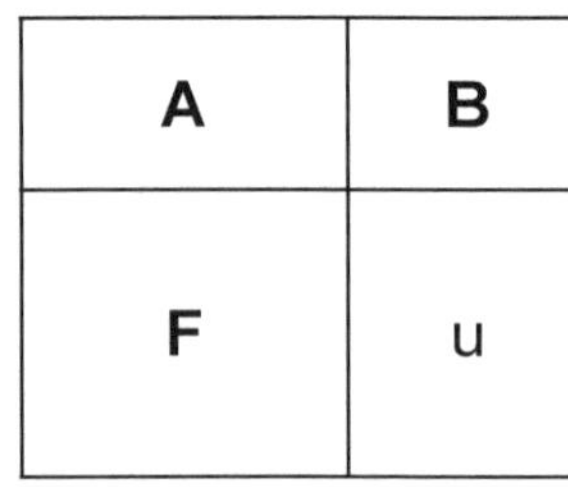

Bull in a China Shop - overuses self-disclosure and lacking in feedback, dominated by "blind spot." Gives feedback but does not solicit feedback. May not value the opinions of others or may feel their own opinions are more accurate. May criticize the group and seem insensitive. May be a poor listener or insecure. Will persist behaving ineffectively because of unawareness of what needs to be changed.

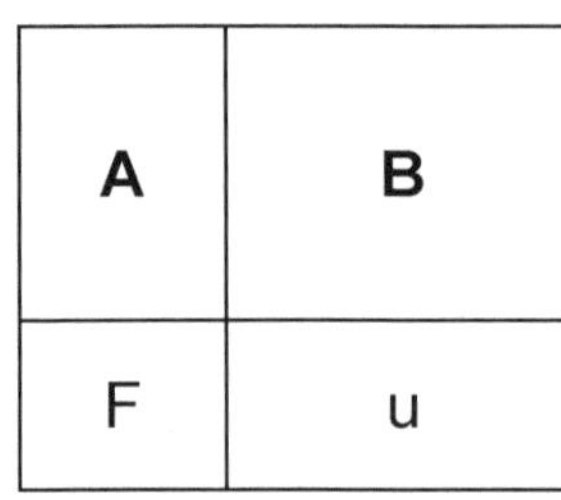

The Turtle - makes minimal use of both self-disclosure and feedback. The "unknown" region dominates. May be the silent member or observer who neither gives nor asks for feedback. Risk avoider, anxious in interpersonal situations, and uncommunicative.

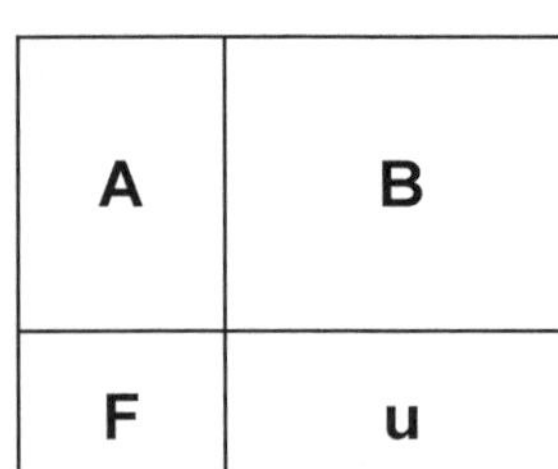

The Arena: Ideal Situation

Engaging in a balanced and extensive use of both soliciting feedback and self-disclosing feedback tends to increase the size of the Quadrant I Arena. This is considered the "ideal window" for everyday leaders. The size of the arena increases as the level of trust in the group increases and the norms that have been developed for giving and receiving feedback facilitate this kind of exchange. As a consequence, there is less likelihood of misunderstanding and fewer projections of personal meanings. Very little guesswork is needed to understand what a person is trying to communicate when his interactions are open both in terms of soliciting and giving feedback.

It is not necessary to have a large arena with everyone. The persons with whom you have a casual acquaintance may see this kind of openness as threatening or inappropriate. However, when individuals make their feelings, perceptions, and opinions public in significant groups or relationships, then game behavior is reduced or eliminated.

The Facade

An individual who overuses feedback while underusing self-disclosure has a style dominated by the "facade." He or she is called the interviewer. Persons with this style tend to respond to the expectation of maintaining a reasonable level of group participation by soliciting information. Their communications are marked by "Tell me what you think about . . ." or "Give me your ideas on . . .," while rarely, if ever, saying such things as "I think . . .," or "I feel . . ." This is because they want to know where other people stand before committing themselves to an issue.

Since these individuals do not commit themselves to a group, it is hard to know where they stand. As a result, they appear to distrust others and may be seen as manipulative or superficial.

Other members of the group may confront them with: "You are always asking me how I feel about what's going on, but you never tell me how you feel." This style, characterized as the "interviewer," may eventually evoke reactions of irritation, distrust, and withholding on the part of the other group members.

The Blind Spot

On the other hand, the individual who overuses self-disclosure and underuses feedback has a style dominated by a "blind spot." This style comes across as a "bull-in-a-china-shop." This person maintains his or her own level of interaction primarily by self-disclosing or giving feedback, but rarely solicits feedback. He may not value the opinions of others or may feel his own opinions are more accurate and that others don't have any information to add that he or she doesn't already have. Here communications take the form of *"I think . . .,"* or *"I feel . . .,"* and rarely include *"How do you feel?"*

These individuals may see themselves as being open and above board and yet may criticize the group as a whole or even lash out at individual members. Generally, they may appear insensitive to the feedback given or not open to it at all. They can be poor listeners, insecure, or may respond to feedback in a way that makes group members reluctant to continue to provide the feedback. As a consequence, these individuals do not appear to utilize the corrective functional reality of group feedback and many of their reactions or self-disclosures appear out of touch, evasive, or distorted. The result of this one-way communication is that the individual persists in behaving ineffectively because he does not know the behaviors that need to change. Further, the group members may feel cut-off, unvalued, or of little interest to the person whose "blind spot" dominates the interpersonal relationship. The group may respond by withholding even more information, thus further increasing the size of the individual's "blind spot." He or she is then seen as a "bull-in-a-china-shop."

The Turtle

When an individual minimizes the use of both self-disclosure and feedback, the "unknown" region dominates. He or she may be the silent member or the "observer" in the group who neither gives or asks for feedback. He is a mystery because it is hard for others to know where this person stands. The person with this style is a risk-avoider, highly anxious in interpersonal situations, and generally uncommunicative. When confronted about this lack of participation, he or she may respond with "I learn more by listening." As we have seen above, listening is critical but must be accompanied by these other skills.

Group members who do not participate get very little feedback and do not provide the group with any data to which they can react. Actively involved group members expose more facets of themselves and provide the group members with more information about which they can give feedback. While this kind of exchange may give the active participant some discomfort, he learns considerably more than the low-profile participant who does not give or solicit feedback. This is a "turtle" profile and takes considerable energy to maintain because of the group pressures to interact.

Insight and Inspiration

The goal of soliciting feedback and self-disclosure or giving feedback is to move information from the blind spot and the facade into the arena where it can be available to everyone and used to improve performance. In addition, through the process of giving and receiving feedback, new information can move from the unknown into the arena. A person may have an "a-ha" experience when he or she suddenly perceives a relationship between a hereand-now transaction in the group and some previous event. Movement of information from the unknown into the arena can be called insight or inspiration.

Lewin's Principles

Lewin[148] added the conceptual tool of tension between the person and the environmental constructs. Being a social scientist (phenomenologist), Lewin stressed the psychological ecology, or the factors in the environment, such as behavioral settings surrounding the individual at work. Here Lewin hoped to identify the immediate determinants of action. Lewin's tools were both practical and ethical.

The principles from the Lewin readings[149] that are important and relevant to the practice of everyday leading include the following:

Individual Workers and the Environment

Understanding the interplay between the work environment and the individual worker is critical for everyday leadership in organizations. Any change in personal growth of individuals within a work group, due to training, for example, should have a correlated effect on social and cultural change within the entire organization. If there is no attempt to change both individuals and the environmental culture of an organization, any change is not likely to succeed. That is why one training session is not likely to bring about significant organizational change. This principle is reflected in the formula B = f (p,e), where behavior (B) change is the function (f) of the person (p) and the environment (e).

Understanding Action Research

To comprehend the system, you must first seek to lead in it through your sphere of influence. Lewin called this *action research.* Accurate measurement of environmental and individual perceptions helps to clarify false perceptions and create correct knowledge about problems blocking the performance of individuals. Gathering, measuring, and evaluating this evidence of perceptions must involve all who create the perceptions.

Action Research and Democratic Values

Scientific thinking (action research) should be combined with democratic values for everyday leadership. Democracy in the practice of change is critical because every work system is a value system as well. It is not possible to have a value-neutral work system. Whereas action research allows for the practice of accurate inquiry and measurement, democracy encourages participants to clarify their own feelings of ambivalence or frustration as well as their own perceptions of what would or would not work. The combination of action research and democracy creates new energy around accepting new values at work as well as the cohesiveness necessary for change in organizations. The more cohesive the group, the greater the readiness for members to influence and be influenced by others.

Lewin[150] contended that is very difficult to be productive if you do things *to* other people. It is better to do things *with* them. His re-educative approach was sometimes called an *action research approach,* which is only a partial use of the principles stated above. A re-educative approach involves those with a stake in the problem helping to accurately define it and solve it. The more involved those who are affected are in the problem-solving process, the more likely a long-lasting solution will be devised. In the first part of this book, a re-educative approach to everyday leadership was suggested.

This approach is based on the idea of systems changing themselves through a communal effort by the people affected by the change. It is repeated here in the context of understanding an everyday leader's sphere of influence.

Other Learning Assumptions

Weisbord and Janoff[151] recalibrated the principles of Lewin and tips of Trist and Emery into the following learning assumptions:

- Each person has a unique learning style. Some learn best by reading, others by doing, still others by discussing or listening. All will benefit by taking action in any way they can.
- Each person learns at a different rate. Hence some may be confused or lost in the early stages. It is okay not to get it the first time you hear it. Try to be patient with yourself and others.
- Each person learns different things from a common experience. Hence we encourage the trading of perceptions and acceptance of different feelings and views.

- Each person learns best from his or her own experience. Hence we urge testing ideas against your own situation and support a healthy skepticism toward a single best way to process change in organizations.

Allowing Leadership to Emerge

A modification of Maslow's criteria to self-actualize helps the everyday leader prepare to lead in his or her sphere of influence. For example:

- Become aware of what is going on between and within individuals
- See life as a process of choices having positive and negative consequences with the end goal being growth
- Be in touch with your essential inner nature, including your values, tendencies, and character tastes
- Be honest about your needs and take responsibility for them
- Learn to trust your own judgment
- Develop your potentialities
- Notice the experiences where you are more aware and you think, feel, and act more clearly; these are the signposts to our strengths
- Recognize your defenses and the way you distort your self-image and the image of the world

No one individual is everyone's leader, but anyone can lead within their sphere of influence with their uniqueness and without being antagonistic. Managers can no longer try to do it all. Managers must share responsibility with subordinates and subordinates need to take action to lead. Men and women in leadership positions can no longer just be at the top of an organization, they must be everywhere in any system of work.

Peter Drucker[152] (1988) suggested in a Harvard Business Review, September–October article entitled "Management and the World's Work" that a system of work is comprised of people with different skills and knowledge doing many different kinds of work. Communication, taking responsible action, clear ethical thinking about consequences, and a show of respect are essential. The aims or goals to be accomplished need to be thoroughly considered and understood by everybody. Each has to know what is owed to the others and what is needed. Others need to know what is expected of them. Clearly, Drucker is saying that relationships and influence are essential.

CHAPTER 5 REVIEW

Answers to the review questions and self-test questions are found in the back of the textbook.

Review Questions

5-1 Briefly describe the quadrants of the Johari Window.

5-2 What kind of reaction from the group does the "interviewer" style evoke? Does this style help, hinder, or have no effect on the growth of the group?

5-3 In what ways does disclosure expand a leader's sphere of influence?

Self-Test Questions

T F 5-1. Providing and receiving information in a relationship increases trust and helps both sides attain aspirations.

T F 5-2. Greater knowledge of oneself in relation to others leads to greater self-esteem and self-acceptance.

T F 5-3. The Johari Window is a tool that can be used to improve the way we influence others around us.

T F 5-4. According to Lewin, it is more productive to do things *with* others than *to* them.

CHAPTER 6

Fundamental Six: Driving Incremental and Radical Change at Work

Learning Objectives

6-1. Understand the implications of incremental and radical change
6-2. Recognize how organizational change influences individual change
6-3. Distinguish the influence of human and environmental factors on the organization
6-4. Identify factors to consider in a changing system
6-5. Understand the design that emerges from different organizational vantage points
6-6. Appreciate the need for systems thinking when dealing with change
6-7. See how the change impacted health care starting in the 1960s
6-8. Identify the kinds of organizations that emerged from the changes to health care
6-9. Understand the terms used when addressing organizational design
6-10. Understand the importance of learning and relearning in a complete system

CHAPTER OUTLINE

Introduction
Change Leadership
Need for Systems Thinking to Address Change
The Organization as a System
A World of Changing Systems
A Tolerance for Learning

Introduction

This chapter discusses the value of understanding how to influence systems for everyday organizational leaders. Organizations are dynamic and complex social systems formed to accomplish goals. Organizational design is a field of study that focuses on the viewing of the organization as a system and how the framework of that system interfaces and influences the performance of the individual. Everyday leadership combines systems thinking with qualitative and quantitative organizational analysis to help choose the best strategy for change with the understanding there is no one best design.

Work Systems

Change Leadership

Leadership of change in an organization emerges when a company of everyday leaders is able to compete successfully by continuously aligning the strategy, structure, processes, and learning to deal with the needs of incremental change while simultaneously preparing for radical change caused by the discontinuous pressure of the external market.

Only people acting as everyday leaders can be involved enough to do this successfully. This requires that the organization be designed to account for *competition* in a mature market where cost, efficiency, and incremental innovation are vital while developing *new products and services* where speed, flexibility, and radical change are critically important.[153] Both of these notions are easily understood, yet focusing on one at the expense of the other may create short-term success but will eventually lead the organization to long-term failure.

Everyday leaders leading organizations proactively align their strategy, structure, processes, people, and culture through incremental evolutionary change. This change is punctuated by radical and discontinuous change that requires simultaneous shifting of the strategy, structure, processes, people, and culture to deal with sudden changes in technology, regulatory events, changes in the political environment, economic conditions, and competitive shifts in the market.[154] It is the knowledge of some kind of a self-designing process that is required to deal with this phenomenon.[155]

Need for Systems Thinking to Address Change

All decisions to deal with system change depend upon the performers acting as everyday leaders both in the organization and in the process they are allowed to use, enabling them to deal with both kinds of change, incremental and discontinuous. Attempting to adapt to discontinuities through incremental adjustments is not likely to succeed. Attempting to go it alone is also not likely to lead to success. If you influence the design of the organizational system, you influence that system, which has a direct influence over individual performers. Using systems thinking for the entire organization will result in success if the members see themselves as everyday leaders. When members act as everyday leaders, companies better organize themselves and deal with the complexities of large organizational life. Everyday leaders must have knowledge of systems thinking and processes, such as the *probe learning, team learning, action research,* and *large group interventions.* These processes help the everyday leader in self-designing the inside of a system in order to help lead the changing destiny of an organization.

The Organization as a System

Organizations are dynamic and complex social systems formed to accomplish goals. Organizational change focuses on the viewing of the organization as a system and how the framework of that system interfaces and influences the performance of the individual.

Factors and Behaviors in Changing Systems

Recognizing there is no one best design, one approach to change is to combine systems think theory and qualitative and quantitative analysis to help choose the best strategy for change. However, anyone can attempt to bring about the best interface of the key factors in an organization in their own sphere of influence.

Factors considered in changing systems include the people performing their jobs; the measurement of the performance; the processes that make up the tasks the people perform; the systems that comprise the processes; the arrangements of the hierarchy and reporting relationships that make up the formal structure; the informal structure professionals create for themselves; and how the strategy of the organization aligns itself to all the aforementioned factors.[156] These factors are underpinned by the following organizational behaviors of everyday leaders: recognition of individual differences in workers, accurate perception of performance, correct assumptions about the motivation of workers, the information technology of organizational communication, the influence of conflict, and collaboration on both group and team dynamics.[157]

In addition, change systems involve developing a process to support both organizational learning and individual learning.[158] The qualities central to changing systems are interpersonal communication, equity, fairness, free speech, teamwork, learning, and re-learning. These are core qualities for the motivation of an everyday leader.

A World of Changing Systems

Today, the words organization and change are closely linked because designing the workplace environment is a complex and never-ending process. The challenges of change in business today are global in scale. These challenges range from sophisticated global competition and cooperation and demands for improved quality to the pressure to reduce the time it takes to communicate, produce, deliver, and respond to cost-cutting and downsizing agendas. Global enterprise requires that organizations move toward adaptive systems capable of creating change and maintaining organization.

This will only happen with a team where all act as everyday leaders. These are among the realities of today's world. These and other socio-political and economic forces drive the need for change in organizations. The swift and demanding currents of change exist in the public and the private sectors. They are constantly negotiated and renegotiated in response to immediate crisis and the practicalities of change.[159]

Because organizations are complex social systems and the external challenge to these social systems add more complexity to understanding leadership, everyday leaders should equip themselves with the systems effect on individuals at work.

A Tolerance for Learning

The "learn how" of an organization is crucial for good organizational design. According to de Geus,[160] enterprises die because managers focus only on the economic activity of producing goods or services and they forget that their organizations' true nature is that of a community of humans who are able to learn and adapt. A study performed in Royal Dutch/Shell Group[161] found that the ability to return investment to shareholders seemed to have little to do with longevity. Profits were necessary for short-term cash flow and to focus the company but were not a predictor or determinant of corporate health. De Geus[162] suggested that profits were a symptom of health and not the root cause. He suggested that the root cause was the company's ability to grasp the need for change and adapt to it. De Geus went on to suggest that a key to survival was an organization's tolerance for learning. That translates into giving employees a certain amount of freedom and space to improve the business operations without fear of reprisal. This suggests people should be free to improve on the efficiency of tasks. In addition, the organization is designed so that learning can be disseminated quickly and occur going up, down, and laterally across the functions of an enterprise.

Optimizing Organizational Design

Inflexibility in organizational design brings about rigid assumptions about power and risk avoidance in communication. These are old habits that will not work anymore. Hammer and Champy[163] suggested that this inflexibility comes from the fragmentation of the workforce through specialization, rigid hierarchy, and the control of work not being in the hands of the workers. To deal with the inflexibility of these organizations, Kochan and Useem[164] suggested continuous, systemic organizational change that is integrated and consistent among an organization's major components and a long-term orientation to provide a more suitable foundation for cooperation, learning, and innovation.

Galbraith and Lawler[165] stated that organizations would need to design themselves through innovation and process improvement. They went on to suggest that the successful organizations would be those that can better design their organization to meet the new realities of business. Kochan and Useem[166] suggested that learning and learning how to learn are the essential capacities for an organization to better design itself. Gilbert[167] and Dean[168] suggest that organizational design emerges from individuals operating from different levels of vantage within an organization. These are the different contexts in which one could look at what happens with the organization and, therefore, subsequent changes to design occurring from these vantage points would be more effective. They include the following:

- Philosophical: the ideals under which the organization operates
- Cultural: the larger environment in which the organization exists

- Policy: the vision and missions that define the purpose of the organization
- Strategic: the plans designed to carry out the mission
- Tactical: the specific duties that achieve the strategies
- Logistical: the support system (resources, information, incentives, etc.) that enables workers to carry out duties

Whatever the suggestions for design and change from the many vantage points of an organization might be, one idea begins to become more clear and loom large as a critical need.

Design and Performance

Attempts at organizational design are often limited. Why? Failure often results from a phenomenon that exists as a fundamental attribution error in everyday inferences about cause-effect relations, according to Jitendra Vir Singh[169] of the Wharton School, the University of Pennsylvania.

The fundamental attribution error predisposes individuals to overemphasize humans as the cause of the problem and underestimate the role environmental factors play in causing resistance to plans for change. This results in managerial decision-makers trying not to influence behavior in the workplace by designing organization contexts but by trying to fix the individuals in the workplace. In the past, performance was perceived as separate from the environment within which the performance occurred. There was no concept that how the direction of the company was framed or structured could impact the work and the people. Far less was the idea that the work environment could be a source of revival, renewal, and recreation of energy.

As Singh[170] (1998) suggested above, organizational design decisions directly impact the performance of work. Organizational design, utilizing a performance improvement mental model,[171] speaks to the total system within which physician leaders make decisions about the configuration or architecture of the design factors in the formal organization, including the formal structures, processes, and systems. This sets the tone for how the work gets done, the way the people perform their job, and the morale of the workplace. For example, an excellent leader would work with the distribution of information processes, such as an electronic performance support system,[172] to do the following:

- Effectively communicate expectations
- Continuously feedback the results of performance
- Objectively allocate resources for task support such as tools, materials, equipment, supplies, and, especially, time to do the work
- Consistently base the rewards, recognition, and incentives on the actual work performed

The decisions about the design of an organization have a direct bearing on individual performance. Knowledge of performance improvement models, methods, and measures[173] can be "useful for the diffusion of the design within the organization."

Health Care: An Example of Changing System

In the past, fee-for-service transactions allowed health care professionals to provide services with patients contributing as much of the fees for these services as they could. The fee-for-service model changed during the 1960s and 1970s when the federal government and employers began to pay for health care coverage. As employers began to increase the amount of health care benefits, they began to forecast how much money should be set aside for future health care bills. Designing the organization around these changes challenged health care leaders. Insurance companies responded to this need by offering indemnity policies to employers. The insurance policies were set up so the employer paid a fixed fee to an insurance company, the health care professional provided services, and the insurance company paid usual and customary fees for services.

Employers were willing to prepay a fixed fee to an insurance company to limit their financial responsibility. The insurance company assumed all of the risk associated with the health care bills of those employees for that year. The fee charged by the insurance company was typically calculated by taking last year's costs and adding a profit margin. In this situation, the physician was paid directly by insurance companies and not the patient. If the insurance company experienced rising costs, the premium of the following year's insurance would go up.

The design of this system had cascading effects and may have affected patient care in an adverse way, increasing the cost of health care to the people. Also, new technologies contributed to the rising costs of health care.

A System Changed by Rising Costs

In response to these rising costs, a new way to manage costs emerged in the marketplace: managed care. There was an even greater challenge for those designing organizations and trying to balance patient care and profitability. Managed care made it difficult to focus the design of organization systems totally centered on patient care.

Managed care allows the employer to pay a fixed fee to a managed care company, the health care professional to provide services at a discount, the patient to pay a co-payor deductible, and the managed care company to pay remaining fees for services.

Managed care became a way of providing health care services within a defined network of health care providers who are given more responsibility to manage and provide quality, cost-effective care. In the early years of managed care, there existed a slowing down of health care costs. With the evolution of health care plans and with employers becoming more demanding, the creators of health care plans had to better design ways of eliminating unnecessary and redundant services. This resulted in a consequence where physicians had to think twice about which services to provide in each patient interaction.

Full-risk transactions consist of the following: the employer pays a fixed fee to the managed care company; the managed care company pays a fixed fee to a health system; the health care professional provides services; and the health system pays salary or capped fee to health care personnel. It is possible that by moving from managed care to full-risk contracts, the physician will have more control over how medicine is practiced.

Changes like these require a rethinking, redesigning, and restructuring of the health care enterprises that provide patient care. For this reason, it is important for physician leaders to have knowledge about the field of organizational design.

How Organizational Design Helps Adapt to Change

Information about organizational design can help health care leaders use systems thinking in the design of organizational factors, such as strategies, policies, structures, processes, systems, and tactics.

Organizational design[174] is critical for health care to address the complex issues change now presents. Whether it is a multinational corporation, small business, hospital, HMO, government agency, or religious organization, the design of the organization matters in the overall organizational (and individual) performance. What kind of a shift is needed for an organization to achieve faster innovation and flexibility and to become a learning organization[175] as well as to achieve improved organizational and individual performance?[176] The shift must move from the traditional, closed organization system with a rigid hierarchical structure that stresses centralized control and fixed boundaries to a more open, flexible hierarchy with a participative learning system.[177] It is in this kind of organization where physician leaders and health care professionals foster two-way communication, decentralized decision making, informal networks crosscutting formal boundaries, reciprocal information sharing, shared commitment to sustained cooperation and involvement, and a common set of values.[178] All of these features should be housed within a self-designing learning organization.[179]

Organizational Design and Individual Performance

The following description of organizational design and its influence on individual performance was mostly drawn from Dean,[180] Robey and

Sales,[181] Nadler and Tushman,[182] and Dean and Ripley.[183] Organizational design involves the total system of formal arrangements housing the interaction of the structure, processes, and systems for the purpose of optimal learning. This total system interfaces between humans and the work the enterprise sets out to accomplish. The design of these arrangements can either enhance or hinder accomplishment of the shared purposes of the enterprise. The organizational designer develops these arrangements in such a way as to lead to the alignment among the broad organizational factors of organization, process, and the behavior of the performer.[184] Organizational design manifests through its operations. Charles Noon has shown how the operations manager implements the operational design. Further, the design also needs to include a subsystem of arrangements involving and impacting the immediate work environment, the job, and the health care provider.

The Nature of Organizational Design

The terms used when discussing organizational design are:[185]

- Strategic vision reveals how the organization acts to survive in the marketplace.
- Structure arranges how tasks are divided and coordinated using specialization and integration as well as decentralization and centralization and formal patterns of relationships between groups and individuals.
- Processes are specifically defined and measured using a sequence of steps, activities, and methods to produce a specified goal, result, or consequence for meeting the need of a particular internal/external customer or market. For example, in health care, the different kinds of processes include the following: patient-care processes, task support processes, and information processes.
- Systems include all the procedures for budgeting, accounting, and training that make the organization run using a particular set of procedures/rules, policies, devices, guides, and practices

that are designed to control processes in a predictable way. Examples from a staffing system might include the following:

- o patient application forms
- o patient reference checks
- o patient exit interviews
- o procedure for posting jobs
- o applying for a transfer, etc.

Cooperative learning of physician leaders and health care professionals requires working together for an integration of goals, policies, procedures, standards, information and feedback systems, incentive systems, training, and budget. Healthy alignment of these organizational factors in a balanced design brings about high-quality patient care and a competitive advantage.[186]

Organizational design engages a physician leader to align functional groupings of the formal structures of the health care organization. This alignment requires asking such questions as the following:

- What departments report to what divisions?
- What is the degree of centralization and decentralization?
- What are the budget structures and procedures?
- How is decision-making authority set up?
- How are jobs designed?
- What are the control and coaching mechanisms for performance improvement?
- What is the role of human resource management systems?
- How does the physical location affect the ergonomics of work?

The processes and systems, or the sequence of tasks involved in implementing answers to these questions, must be consistently and flexibly arranged based on their value-added contributions to the health care organization. The explicit and implicit aspects of collaborative learning focus on the work itself. These aspects include the capacity, skill, and knowledge the worker must have, aligned with the provisions of the organization to inform, communicate, support, and recognize the worker's accomplishments. The opportunity to collaborate with fellow coworkers to improve their own performance also is important.

A Complete System

All the structures, systems, and processes, and "learn-how" of the members of the organization, aligned with the strategy of the health care organization, must be considered as part and parcel of one connective system. Without learning and relearning, the system will become closed and unresponsive. Without continual process and systems redesign based on market demands, the system will not be connected with itself or the market demands. Without leadership, the structure will not be designed in a way to compete effectively in the marketplace. Physician leaders who take on organization design in health care enterprise are taking on one of the most critical endeavors for the life cycle of the business in these rapidly changing times of the global market.

CHAPTER 6 REVIEW

Answers to the review questions and self-test questions are found in the back of the textbook.

Review Questions

6-1. According to de Geus and the Royal Dutch/Shell Group Study, what are the most important predictors of corporate health?

6-2. What is the attribution error that often causes organizational design to be limited or even fail?

6-3. Why are attempts to adapt to change incrementally unlikely to succeed?

6-4. Describe the different vantage points or contexts when optimizing organizational design.

6-5. In the health care example of organizational design, what are examples of questions that need to be asked when aligning functional groupings?

6-6. What are examples of factors and behaviors in a changing system? Why is each important?

6-7. In the health care example, what information would an excellent leader include in a performance support system?

Self-Test Questions

T F 6-1. Organizational design is the field of study that focuses on the viewing of an organization as a system and how the framework of that system interfaces and influences the performance of the individual.

T F 6-2. In the health care example, cooperative learning of physician leaders and health care workers requires working together on the integration of items such as goals, policies, and procedures.

T F 6-3. An essential tenet of organizational design is to respond to change incrementally and individually.

T F 6-4. Individuals often overemphasize the role humans play and underestimate the role environmental factors play in causing resistance to plans for change.

T F 6-5. Someone viewing an organization from a cultural vantage point will address the support systems that enable workers to carry out duties.

T F 6-6. Strategic vision describes how the organization acts to survive in the marketplace.

T F 6-7. Singh suggests that managers, incorrectly, often attempt to influence workplace behavior via organizational change rather than through individuals in the workplace.

CHAPTER 7

Fundamental Seven: Leading by Probing Systems at Work

Learning Objectives

7-1. Understand the Behavioral Engineering Model and its six factors
7-2. See how Probe Learning can help identify the work environment that impacts ethical performance
7-3. Explain Strategic Profiling and how it relates to the original PROBE questionnaire
7-4. Recognize the Six Facets of Behavior and how they can help determine leverage points
7-5. Understand the categories of behavior represented in PROBE
7-6. Identify the management implications of behavioral transactions such as "motive and capacity errors"

CHAPTER OUTLINE

Introduction
Systems Learning
Everyday Leaders and System Learning
PROBE Learning
Need for Change
Strategic Profiling
Six Facets of Behavior
Behavioral Leverage in Practice
The General Model
Behavioral Transactions
From Model to PROBE
Chapter 9 Review

Introduction

In the late 1970s, Tom Gilbert and B. F. Skinner, a professor of psychology at Harvard, worked with over three hundred Fortune 500 companies, applying a model put together from the work of Taylor, Lewin, Trist, and Skinner.

Tom Gilbert and Peter Dean worked together at Penn State University for five years before his death in 1996. The author's book, *Performance Engineering at Work,*[186] uses Gilbert's work to create tools to diagnose, prioritize, and plan performance-improvement solutions during change. Gilbert used the work of Taylor, Lewin, Trist, and Skinner to put together his model.

In this chapter, we'll address the Behavioral Engineering Model and review probe learning, strategic profiling, behavioral transactions, motivation issues, and leverage points.

Everyday Leaders and System Learning

Gilbert, in his Behavioral Engineering Model (see figure 7-2), identifies six factors of the interaction between the person and environment that, if aligned, can carry a guarantee of higher performance as long as managers deliver these factors with clear expectations of the role.

Information, Resources, and Incentives

The three top cells of the model are the systems that surround the individual (data, instruments, incentives) – or environmental factors. These include: information on job expectations and feedback; access to managers and resources (tools, time, and materials to do the job); and incentives (financial incentives and nonmonetary rewards).

Training, Capacity, and Motives

Gilbert believed that with these three above mentioned environmental factors in place, the other three lower cells in the model (training, capacity, and motives) would then fall into place. Gilbert believed in the careful selection and development of people, training, performance-based incentives, proper task support, clear goals and a system of feedback. All of these six factors must be considered by management and worker cooperation.

Taylor, Lewin, Trist, and Skinner

Gilbert models on Taylor but packages the work in a system involving the individual worker interacting with the environment that management creates. This is Lewin's interpersonal aspects of life space, which enacted social values that Taylor reached for but could not hold on to. With the point about managing the boundaries of work and supporting the worker's effort and removing the parent-child relationship, Gilbert's model also encompasses Trist's work. Also, the extrinsic conditions of employment due process (expectation, feedback, and access to managers), health and safety (proper task support), fair and adequate pay and benefits (incentives), and job security (motives) are all part of the Gilbert model. Skinner's stimulus, response, and consequence ideas of operant conditioning move across the model from left to right on both levels.

Vantage

Gilbert's work helps individuals see the levels of vantage within an organization. These are philosophical, cultural, policy, strategy, tactical, and logistical.

PROBE Learning

If the organizational culture is reinforcing the standards from all six levels of vantage described in the previous section, then professionalism and productivity abound. If a professional wants to know what kind of culture is reflected in their organizations, the following questions would help them determine how these standards might be used.

The questions focus on expectations, feedback, task support, and incentives for your performance and are designed to begin to uncover the culture of a system of work.

The following PROBE questions are designed to identify the kind of work environment that might affect the ethical performance of stakeholders. The responses are "yes" or "no" to each item. For each "no" response, please explain your perception.

Questions for PROBE Learning

- Are expectations for your performance readily available to assist you to perform well?
- Are expectations clear enough to assist experienced employees to perform well?
- Are expectations and directions accurate?
- Are directions given in a timely manner?
- Do you have all the information you need to do your job well?
- Are clear and measurable performance standards communicated to you so you know how well you are supposed to perform?
- Do you believe the standards are reasonable?
- Does your work-related feedback provided by your direct report describe results consistent with the above standards?
- Is feedback immediate and frequent enough to help your performance?
- Is feedback selective and specific-limited to a few matters of importance and free of "data glut" and vague generalities?
- Is feedback educational-positive and constructively informative so that you can learn from it?
- Are the necessary implements available for the job?
- Are they reliable and efficient?
- Are they safe?
- Are procedures efficient and do they avoid unnecessary steps?
- Are they appropriate to the job and skill levels?
- Are materials and assistance usually available to do the job well?
- Are materials appropriate to the job?

- Is time sufficient to do the job well?
- Do trainees/employees complain about tools, equipment, and facilities? If so, what do they complain about?
- Is the pay for the job competitive?
- Are bonuses or raises given based on good performance?
- Does good performance bear a clear relationship to career advancement?
- Are meaningful nonpay incentives given based on good results, not just completion of assignments?
- Are nonpay incentives not so frequent, or infrequent, as to be meaningless?
- Is good performance free of punishing consequences such as peer pressure on employees who are successful or being asked to "pick up the slack" for someone else when they have finished a project early?
- Is environment free of incentives to perform poorly such as praise for completion of task without regard to outcome?
- Do employees clearly understand the consequences to others and to the organization for both good and poor performance?
- Do they grasp the essentials of performance? Do they get the "big picture" of what it takes to achieve the expectations of their jobs?
- Do employees have the technical concepts needed to perform well?

If these questions have "no" for answers, then it opens the door to explore the actual culture that does exist and gives directions as to ways in which one might seek to change the culture to better reflect the standards.

Need for Change

The need for incremental change originates from attempts at cost containment, efficiency improvements, and local-level innovation. Incremental change requires systems and processes that can undergo continuous change. Yet incremental change and the resulting continuous change are punctuated by the need for discontinuous change, which requires a simultaneous shift in strategy, structure, process, people, and learning. The major drivers for discontinuous change include organizational performance problems, technological advances, competitive shifts in the market, regulatory events, and political events. The Future Search process allows the organization to deal with both kinds of change by allowing the entire system to adapt with speed, flexibility, and radical innovations.

Inflexibility

Inflexibility in organizational design leads to rigid assumptions about power and risk avoidance in communication. These are old habits that will not work anymore. Hammer and Champy[187] suggest that this inflexibility comes from the fragmentation of the workforce through specialization, a rigid hierarchy, and the control of work not being in the hands of the workers. To deal with the inflexibility of these organizations, Kochan and Useem[188] suggest continuous, systemic organizational change that is integrated and consistent among an organization's major components and applied over the long term to provide a more suitable foundation for cooperation, learning, and innovation. Galbraith and Lawler[189] state that organizations need to design themselves through innovation and process improvement. They also suggest that successful organizations will be those that can better design their organizations to meet the new realities of the business environment.

Kochan and Useem[190] believe that "learning" and "learning how to learn" are the essential capacities for an organization to better design itself. Gilbert[191] and Dean[192] suggest that organizational design should emerge from individuals operating at different levels within an organization.

Organizational Needs and Change Opportunities

From these different contexts, a more accurate overall perspective of organizational needs and change opportunities can be gained and therefore subsequent redesign would be more effective. These varied perspectives include:

- Philosophical – the ideals under which the organization operates
- Cultural – the larger environment in which the organization exists
- Policy – the vision and missions that define the purpose of the organization
- Strategic – the plans designed to carry out the mission
- Tactical – the specific duties that achieve the strategies
- Logistical – the support system (resources, information, incentives, etc.) that enables workers to carry out duties

Whatever the suggestions are for design and change from these many vantage points, a central idea will emerge and loom large as a critical need. By ambitiously attempting to create an enterprise that is aligned on all of these variables, Future Search facilitators hope to harness the individual value-added aspects listed above. The organization as a consequence will then perform better and compete more successfully in the global marketplace. Improved performance comes about because the community of humans are learning and adapting to change.[193] Future Search is one practice by which to accomplish this.

Strategic Profiling

This author has found that for strategic profiling of behavior, some fifty to sixty questions nearly exhaust those ever worth asking. Figure 7-1 is an adaptation of the PROBE questions. Although some of the questions were revised slightly to address the work environment of corporate trainers, all the items in the original PROBE questionnaire are represented. Not all questions are relevant to every job or accomplishment. Questions may be answered "yes" or "no." The "no" answers to relevant questions are those of concern, since they reveal possible barriers to excellent performance. An irrelevant question is one that can be answered, "No, but it doesn't matter." Obviously, as many questions as are useful can be added to the list. Some belong in "performance audit" models: "Is efficient or cost-effective training available?" "Are the duties appropriate to the job?" and "How good are the performance standards?"

FIGURE 7-1
PROBE Questions

E-QUESTIONS ABOUT THE BEHAVIORAL ENVIRONMENT

A. Directional Data

1. Are there sufficient, readily accessible data (or signals) to direct an experienced person to perform well?
2. Are they accurate?
3. Are they free of confusion— "stimulus competition" —that slows performance and invites error?
4. Are directions free of "data glut" —stripped down to the simplest form and not buried in a lot of extraneous data?
5. Are they up-to-date and timely?
6. Are good models of behavior available?
7. Are clear and measurable performance standards communicated so that people know how well they are supposed to perform?
8. Do they accept the standards are reasonable?

B. Feedback

1. Is feedback provided that is "work-related" —describing results consistent with the standards and not just behavior?
2. Is it immediate and frequent enough to help employees remember what they did?
3. Is it selective and specific, limited to a few matters of importance and free of "data glut" and vague generalities?
4. Is it educational-positive and constructively informative so that people learn something from it?

C. Tools and Equipment

1. Are the necessary implements usually on hand for doing the job?
2. Are they reliable and efficient?
3. Are they safe?

D. Procedures

1. Are procedures efficient and designed to avoid unnecessary steps and wasted motion?
2. Are they based on sound methods rather than on historical happenstance?
3. Are they appropriate to the job and skill level?
4. Are they free of boring and tiresome repetition?

E. Resources

1. Are adequate materials, supplies, assistance, etc., usually available to do the job well?
2. Are they efficiently tailored to the job?
3. Do ambient conditions provide comfort and prevent unnecessary interference?

F. Incentives

1. Is the pay for the job competitive?
2. Are there significant bonuses or raises based on good performance?
3. Does good performance have any relationship to career advancement?
4. Are there meaningful nonpay incentives (recognition and so on) for good performance (based on results and not behavior)?
5. Are they scheduled well or so frequently as to lose meaning and so infrequent as to be useless?
6. Is there an absence of punishment for performing well?
7. Is there an absence of hidden incentives to perform poorly?
8. Is the balance of positive and negative incentives in favor good performance?

P - QUESTIONS ABOUT BEHAVIORAL REPERTORIES

G. Knowledge and Training

1. Do people understand the consequences of both good and poor performance?
2. Do they grasp the essentials of performance—do they get the "big picture"?
3. Do they have the technical concepts to perform well?
4. Do they have sufficient basic skills—reading and so on?
5. Do they have sufficient specialized skills?
6. Do they always have the skills after initial training?
7. Are good job aids available?

H. Capacity

1. Do the incumbents have the basic capacity to learn the necessary perceptual discriminations with accuracy and speed?
2. Are they free of emotional limitations that would interfere with performance?
3. Do they have sufficient strength and dexterity to learn to do the job well?

I. Motives

1. Do incumbents seem to have the desire to perform when they enter the job?
2. Do their motives endure, e.g., is the turnover low?

There Are No Bad Answers

Every question listed can also be refined into subsets. For example, a "no" answer to the question "Are there sufficient specialized skills?" (question G-5 in the example) can lead to all the questions we might ask to identify specific skill training needs, or to the kinds of job aids that are appropriate. But PROBE isn't intended for use at this level. Its purpose is to profile the barriers to behavior and to help us plot a balanced strategic approach to overcoming them. The questions are designed with sufficient generality to avoid distractions of detail. Highly refined questions are premature and sometimes misleading until the profile is completed.

Battle Strategies

Plotting performance strategy is not unlike planning battle strategies. You first want to profile all of the enemy's strongholds before you attack the most obvious one. It happens sometimes that crippling a minor partition can destroy the effectiveness of the main one. Mindless frontal attacks in battle are not unlike the rush to solution in the human resource business. For example, if the data that direct performance are inadequate and people have poor skills in using them, we would want to examine how improved data might affect the skills before beginning a detailed analysis of training requirements. With better data, we might need very little skill training. Obviously, experience is needed in asking the questions and clearly knowing what you mean by them.

For example, what you mean by the question "Are clear and measurable performance, standards available to people?" (question A-7 in the example) will largely determine your answer. The user will have to establish standards for determining whether a "yes" or "no" answer is appropriate for each question.

It is useful to reword each question carefully (often with examples) to suit the experience and language habits of client users, as well as to match the specific situations in question.

In all but chaotic work situations, a few answers should be "no." But the number of "no" answers tells us little about their importance. For example, asking these questions about the job of a fabrication supervisor produced just two "no" answers. One was to question A-7 above, regarding clear and measurable performance standards and the other was to question F-4: "Are meaningful nonpay incentives given based on good results, not just completion of assignments?" These "no" answers revealed a critical problem. Supervisors are unwittingly encouraged to scrap material because management discusses with them and rewards them only for the control of labor hours.

The method for selecting and classifying these questions will become clear with an explanation of the theory of behavior on which PROBE is based.

Six Facets of Behavior

There are many legitimate ways to look at human behavior. The PROBE questionnaire was developed for its usefulness in engineering more competent performance in the world of work. To understand it, we need to see that we can look at behavior from two points of view. One is: Where is the behavior "located"? Or: Where do we go to "fix" it? The other is: How does it function? Or: What about it do we "fix"?

We often think of behavior as something that occurs within people, almost independently of their environment. It may be more useful to think of it as a product of people's repertories (skills, perceptions, emotions, etc.) and their environment. For example, the behavior of cutting wood requires a repertory of skill, capacity, and motive to handle the ax, as well as an environment consisting of an ax, the wood, data about what wood should be cut, and so on. My performance can suffer if my skill is poor, if my ax is dull, if my motive is weak, or if I am rewarded for cutting the wrong trees. Thus, we can improve or downgrade performance by changing people's behavioral repertories or their environments—or both.

Functional Flow

Another way of looking at behavior is in terms of its functional flow. To maintain behavior, we must receive information (or what psychologists call "stimuli"), act upon it (make a "response"), and be motivated to continue ("reinforced" by the consequences of our actions). We can improve or downgrade performance by changing any of these functions: by changing the "stimuli (SD)," the "responses (R)," or the "reinforcement (SR)," as psychologists put it.

These ways of looking at behavior can be illustrated in an example that should be convincing. We can use an example of assembling a child's tricycle.

My behavior can be altered, that is, my performance improved or downgraded, by changing the following:

- The data that the manufacturer has provided me as the instructions for assembly, by making them clearer or more confusing: All manufacturers whose products I have bought wrote confusing instructions. (El)
- My skill in using that data: My training in reading mechanical instruction was sadly inadequate. (Pl)
- The instruments to do the job: Last Christmas the manufacturer forgot to supply the small wrench that its packing list promised. (E2)
- My capacity to make the required responses: My fingers, eyesight, and temper are all too short. (P2)
- The incentive of a beautifully finished product: Or, sooner or later you'll give up. (E3)
- The motives to do the job. (P3)

Notice that these are not six separate "pieces" of behavior, just six different ways of looking at the same "task."

One could look at the same behavior in many other ways. One could worry about its history, its "deep dynamics," its neurological basis, or its esthetic beauty. Why are these six included? Because they represent largely observable aspects of behavior that we can do something about with reasonable ease. In the world of work, if all of these aspects are maintained at peak efficiency, we won't have to worry about history, neurology, "dynamics," or aesthetics, none of which we do much about anyway. And, if any one of these six factors fails seriously, performance will suffer.

These six also help us sort out the leverage points for modifying behavior. Behavior doesn't have to be at perfect peak efficiency in order for performance to be excellent. On the other hand, any defects in otherwise excellent behavior can make performance an absolute disaster. To see this, let's look again at my cycle-assembly performance.

Behavioral Leverage in Practice

In the example, behavior was not at peak efficiency in any of its six aspects. But each of these aspects does not offer an equal opportunity for improvement in performance. For example, my capacity was largely adequate—

and difficult to improve. Longer fingers would not have resulted in more efficiency, and my emotional capacity for this work—my "temper"—was adequate.

Further training to read and understand mechanical instructions would definitely improve performance, but it would be a long and costly effort. A makeshift replacement for the missing wrench was found. One thing would have helped: improving the data represented by the instructions. Moreover, changing this one aspect of my behavior would have considerable effects on others. With better instructions, my skill requirements would be reduced and motivation heightened.

In other words, if PROBE questions were applied, the following questions would receive "no" answers:

- "Are the directions free of confusion?" (A-3)
- "Are the directions free of data glut, stripped down to the simplest form?" (A-4)
- "Are necessary implements available for the job?" (C-1)
- "Are procedures appropriate to the job and skills levels?" (D-3)
- "Do the performers have adequate specialized skills?" (G-5)

But only questions A-3 and A-4 reveal important opportunities to improve my performance once we analyze the situation. Transfer this concept of leverage from my living room to a tricycle assembly line. The leverage points might change. Now, the beautifully finished product is no longer sufficient incentive. Somebody will have to pay me! Investment in some skill training may become worth it. Working through the poor instructions a couple of times, I may no longer need them, so improving them would have little leverage.

In short, the leverage of each aspect of behavior of improving performance varies from one job to another, from one type of behavior to another and even from one person to another. Each aspect exists in every kind of performance and in every kind of job in the world. One of our tasks in finding ways to improve performance is to sort out the high leverage points in human behavior, PROBE provides a tool for making this analysis.

The General Model

My next step is to help you generalize the PROBE questionnaire beyond the behavior of tricycle assembly by examining the Behavior Engineering Model in figure 7-2. The first row (E) represents the environmental aspects of behavior; the second row (P), people's repertories.

FIGURE 7-2
Categories of Behavior Represented in PROBE

INFORMATION	INSTRUMENTATION	MOTIVATION
Cell 1 - E Data	Cell 2 - E Instruments	Cell 3 - E Incentives
• Direction • Confirmation/feedback	• Tools • Procedures • Resources	• Pay incentives • Nonpay incentives
Cell 4 - P Knowledge	Cell 5 - P Capacity	Cell 6 - P Motives
• Inductive • Concepts • Skills	• Physical • Mental • Emotional	• Intrinsic • Induced

The columns in figure 7-2 are called Information (the Stimulus), Instrumentation (the Response), and Motivation (the Reinforcement). Each of the six cells of the table and their major categories are named.

Cell 1 - Data

Cell One represents data—the environmental aspect of the stimulus—which has two major functions: to give us direction and to give us confirmation (feedback), i.e., "What are we supposed to do?" and "How well did we do it?"

Cell 2 - Instruments

In Cell Two, instruments—the environmental aspect of the response—we have identified three categories: the tools we use, the procedures we follow, and the other response supports called resources.

Cell 3 - Incentives

Cell Three, incentives—the environmental aspect of reinforcement—recognizes two kinds of incentives we can provide at work: contract (pay and benefits) and noncontract (recognition, bonuses, and so on).

Cell 4 - Knowledge

Regarding the aspects based on people's repertories, the first is Cell Four, which is called knowledge—the reportorial aspect of the stimulus. It comprises inductive knowledge, meaning things such as understanding the context, and "whys" of performance; concepts, or the generalizations or theories needed to perform; and skills, or the discrimination that behavior requires. For example, in order to operate a piece of production machinery, we should understand what it does and the consequences of good and bad performance on our part (the inductive), have at least some useful theory of how it works (the concept) and be able to discriminate what the gauges say or which buttons to push (skill).

Cell 5 - Capacity

Cell Five, capacity—the reportorial aspect of the response, is classified as perceptual, physical, and emotional. For example, to climb a power pole well, one needs to be able to see, to have (or be able to develop) the strength and adroitness required, and to be able to overcome my fear of heights.

Cell 6 - Motives

Finally, Cell Six recognizes two kinds of motives—the reportorial aspect of motivation: those we bring to a situation (intrinsic) and those that can be induced by inspiration, drugs, "brainwashing," fear, or other means.

Behavioral Transactions

Now we need to take one final conceptual step to understand how the six cells are parts of a unitary behavioral transaction.

Look at column 1 of figure 7-2, which is called "information," and the cells in the column, which are called "data and knowledge." This is no arbitrary distinction. It is one that is critical to efficient performance analysis. One feature of this model, in fact, is to help us make important distinctions, which, although obvious when they are specifically pointed out, are often blurred in our minds. This model says that information and data are two different things. It points out that they are only the environmental aspects of information. To be truly informed, we must have knowledge of what the data say.

It makes no sense when I say, "I gave them the information, but they didn't understand it." What I really mean is "I gave them the data which didn't inform them." The first statement implies that the employees are somehow lacking. In the second statement, the suspicion is shifted to the environment. For there to be information, the data must be clear and understandable to employees.

Motivation Issues

Similarly, often people say they aren't motivated, suggesting, again, that the problem lies within the employees. Motivation requires both the incentives in the environment and the motives in people (their "desire," "drive," "need"—or whatever you want to call it). So rather than, "I didn't give them adequate incentives," the burden of performance is shifted to the environment. The rat in the Skinner box can help clarify this too-often-blurred distinction. If the hungry animal presses the bar and no food incentives appear, it will soon quit pressing because the environment isn't supporting the motivation. But an abundance of food pellets won't get it to press the bar if it's not hungry—the repertory doesn't support the motivation. Both the incentives and motives must be present for the rat to eat and for people to perform.

Understanding that information is a product of data and knowledge and that motivation is a product of incentive and motive helps stay the rush to a solution. If people don't receive the information they need, perhaps training will help. Improving the data may help even more and often cost less. Or perhaps the greatest leverage requires a little of both.

Management is frequently guilty of what can be called "motive and capacity errors." One error is the easy assumption that the important cause of low motivation lies in employees ("They don't give a damn") and not in the incentives that managers should create. The other is that behavior is inadequate because the employees are "dumb," and not because the manager has supplied inadequate tools, procedures, incentives, training, directions, or feedback.

Leverage Points

The more we use PROBE, the more we find that the great leverage points most frequently lie in the environment—and in training. Seldom do we find much leverage in trying to improve on capacity and motives. That doesn't mean they aren't important; they are vital to good performance. It means that most employees have adequate motives and capacity to do an excellent job if we train them well and provide an efficient working environment. Moreover, the only thing most of us know about capacity and motives is how to select and to recruit people. Unfortunately, we have neither science nor art to do either of these well.

The boss had better hope that he or she has an HRD department that can quickly ask the right questions and find the smartest way to provide the needed behavioral supports. Nothing can mess the boss up more than a rush to a solution, say, a battery of selection tests or a motivational lecture.

From Model to PROBE

Going from the model depicted in figure 7-2 to the PROBE questions in figure 7-1 is a fairly easy step. For example, note that one aspect of behavior in the model is "procedures." We ask questions about procedures such as whether they are "efficient" and "free of task interference." About "directional data," we know they should be accurate, nonconfusing, timely, etc. Confirmation (or "feedback") should be work related, frequent, selective, and specific. These requirements prompt another set of questions. Depending on how deeply we want to probe, we could ask hundreds of questions. For strategic planning, the questions in figure 7-1 nearly exhaust those worth asking.

With these rudiments of the PROBE concept, we can begin to ask questions that will help us find strong behavioral leverage points, which is another way of saying "cost-effective ways to help people."

CHAPTER 7 REVIEW

Answers to the review questions and self-test questions are found in the back of the textbook.

Review Questions

7-1. Why are the Probe Learning questions important? What do they reveal?

7-2. Provide two to three examples of how a "battle strategy" might be designed knowing a competitor's strategic profile.

7-3. Identify the six factors Gilbert identified that can guarantee competence if delivered with a clear mission.

7-4. What do we mean by "functional flow" in the context of behavior?

7-5. Why are there no "bad" answers when responding to Probe questions?

7-6. How do the strategic profiling questions (figure 9-1) relate to the original Probe questionnaire?

7-7. Identify components of the behavioral engineering model and describe how it is part of the unitary behavioral transaction.

7-8. When reviewing behavior, what is meant by "leverage points"?

Self-Test Questions

T F 7-1. The six levels of vantage described by Gilbert include training, capacity, and motives.

T F 7-2. For strategic profiling, it is helpful to reword PROBE questions to match the specific situations being addressed.

T F 7-3. Leverage of each aspect of behavior of improving performance varies from one person to another.

T F 7-4. In strategic profiling, "no" answers are critical because they show a predilection to organizational change.

T F 7-5. PROBE offers a way to analyze tasks and find ways to improve performance by sorting out the high-leverage points in human behavior.

T F 7-6. Instruments are the environmental aspect of a response.

T F 7-7. PROBE questions are designed to uncover the logistics and data system support of an organization.

T F 7-8. Something can be done, with reasonable ease, to improve or downgrade performance by changing the task data, knowledge, instruments, capacity incentives, and motives.

CHAPTER 8

Fundamental Eight: Leveraging the Impact of Systems on the Individual

Learning Objectives

8-1. Appreciate the effect of the organizational environment, its processes, or the job performer on improving individual performance.
8-2. Appreciate the linkage of the Rummler and Brache models and the Gilbert model.
8-3. Identify Gilbert's contribution in terms of the six factors influencing performance and his performance engineering.
8-4. See how "quality at the source" contributes to improving performance.
8.5. Distinguish among behavior, performance, and accomplishment.
8-6. Recognize the elements of the "Where's My Biggest Performance Block?" group exercise.
8-7. Appreciate the conclusions of the "Where's My Biggest Performance Block?" group exercise.
8-8. Be familiar with elements of the Performance Improvement Process and the Human Performance System Checklist.

CHAPTER OUTLINE

Introduction

The challenge of improving performance is complicated by uncertainty over whether it is best accomplished by individual development, process redesign, or by organizational change. The underlying question is to what effect does the organizational environment, its processes, or the individual job performer exert greater influence on improving individual performance.

Using results of an exercise based on Gilbert's Behavior Engineering Model and Rummler's Human Performance System Model, this chapter contributes to this area of research. It is an attempt to bring a partial answer to this question by identifying where people perceive blocks to bettering their performance—in the work environment, or within themselves.

Performance Improvement Professionals continue to research which force—the environment, the process, the individual, or the interaction of all three—has the greatest influence on employee performance and thus organizational effectiveness. The findings of any and all research are important because it determines the focus and success of attempts at dealing with organizational change for companies to remain competitive. By suggesting that it is individual transformation alone that leads to organizational transformation, recent authors like Senge[194] seem to fall short of a key theme of the human performance improvement message, that it is essential to first look to the environment and its processes for optimizing change before trying to change the behavior of the person on the job, not to mention the person him or herself.

This chapter contributes important information to these areas of research by documenting people's perceptions of two of the three forces. Initial findings of participants' perceptions of where blocks to better performance originate focus on the environment and on individual repertories.

The findings are based on data from a study by Dean and Rebalsky,[195] which used an exercise based on Gilbert's Behavior Engineering Model and subsequent samplings by Dean using Rummler's Human Performance System Model. The research question used was based on the following concept, which is a combination of Rummler's and Gilbert's work: "Are people more likely to perceive blocks to better performance in the environmental factors of":

- Exchange of information (specification of work expectations and timely, accurate and relevant feedback about the outcome)
- Resources of time, tools, logical workflow, etc., for task support
- Consequences of the alignment of adequacy of exchange of information, allocation of task support, meaningful and timely pay and nonpay incentives, or the individual factors of
  - Knowledge and skills
  - Physical, mental, and emotional capacity
  - Intrinsic motivation

This chapter also reveals the connection between the Rummler and Brache model and the Gilbert model. It was Rummler who first saw the importance of the process level of work in an organization during his own research and application back in the 1970s. His assessment checklist for bettering the Human Performance System[196] is provided.

Gilbert's Contributions

In *Human Competence,* Gilbert[197] introduces the Behavior Engineering Model, which identifies six factors influencing performance. Three of the factors are related to the environment surrounding the employee: information, resources, and meaningful incentives provided. The remaining three factors are related to what employees bring to performance from their own repertories: their knowledge, capacity, and motivation.

FIGURE 8-1
Gilbert's Behavior Engineering Model

Stimulus	Response	Consequences
Cell 1: Environment **Information**	Cell 2: Environment **Resources**	Cell 3: Environment **Incentives**
• Description of what is expected of performance • Clear and relevant guides on how to do the job • relevant and frequent • feedback on adequacy of performance	• Tools, resources, time, and materials designed to • achieve performance needs • Access to leaders • Sufficient personnel • Organized work processes	• Adequate financial incentives contingent upon • performance • Nonmonetary incentives • Career development opportunities • Clear consequences for poor performance
Cell 4: Individual **Knowledge**	Cell 5: Individual **Capacity**	Cell 6: Individual **Motives**
• Systematically designed • training to match requirements of exemplary performers • Opportunity for training	• Match between people and position • Good selection processes • Flexible scheduling to match peak capacity of workers • Prostheses or visual aids to augment capacity	• Recognition of worker's willingness to work for • available incentives • Assessment of worker's motivation • Recruitment of workers to match realities of work • conditions

Source: © Human competence 1978, 1996. Used with permission from T. F. Gilbert.

Gilbert's additional contribution, which he called *performance engineering*, was to be able to understand how to engineer performance using the following guidelines. As performance improvement professionals, we must be able to:

- Identify the ultimate mission of the organization and determine whether the accomplishments of the organization and its people are aligned with the mission.
- Redefine accomplishments at all levels of the organization to support the mission of the organization

- Establish accomplishment standards based on the performance of exemplary employees
- Determine whether improving the performance of the average employee to the level of the exemplary employee on a specific accomplishment would be value-added to the organization.
- For those accomplishments for which improvement of employee performance is value-added, identify the causes of performance deficiencies.
- Suggest performance-improvement solutions for targeted accomplishments.

Performance Improvement: At a Glance in Today's Workforce

Some organizations are committing themselves to radical change through reengineering and/or process redesign, believing that is the only way a true paradigm shift can be achieved. Some organizations are opting for incremental change. Certain practices remain the same in either case, however. One of these is "quality at the source." This involves making employees responsible for the quality of their accomplishments by providing them with the resources and freedom of action to identify and solve work process problems as they occur. It also requires that employees monitor their own progress against a predetermined standard and make the adjustments necessary to meet the standard.

In order for "quality at the source" to be successful, managers must assure that employees have the knowledge and skill necessary to perform, as well as the information (input and feedback), tools, resources, processes, and incentives necessary for exemplary performance. This is a shift from the command-and-control style characteristic of the old management paradigm. John Martin, the CEO of Taco Bell, transformed it from a $500 million regional company to a $3 billion national company in ten years through a variety of reengineering strategies. One of these strategies was eliminating a supervisory level and creating the new position of market managers.

"Successful market managers in the new Taco Bell manage by exception, which means they must work only to solve problems, not create them. Equally important, they have to completely reject the old command and control style in favor of a model that promotes flexibility, relies on the most advanced management information systems in business, encourages innovation, and empowers the people around them to do their jobs.

The new market manager position prompted a shakeout. Some former area supervisors rose to the new challenge, others switched to restaurant general managers and became very productive, while still others left Taco Bell for the more comfortable confines of our competitors."[198]

Implications for Managers

The implications are clear. Managers in today's changing organizations will have to know the knowledge of the performance improvement profession.

Another condition of business today that helped to bring about the new paradigm is the continual change of job responsibilities at all levels of the organization. These changes necessitate training and retraining. They also require adjustments in the work environment to guarantee effective performance. For instance, clear performance expectations are a must for employees given new tasks and responsibilities. This is especially essential if employees are being asked to monitor their own performance. They must have standards against which to compare themselves. Providing well-defined, accomplishment-based expectations is one of the responsibilities of management.

Managers retain the ultimate responsibility for productivity and performance. Thus, they must have sufficient knowledge to participate, with performance improvement professionals, in identifying the root causes of performance needs and problems and selecting the appropriate solutions. They must also recognize performance improvement opportunities. With this knowledge, they can provide leadership for the performance improvement of those for whom they are responsible, whether they are actively involved in the performance improvement efforts or not.

The activity described below helps describe the need in a reliable way using the perceptions of the managers themselves. Managers need to understand and use the following ideas:

- Put a good performer in a bad system and the system will win.[198]
- Top performers are exemplars; let them be your guide for the facilitation of change. Too often, the average performer of a group is taken to represent the expected standard of performance, leading to a complacent work system. That is why exemplars need to be the focus.[199]
- Once deteriorated, individual performance is increasingly resistant to any and all efforts to bring about improvement.
- Performance can be improved and stay improved if there is system support from the environment surrounding the performer.
- Training to improve performance is one solution of many performance supports but it tends to be overused, improperly designed, and poorly delivered.[200]
- Management must learn the essential value of using behavior plus accomplishment equals performance.[201]

Behavior + Accomplishment Equals Performance

According to Gilbert[202] behavior is often confused with performance and accomplishment. *Behavior* plus *accomplishment* equals *performance* was one of his favorite ideas. Accomplishments are the important, positive outputs that a manager wants to happen as a result of the behavior of his or her employees. These are important distinctions because unless you can describe a performance in detail and create the proper system via input, feedback systems, resource allocations, and incentive systems, you will have a hard time changing it. Let's elaborate the distinction between behavior and accomplishment.

FIGURE 8-2 **Performance as a Combination of Behaviors and Results**	
Behaviors	**Accomplishments**
What you see people do when they are working	*What you see after people stop working*
Commonly described as: • Input • Process • Activity • Process • Means	Commonly described as: • Output • Outcome • Product • Achievement • Ends
Examples: • Inspecting • Designing • Conducting meetings • Reinforcing • Giving feedback	Examples: • Production • Yield • Run time • Milestones met • Suggestions

Performance is a combination of behaviors and the results that they produce.[203]

Within the behaviors described above are many, more specific behaviors—some of which contribute to the accomplishment, some of which may not. One aspect of performance improvement is to be able to identify which of the specific behaviors contributes no value to the accomplishment, and thereby contributes no value to the organization. These are behaviors that can be eliminated, especially if they consume personnel and material resources[204] or are reinforced by management. In order to make this determination, we must identify the accomplishments that are of value and backtrack to the behaviors that yield these accomplishments.

How do we do this? First, we list the result we are trying to achieve. To verify that we have identified the true accomplishment, we ask: "Is this what is left after the behavior has ceased and the employee has left the scene?" and "Is this the end purpose of the job, task, or function?" If the answer is yes to both questions, we then apply three criteria of an accomplishment. It must be measurable, observable, and reliable.

Attempting to measure the behaviors described in the examples above is difficult compared to measuring the accomplishments. The categories of accomplishment measures include:

- Quality: accuracy, class, and novelty
- Quantity: rate, time, and volume
- Cost: labor, materials, and management

We can use as an example a book in a bookstore. We can use the critical reviews and how long the book was on a best-seller list as a measure of quality. Quantity could be measured by the time in which the book was written and the number of books printed and sold. Cost would be represented by the total cost of production compared to profit. The data related to quality and quantity could be used as feedback to the author regarding the effectiveness of his or her performance. If the performance was ineffective, the data would provide clues as to what could be done to improve the performance in the future. For instance, some authors attend writing workshops to hone their writing skills. Without the feedback from the critics regarding the quality of the writing, the author would not know what needed to be improved—and the time in the writer's workshop would be wasted.

The second criterion of an accomplishment is that it must be observable, so it can be measured. For instance, the time it takes from design to production of a new product is observable in terms of hours, days, weeks, and/or months. The amount of rework required in a production line, the number of repeat customers, the net sales per month, the number of hand-offs of a product, the number of times data are handled are all observable measures.

Establishing reliability is the third criteria of an accomplishment. This is done by obtaining observations from two or more independent observers. If they agree regarding the measures of an accomplishment, you most likely have accurately identified your accomplishment. If there is some disagreement, there may need to be some clarification of exactly what the accomplishment of the job, function, or team is. Although it is not necessary to have 100 percent agreement on an accomplishment and its measures, the general agreement is important as we shall see.

Before we go on to examine the different ways we use performance measures, more clarification is necessary. Although we do not consider beliefs, perceptions, or attitudes as performances, such abstracts as motivation, morale, teamwork, communication, and rapport are factors that are often examined in relation to performance. The research on performance assessment in business and education settings, indicates that these factors can be inferred from measurable, observable, reliable behaviors and/or accomplishments. For instance, listening skills can be inferred from how frequently a listener's communications address the expressed interests, concerns, or needs of the speaker or by the number of times a listener responds to the speaker as compared to the number of responses that relate to the listener's interests and agendas.

The Exercise

Being able to identify the specific behaviors and accomplishments that represent performance is essential to managers who are required to either establish performance expectations or provide feedback intended to improve performance.

Initially, Dean[205] used Gilbert's Behavior Engineering Model as the basis for an experiential group exercise, "Where's My Biggest Performance Block?" Dean's exercise asks participants to identify one of Gilbert's six factors as the source of limitations to their own improved performance. Results from the exercise will demonstrate that participants, regardless of their role or level of responsibility, are more likely to identify environmental factors rather than individual factors as holding blocks to better performance.

An analysis of the data demonstrated that these results are not accidental but represent a real trend. In addition, results from testing alternative models of the exercise were developed to avoid the effects of primacy and recency and to explore the effect of the actor-observer bias.

Methodology

Participants in the "Where's My Biggest Performance Block?" group exercise included managers, staff-level employees, members of professional societies, and students in a graduate management program. Prior to the exercise, participants signed a form consenting to their involvement in this research.

In the exercise, participants were asked: "Improvement in which one of the following six areas would enable you to do your job better?" Participants were directed to choose one of the following six options; each option relates to one of the factors in Gilbert's Behavior Engineering Model (expressed in parentheses):

1. Clear performance expectations and relevant feedback about the adequacy of your performance (Information)
2. Tools, resources, and materials to achieve your performance goals (Resources)
3. Adequate pay and nonpay incentives made contingent upon your performance (Incentives)
4. Systematically designed training that matches the requirements of your job (Knowledge)
5. A match between your skills and the requirements of your job (Capacity)
6. Assurance of job security and social acceptance (Motivation)

For the exercise, a wall chart is positioned at the front of the room, visible to all participants. The wall chart depicts six cells numbered one through six with the first three cells stacked on top of cells four through six. The wall chart thus resembles Gilbert's six-cell behavior engineering model, but the cells are not labeled.

After selecting a response to the question, participants· write the number corresponding to their response on a red-colored self-stick dots. Participants then approach the wall chart and place their colored selfstick dot in the cell corresponding to their selection.[206]

After the participants place their responses on the wall chart, the exercise facilitator explains Gilbert's Behavior Engineering Model and

Rummler's Human Performance System Model and how each response to the exercise question (and each cell of the wall-chart model) relates to a factor influencing performance. The first three options—the top three cells of the model—represent factors in the performer's environment. Options four through six—the bottom three cells of the model—represent factors related to the performer's repertory.

The exercise facilitator asks the participants to comment on the results of the exercise as displayed on the wall chart. The clustering of the selfstick dots reveals whether most of the participants perceive environmental factors (dots clustered on top row) or individual factors (dots clustered on bottom row) as blocking better performance.

Manipulating the Exercise to Avoid Effects of Primacy and Recency

Attendees of a teachers' conference participated in the "Where's My Biggest Performance Block?" exercise under slightly different circumstances than the other groups. In an attempt to avoid the influence of primacy and recency on participants' responses to the question, the order of the answers to the question was reversed. In addition, a color rather than a number was assigned to each answer. In response to the question, "Improvement in which. one of the following six areas would enable you to do your job better?" participants could choose one of the following options:

- Assurance of job security and social acceptance (Yellow)
- A match between your skills and the requirements of your job (Blue)
- Systematically designed training that matches the requirements of your job (Red)
- Adequate pay and nonpay incentives made contingent upon your performance (Green)
- Tools, resources, and materials to achieve your performance goals (Purple)
- Clear performance expectations and relevant feedback about the adequacy of your performance (Orange)

Therefore, the original first response became the last response, the second response became the fifth response, etc. Each participant selected a sticker that was the same color as the color corresponding to the answer selected, and then placed their stickers on the six-cell wall chart. Each cell of the wall chart was labeled by color, but the cells were labeled according to their original order. For example, the original first response (for the participants, the last response labeled "orange") was assigned to the first cell.

Identifying Blocks to Better Performance in Others

Attendees of the teacher's conference participated in the exercise a second time. The answers to the exercise question were still reversed and color-coded; however, instead of examining the question from the viewpoint of their own performance, participants were asked to answer the question in terms of their students' performance. The question and answers were rewritten as follows: "Which one of the following six areas do your students need to improve their performance in the classroom?"

- Assurance of social acceptance and security in the classroom (Yellow)
- A match between their skills and their grade level (Blue)
- Systematically designed instruction that matches the requirements of their grade level (Red)
- Adequate incentives made contingent on their classroom performance (Green)
- Tools, resources, and materials to achieve their classroom performance goals (Purple)
- Clear expectations and relevant feedback about the adequacy of their classroom performance (Orange)

Results

Dean's "Where's My Biggest Performance Block?" experiential group exercise has been conducted with more than 1,500 participants over the past four years. Results show that typically, over two-thirds of participants choose options one, two, or three; they identify environmental factors—information (input and feedback), resources, or incentives—as the areas needing improvement in order to enable them to perform better. Initial results were published in *Performance Engineering at Work*.[207]

To measure the results as published in *Performance Engineering at Work* of the exercise, participants' responses for each cell were tallied. Percentages of total participants selecting each cell were also calculated. Also, the sum of percentages of the top three cells was compared to the sum of percentages of the bottom three cells to determine which set of factors—environmental or individual—were selected by the majority of participants.

Results were categorized according to the type of participant: stafflevel employees, managers, members of professional societies, or graduate management students. Results were categorized in this manner in order to determine if participants with different roles (i.e., manager, employee, or student) would respond differently to the exercise. Results were also determined for the teachers' conference attendees, who participated with alternative models of the exercise.

The following are results according to the type of participant.

- **Employees**: A total of 110 participants were staff-level employees. Of these employee participants, 39% selected cell one (information); 25% selected cell two (instruments); 18% selected cell three (incentives); 8% selected cell four (knowledge); 7% selected cell five (capacity); and 3% selected cell six (motives). Overall, 82% selected the environmental factors in cells one through three, and 18% selected the individual factors in cells four through six. Thus, more than two-thirds of the stafflevel employee participants selected environmental factors.
- **Managers**: Of a total of 48 managerial participants, 38% selected cell one (information); 27% selected cell two (instruments); 2% selected cell three (incentives); 19% selected cell four (knowledge); 6% selected cell five (capacity); and 8% selected cell six (motives). Overall, 67% selected the environmental factors in

cells one through three, and 33% selected the individual factors in cells four through six. Again, these results show a majority of participants selecting environmental factors as blocks to better performance.

- **Employees and Managers**: A total of 409 participants were groups of staff-level employees and managers undergoing the exercise together. Of these participants, 29% selected cell one (information); 21% selected cell two (instruments); 29% selected cell three (incentives); 11% selected cell four (knowledge); 7% selected cell five (capacity); and 2% selected cell six (motives). Overall, 80% selected the environmental factors in cells one through three, and 20% selected the individual factors in cells four through six. Thus, more than two-thirds of the staff-level employee and managerial participants undergoing the exercise together selected environmental factors.
- **Attendees of meetings of professional societies:** A total of 191 participants were attendees of meetings of professional societies. Of these participants, 40% selected cell one (information); 36% selected cell two (instruments); 7% selected cell three (incentives); 4% selected cell four (knowledge); 10% selected cell five (capacity), and 3% selected cell six (motives). Overall, 83% selected the environmental factors in cells one through three, and 17% selected the individual factors in cells four through six. Thus, more than two-thirds of these participants selected environmental factors.
- **Graduate management students:** A total of 40 participants were graduate management students. Of these participants, 30% selected cell one (information); 30% selected cell two (instruments); 10% selected cell three (incentives); 13% selected cell four (knowledge); 8% selected cell five (capacity); and 10% selected cell six (motives). Overall, 70% selected the environmental factors in cells one through three, and 30% selected the individual factors in cells four through six. Thus, more than two-thirds of the graduate student participants selected environmental factors.

- **Teachers group-manipulated exercise:** Despite the changes to the exercise, the results from these participants resembled results from participants who were given the original exercise. Of the 59 participants, 37% selected cell one (information); 34% selected cell two (instruments); 2% selected cell three (incentives); 8% selected cell four (knowledge); 7% selected cell five (capacity); and 12% selected cell six (motives). Overall, 73% selected the environmental factors in cells one through three, and 27% selected the individual factors in cells four through six. Even using an alternative model of the exercise, more than two-thirds of the participants selected environmental factors as the areas needing improvement in order for them to improve their own performance.
- **Identifying blocks to better performance in others:** When answering this question in terms of their students and not themselves, participants' responses differed greatly. Of 58 participants, 22% selected cell one (information); 10% selected cell two (instruments); 9% selected cell three (incentives); 0% selected cell four (knowledge); 5% selected cell five (capacity); and 53% selected cell six (motives). Overall, 41% selected the environmental factors in cells one through three, and 59% selected the individual factors in cells four through six.

Departing from the usual trend of the majority of responses favoring environmental factors, in this exercise, the majority of participants identified individual factors as limiting performance.

Summary and Conclusions of the Exercise

For all categories of participants undergoing the original "Where's My Biggest Performance Block?" exercise, results consistently show that at least two-thirds select the environmental factors of information, resources, and incentives as needing improvement in order to enable them to improve their own performance. Even when the exercise was changed to avoid the tendency of participants to select either the first or last response, results still favored environmental over individual factors. A chi-square analysis provided statistical support for the premise by demonstrating that these results are not accidental, but reflect an actual trend. Subsequent use of the activity has revealed similar results since the publication of *Performance Engineering at Work.*

When the exercise was modified to elicit participants' responses about the performance of others, rather than themselves, however, the trend reversed. A group of teachers, which had identified environmental factors as limiting their own performance, largely identified individual factors as blocking better performance from their students. These results probably reflect the actor-observer bias as identified by Jones and Nisbett, who "suggest that actors focus their attention upon the environment, but observers concentrate on the actors and their behavior."[208] The presence of the actor-observer bias may further complicate the debate over which force—the environment or the individual—has a greater influence on performance. Are environmental factors truly blocking better performance? Or do people falsely identify environmental factors as blocks because they are naturally blinded when examining themselves?

Rather than propose an answer to these questions, this paper demonstrates the importance of people's *perceptions.* Results of the exercise show that people clearly perceive environmental factors, rather than individual factors, as limiting their performance. Perceptions are powerful and cannot be ignored. If people believe that the work environment limits their performance, then this belief must be addressed by human resource development professionals. If instead, we focus on individual training and development, then we are not giving employees what they think they need.

How to Translate the Support of the System and the Significant Power It Has Over Individual Performance

Analyzing the Performance System

Regarding the Gilbert model using their dots, one can go on to explain Rummler's model, which would simply add a seventh cell.

Gilbert's cell one is labeled *information,* meaning communicating and receiving feedback. The seventh cell using Rummler's model simply takes Gilbert's cell one and creates cell one and cell two with the respective labels of input (that is specifying expectation) and giving relevant feedback, respectively. This shows the connection between Rummler's and Gilbert's work.

FIGURE 8-3
Gilbert's Behavior Engineering Model as Modified by Rummler's Approach

Cell 1: Environment **Input**	Cell 2: Environment **Feedback**	Cell 3: Environment **Resources**	Cell 4: Environment **Incentives**
Cell 4: Individual **Knowledge**	Cell 5: Individual **Capacity**	Cell 6: Individual **Motives**	

It is Rummler's contention as well that accomplishments can—and should—be identified and measured at all levels of the organization. This is necessary in order to assure congruence across levels (performer, process, and organization), that is to assure that all employees at all levels are actually furthering the accomplishment goals of the organization. A lack of congruence across or within levels is the cause of many a performance problem. Identify this lack of congruence to pinpoint performance problems.

In the new management paradigm, which emphasizes processes (instead of departments) and cross-functional work teams, the department, function, and process systems are less distinct than in the old paradigm. This is designed to achieve a greater focus on customer needs across all systems and reduce the focus on the needs and management of separate departments, functions, and process systems. No matter how the organization is structured and what labels are given to its levels, the important thing is that the organization can define its accomplishments at its different levels and that the accomplishments all contribute to achieving the mission of the organization.

Rummler and Brache's answer to that issue was to include the *process level* of the organization between the levels of individual performance and the organization systems effect.

They describe the *Performance Improvement Process,* which starts at the organization level, with concern for identifying processes with performance payoffs. It then moves to the process level, specifying process improvement steps and identifying jobs with performance payoffs. Finally, the process moves to the performer level where job improvement actions are specified.

At this level, the *Human Performance System Checklist* is used to assess the environmental and individual factors that bear on the performance of a particular performer. Following this set of troubleshooting questions, the performance system solution would be determined, along with the person responsible. Specific action steps are itemized, with target dates and priority orders.

Conclusion

This chapter reinforces the importance of the work environment in people's perceptions and underscores the need for the human resource community to continue to acknowledge the dual role of the individual and the environment in influencing performance. With this understanding, performance improvement professionals can continue to expand their repertories beyond well-designed individual training to include organizational system change.

CHAPTER 8 REVIEW

Answers to the review questions and self-test questions are found in the back of the textbook.

Review Questions

8.1 What are the six factors influencing performance according to Gilbert's Behavioral Engineering Model?

8.2 What does the Taco Bell example tell us about "quality of source" and how it relates to reengineering strategies?

8.3 "Behavior plus accomplishment equals performance." What does Gilbert mean by the formula?

8.4 Describe the three criteria of an accomplishment and what is meant by each.

8.5 In general terms, what does Dean ask participants to identify in the exercise "What's My Biggest Performance Block?" What does the outcome demonstrate?

8.6 Compare the outcome of the Performance Block exercise when participants were asked to distinguish their own performance from the performance of others.

8.7 Describe the three levels of Rummler and Brache's Performance Improvement Process.

8.8 What factors does the Human Performance System Checklist assess?

Self-Test Questions

T F 8-1. "Quality at the Source" requires employees to strictly evaluate and control the performance of managers.

T F 8-2. According to Rummler, accomplishments should be measured at all organizational levels.

T F 8-3. The Human Performance System Checklist assesses environmental and individual factors that influence performance.

T F 8-4. Establishing the reliability of an accomplishment requires observations from two or more independent observers.

T F 8-5. Gilbert suggested six performance engineering guidelines including establishing standards based on the performance of exemplary employees.

T F 8-6. Results from the Performance Block exercise show individual factors playing a more important role than environmental factors.

CHAPTER 9

Fundamental Nine: Identifying Needs to Improve Engagement

Learning Objectives

9-1. Recognize how a needs assessment can identify factors required to improve employee performance.
9-2. Appreciate the problems that may be encountered implementing a professional development program.
9-3. Recognize the evaluation research, nominal group technique, and performance technology model.
9-4. Be familiar with the elements of the research project plan.
9-5. Understand the most important elements of the needs assessment.
9-6. Be able to distinguish the benefits and limitations of a needs assessment.

CHAPTER OUTLINE

Introduction
Background
Method
- Evaluation Research
- Nominal Group Technique
- Performance Technology Model

Our Project
Results
- Solution Categories
- Similarities Across Function Groups
- Differences Across Function Groups

Recommendations
Outcomes
Benefits of the Process

Introduction

The effectiveness of any organization is dependent on its most important resources—people. Systems and techniques abound for the purpose of developing human resources. These are designed to help an organization get the best performance from its people and have frequently focused on providing knowledge and skills through some type of training. Analysis can show what kind of training is most appropriate for achieving improved performance in any human system and also reveal when training is not necessary in order to achieve improved performance. One strategy that accomplishes both of these ends is evaluation research.[209]

This chapter describes a needs assessment we conducted with 280 support staff, faculty, and administrators of a community college. We used the evaluation research strategy[210] as a guideline for planning and implementing the needs assessment. We taught the nominal group technique,[211] a comprehensive data-gathering process for large groups, to representatives from each of these three groups. These representatives facilitated the participation of virtually all employees at the college in identifying a prioritized list of items that would enable these persons to "do their jobs better." Analysis of the suggested performance improvement needs used the performance technology model.[212]

Five categories of intervention emerged from the data:

- High-yield training
- Direction and flow of information
- Resources
- Performance incentives
- Medium-yield training

Analysis of the results showed that improving employee performance required altering information and incentive systems. Without these alterations, traditional training was likely to have minimal effect.

Background

The Professional Development Committee of a mid-sized community college in suburban Philadelphia had responsibility for developing a oneyear professional development plan for the administrators, faculty, and support personnel at the college. Past professional development programs were held on two consecutive days just before the second semester. All employees at the college were mandated to attend. In light of concern voiced over these programs, we were hired as outside consultants to help develop the plan.

After three lengthy meetings with the committee and focus groups with representatives from each of the function areas, we identified seven problems that would have to be dealt with in planning the professional development program. The problems included:

- The commonly held perception that "professional development" automatically means training
- A need to link professional development with performance improvement
- Lack of agreement among committee members as to how to select professional development opportunities, with some members feeling they already knew the needs of each function group
- Limited communication of operating information across function groups
- Negative employee perceptions regarding previous professional development efforts
- Perceived unresponsiveness of decision makers to past employee suggestions related to professional development needs
- Recent loss of incentive due to reduced power and autonomy within the faculty structure

It appeared that a failure to address these problems would reduce the impact of the professional development program. Specifically, the final professional development plan for the 1991–92 academic year had to:

- Involve and empower all employees (stakeholders) equally in identifying professional development needs, regardless of how valid or invalid their perceptions were as viewed by their peers
- Develop a means by which the planning committee itself would recognize that performance improvement can be achieved by nontraining actions and that such actions might be required in order to maximize the effectiveness of the training that is done
- Elicit data that would represent both the perceived wants and needs of the employees of the college
- Elicit accurate data while facilitating a process with 280 participants at one time
- Provide decision-makers with a systematic process for selecting professional development activities that would yield maximum results for the cost and effort invested

In light of the challenges outlined above, the Professional Development Committee agreed to conduct an assessment to identify the training needs of each function group. They asked the consultants to submit a plan for conducting the needs assessment.

Method

The following section outlines the needs assessment plan accepted by the committee. In designing the plan, we not only wanted to address the problems and challenges above but also to shift the focus of the committee from "professional development training" to "performance improvement solutions." This meant involving the committee in each phase of the needs assessment design and implementation so they would have confidence in the accuracy of the data and the systematic way in which it was gathered. It also meant providing them with the technical information they needed to make the right decisions about the data.

We selected the strategies of the evaluation research model to guide this process, the nominal group technique to gather accurate data, and the performance technology model to demonstrate to the committee the difference between training and nontraining performance improvement solutions. The unique application of each of these techniques formed the backbone of our methodology. We now describe each of them in general terms and then describe their specific use in our needs assessment project.

Evaluation Research

Evaluation research is a pragmatic, program-focused research strategy of analysis for decision-makers. Its purpose is to provide data that can enable decision-making, through analysis of pros and cons, through prioritizing, or through the application of decision-making criteria, and other means.

The involvement of stakeholders throughout the research process gives the technique its strength. Input and feedback from the stakeholders influence numerous aspects of a project: feasibility in terms of cost, timeliness, and manner of implementation; and utility, accuracy, and proprietorship in terms of outcome.

Beginning with *Phase One, Selection of Evaluation Research Purpose* (see figure 9-1), the research evaluators and the stakeholders "become collaborating partners in the search for useful information."[213] From then on, collaboration is included in each phase of the process. This provides a means of monitoring the appropriateness and relevancy of each activity and strategy, as well as its feasibility regarding time and resources. As a result, the information gathered is more likely to address the needs of the stakeholders. The collaboration is also more likely to facilitate decision-making through both its accuracy and the way the information is reported. Furthermore, the stakeholders who have helped structure the process and those from whom the data are derived have greater ownership of the results. Their potential buy-in to the recommendations stemming from the research is therefore increased.

A unique feature of evaluation research is its focus on the stated goals and objectives of a program. These may include decisions to be made, problems to be solved, or perceptions about program effectiveness. The data gathered are used to create, maintain, or improve program policy or implementation practices.

<table>
<tr><td colspan="3">FIGURE 9-1
Evaluation Research Model</td></tr>
<tr><td colspan="3">**1. Selection of evaluation research purpose**</td></tr>
<tr><td>• Needs assessment
• Basic research
• Coverage accountability</td><td>• Small-scale testing
• Evaluation
• Input assessment</td><td>• Policy analysis
• Fiscal accountability
• Economic analysis</td></tr>
<tr><td colspan="3">**2. Identify the technique to the used**</td></tr>
<tr><td>• Front-end analysis
• Formative evaluation</td><td>• Program monitoring
• Evaluability assessment</td><td>• Impact evaluation
• Evaluation of evaluation</td></tr>
<tr><td colspan="3">**3. Develop research questions**</td></tr>
<tr><td colspan="3">• What do you need to meet our professional goals and objectives?</td></tr>
<tr><td colspan="3">**4. Establish a collaborative, utilization-focused process**</td></tr>
<tr><td>A. Compose task force</td><td colspan="2">B. Design task force activities</td></tr>
<tr><td>• All stakeholders represented
• Power exists to act on findings
• Time committed
• Process and results valued</td><td colspan="2">• Focus clarification
• Methods and measurement selection
• Review of instruments and strategies</td></tr>
<tr><td colspan="3">**5. Determine research focus**</td></tr>
<tr><td>• Evaluation research with goals</td><td colspan="2">• Evaluation research without goals</td></tr>
<tr><td colspan="3">**6. Determine evaluation research strategy**</td></tr>
<tr><td>• Scientific – hypothetical-deductive</td><td colspan="2">• Anthropological – holistic-inductive</td></tr>
<tr><td colspan="3">**7. Select data collection method**</td></tr>
<tr><td>• Formal instruments (ex. survey)</td><td colspan="2">• Nonformal instruments (ex. structured or nonstructured interview)</td></tr>
<tr><td>**8. Implement research**</td><td colspan="2"></td></tr>
<tr><td>**9. Analyze research**</td><td colspan="2"></td></tr>
</table>

Nominal Group Technique

The nominal group technique[214] uses a structured group meeting conducted by a group leader or facilitator in four steps:

- Generation of ideas
- Sequential reporting of ideas
- Clarification of ideas
- Ranking of ideas by importance

Consistent with evaluation research, one of the advantages of the technique is the involvement of stakeholders. The nominal group technique assures that each person has an equal opportunity to express his or her ideas. It stimulates the generation of ideas through silent writing in step one and the round-robin listing in step two. This prevents closure on ideas before all are equally considered. All participants can reflect on all ideas and have their questions and concerns addressed in the third step. Silent ranking, the fourth step, gives equal weight to each opinion during decision making and reduces peer pressure to support one idea. Furthermore, the nominal group technique is cost and time effective.[215]

Performance Technology Model

The premise of performance technology is that there are a variety of factors in the workplace that have bearing on performance effectiveness and that appropriately adjusting these factors can yield exemplary performance, often without training. Thus, it behooves those responsible for the performance of others to identify environmental and individual factors in a given workplace that will not only improve performance, but also maintain exemplar quality without costly training. These factors, as illustrated by figure 9-2 on the following page, are represented by the Behavior Engineering[216]/PROBE Model[217] developed by Thomas Gilbert, which is the basis of the performance technology model.[218] This model identifies what can be done to improve and maintain performance, one of the goals of any professional development project.

It is Gilbert's claim that any job that is supported in all six of the areas of the model should "carry a guarantee of high competence, provided that management was structured so as to really deliver these things and had a clear focus on the mission of the job in the first place.[219]

FIGURE 9-2
The Behavior Engineering Model

STIMULI	RESPONSE	CONSEQUENCES
Cell 1 Information	**Cell 2 Resources**	**Cell 3 Incentives**
• Descriptions of what is expected of performance • Clear and relevant guides on how to do the job • Relevant and frequent feedback about the • adequacy of performance	• Tools, resources, time and materials designed to • achieve performance needs • Access to leaders • Sufficient personnel • Organized work processes	• Adequate financial • incentives made contingent upon performance • Nonmonetary incentives • Career development opportunities • Clear consequences for poor performance
Cell 4 Knowledge	**Cell 5 Capacity**	**Cell 6 Motives**
• Systematically designed training that matches • requirements of exemplary performers • Opportunity for training	• Match between people and position • Good selection processes • Flexible scheduling of performance to match peak capacity of workers • Prostheses or visual aids to augment capacity	• Recognition of workers willingness to work for • available incentives • Assessment of worker's motivation • Recruitment of workers to match realities of work • conditions

*Source: Human Competence,*1978, p. 88 from T.F. Gilbert.

Research and experience verify that without good needs assessment, training is likely to be the performance improvement intervention of choice. As a result, wants instead of needs are frequently addressed, the value of training yields less than optimal return on the dollar and time investment, and training has little long-term impact on the organization as a whole.

Strategies related to evaluation research and performance technology have proven effective in carrying out "front-end" identification of needs[220] and in deciding how to address the needs so the training that is eventually done will have high yields to both the trainee and the organization.[221] Performance technology helps to show where training is not the best choice of intervention and if training is the best intervention, what kind of training will best meet the need.

Our Project

The needs assessment process we employed illustrates the integration of the nominal group technique and the performance technology model into the strategies of the evaluation research model. By walking through the stages of the needs assessment planning and implementation, this integration becomes apparent.

- *Establish goals.* As described in the introduction, we, along with the Professional Development Committee, determined an assessment was necessary to identify professional development needs and their appropriate solutions. This corresponded with phase one of the evaluation research model, selection of the evaluation research purpose.
- *Design needs assessment techniques.* We selected the nominal group technique[222] as the primary method for collecting data because it addresses the need to involve and empower all employees equally. This fulfilled phase two of the evaluation research model, identifying the technique to be used. The first of the five applications of the nominal group technique occurred at this point. We used it with the Professional Development Committee for two reasons. The committee needed to experience the nominal group technique firsthand in order to "buy into" it. They also needed to achieve consensus on the definition of professional development (versus training) and the purpose of the committee. The nominal question we used with

the committee led them to consensus. We addressed phases two and four of the evaluation research model during this activity.

- *Conduct focus groups.* We then held focus groups with representatives from each of the function areas, (administration, faculty, and support staff) in order to identify any perceptions or problems in the workplace that night have an impact on the professional development program planning. The information we gathered verified problems three through six listed in the introduction and reinforced the need for a collaborative needs assessment process. The perceived professional development needs we identified during the focus groups corresponded with data gathered later during the nominal group technique. The focus groups provided another opportunity for collaboration of the stakeholders. This activity was also part of phase four of the evaluation research model, establish a collaborative utilization-focused process. We carried it out before phase three, develop the research question, because we wanted to use the results of the focus groups in finalizing the research question.
- *Design methodology.* We used the information provided by the Professional Development Committee and the focus group interviews to develop the question that we eventually asked each of the 280 employees of the college: "What do I need to meet my professional goals and objectives?" This completed phase three of the evaluation research model.

Our biggest design challenge was how to do the nominal group technique with 280 people at one time. As the average nominal group technique is conducted with no more than 10 members in a group, we decided to conduct 28 concurrent nominal groups by training group facilitators. Data would be collected through three separate nominal group processes. The first would identify needs, the second would prioritize the needs, and the third would generate solutions to the previously identified needs.

At this point, we selected the performance technology model for analyzing and reporting the data. The design methodology represented phases five, six and seven of the evaluation research model, an evaluation research without goals as the research focus, an anthropological (holistic inductive) research strategy, and a data collection method that involved a nonformal instrument, namely the nominal group technique.

- *Train facilitators.* We trained over forty people, representing each of the three function groups to serve as facilitators during the two-day needs assessment program. This training was the second application of the nominal group technique. The training consisted of information on the technique and a walk-through of the process. Job aids were provided, including directions for the three phases of the needs assessment, tips for facilitators, and forms for reporting the data.
- *Conduct needs assessment.* On the first morning of the two-day program, we introduced the needs assessment process and used icebreaker activities to encourage the free flow of ideas when it came time for the nominal group technique.

After lunch, each of the three function groups met in a different location where they divided into smaller nominal groups of about ten people each. The trained volunteers facilitated the groups through the processes of need identification and prioritization. We collected all the data from the groups and with the help of volunteers from the support staff and some members of the Professional Development Committee, we worked until late in the evening organizing and typing ALL responses.

On the second morning of the two-day program, we gave each of the 280 participants a copy of the responses from his or her function group, as well as the responses of the other function groups. This served several purposes. Each group was encouraged to review responses of all other groups within their function area. This additional information reinforced some groups' ideas. It also helped broaden their focus in some cases and increased the likelihood of constructive solution ideas. The quick turnaround of ideas also demonstrated responsiveness to employee suggestions.

During the morning, each group generated solutions to each of the needs they had identified on the previous day. They were encouraged to consider both training and nontraining solutions.

By lunch of the second day, the project had evolved through the first eight phases of the evaluation research model and used the nominal group technique in three separate contexts: establishing the goals of the project (15 participants); training the facilitators (40 participants); and conducting the needs assessment (280 participants).

Analyze data. The volunteers tabulated the data generated by the needs assessment over a six-week period. They then organized lists of prioritized needs and suggestions by themes in order to facilitate analysis. For instance, they grouped together all needs that had to do with the clarification or revision of policies and procedures (See tables 9-1 to 9-3.) This process of grouping needs and suggestions by theme was conducted separately for faculty, support staff, and administrators. Consequently, we had a unique list of themes for each function group. Next, we had to develop a means of representing these themes that would help the Professional Development Committee decide what training and nontraining activities to recommend. This meant synthesizing pages of data into a summary that was easy to interpret. We created a matrix that would illustrate the need themes on one axis and categories of solutions on the other. The solution categories were high-yield training, information, resources, incentives, and low-yield training (see tables 10-1 to 10-3). Within each cell of the matrix the number of times a particular kind of solution was recommended for a need theme was shown, revealing the priorities placed on themes and categories of solutions. When necessary, the committee was able to refer back to the organized lists of solutions to identify the specific solutions that fell into each solution category.

TABLE 9-3
Responses from Faculty

	High-Yield Dev. Programs	Information	Resources	Incentives	Mod-Yield Dev. Programs	TOTAL NEEDS
Money, resources, budget			**64**	**12**		76
Return to former dept. structure/staff development	8	**25**		**24**		57
Communication						39
• Interdepartmental		18				
• Expectations		1				
• Open forum		5				
• Streamline procedures		6				
• Budget procedures		9				
Equipment needs	3	3	**22**		3	31
Self-determination needs		**24**				24
Faculty/admin. relationship		19				19
Training: PC's, teaching	12	2			5	19
Helping special students	3	4	3		2	**12**
Recognition				4		4
Team building		2			2	4
TOTAL BY SOLUTION	26	188	89	40	12	285

This analysis of results was phase nine of the evaluation research model. In the following section of this paper, we discuss these results and the decisions they prompted.

Results

Solution Categories

Although we had chosen the performance technology model[223] as a means of organizing and reporting the data prior to the needs assessment, we did not "force-fit" responses into the model. The needs identified through the nominal group technique naturally fell into categories according to the type of solution that would meet the need: information, resources, incentives, and knowledge/skills (training).

A review of the data indicated that not all solutions were of equal yield (i.e., cost-to-benefit ratio). For instance, although personal computer training was frequently identified as a need, its yield was minimal because, in many cases, there were a limited number of personal computers in the workplace. The distinction between high- and low-yield interventions was most evident in the knowledge/skills (training) category. As a result, we subdivided train solutions into two categories. We now describe all five categories and the data classified in them.

- *Category One*: High-Yield Development Programs. The needs in this category could be met by effectively designed training that matched the skill and knowledge requirements of a specific job function. Here the benefit from the program was greater than the cost of implementing the program. For instance, communication skills training for administrators was considered high yield. Not only had it been rated as very important by the administrators, there were many needs identified by all function groups that required information solutions. The administrators would need good communication skills to address the needs.
- *Category Two*: Information. Three general solutions met the needs in this category. The first solution was to provide descriptions of what performances were expected. This included job descriptions. The second kind of information solution was clear and relevant guides for job performance in the form of policies and procedures. The third information solution was

relevant and frequent feedback about the level of performance achieved in relation to the expectations.

- *Category Three*: Resources. This category involved needs that could be solved by more equipment, better tools, a more effective working environment, or other solutions that require additional funding.
- *Category Four*: Incentives. Needs that could be met by adequate financial and nonfinancial incentives such as rewards and recognition, fell into this category. Optimally, these incentives should be based on performance. Also, career-development opportunity solutions addressed these needs.
- *Category Five*: Moderate-Yield Development Programs. This category was similar to Category One except for the yield derived from the implementation of the program. The cost of the program would not have been balanced by the benefit. This was probably due to another related need that fell into the Second, Third, or Fourth Categories. For instance, with regard to the need for personal computer training mentioned above, the training would be of little benefit to employees until they had regular access to computers during the workday. A resource need for computers would have to be met before the computer training would be high yield. It was recommended that programs in this category not be implemented until the other related needs were met. Once the related needs were met, however, the yield of the program might change, or the need for the program might be eliminated entirely.

Similarities Across Function Groups

The patterns of suggestions made by the three function groups led to several interesting insights. The support staff, faculty, and administrators all suggested information needs and solutions more than any other. The specific themes for all three groups dealt with the need for information about policies, department structure, decision making, and "what the other person is doing." This is consistent with the experience of many performance technologists who often find, during needs assessments, that information, in the form of clearly defined performance expectations, policies, procedures and feedback, is the greatest need related to performance improvement.[224]

Providing information is less time consuming and less costly than providing training. In some cases, it is also more likely to result in performance improvement. When training occurs but employees are still not clear on performance expectations and do not receive feedback that will help them assess their progress toward performance expectations, they cannot achieve maximum performance improvement. This results in frustrated employees and a frustrated organization.

The second most common needs/solutions identified across the three function groups were resources. Here the administrators' responses focused on the need for more staff; support staff needed more equipment; and the faculty expressed a need for funding to support professional development travel and more equipment.

Differences Across Function Groups

The administrators identified the highest proportion of training needs/solutions. Their particular interest was communication and interpersonal problem-solving skills that would contribute to a more positive organizational climate. This reflected the "feeling of being overworked" that was voiced by many administrators and was consistent with their expressed need for more staff. The faculty, on the other hand, was interested only in training related to their subject-matter area. This may have reflected the sense of alienation the faculty felt during previous professional development programs at the college.

The lack of suggested solutions in the incentives category might lead to the conclusion that employees were highly motivated and felt no need for incentives. However, it appeared that employee motivation was affected by environmental factors that were not directly associated with incentives. For instance, all groups expressed frustration about communication and resource needs. When these kinds of needs are addressed, frustration levels are usually reduced and employees become more motivated.

Recommendations

After identifying the similarities and differences across the three function groups, we made recommendations to the Professional Development Committee. Our nontraining recommendations included:

- Establish a new committee to oversee noninstructional performance improvement solutions
- Present an overview of Performance Technology to the Professional Development Committee
- Review results of both training and noninstructional interventions after one year
- Certain high-yield training was recommended across function groups as well
- Conduct a re-orientation program for all employees to provide information regarding the operation of reach function group
- Use the re-orientation program as the new employee orientation program
- Implement the following high-yield training programs:
    1. Interpersonal problem solving for administrators
    2. Communication skills for faculty and staff
    3. Personal computer teaching methods for faculty
    4. Delegation skills for administrators
    5. Budget planning for administrators

Additional nontraining professional development solutions were recommended for each function group. For instance, we suggested that the faculty division structure be reviewed. This would address their feeling of power loss and alienation as a result of a recent restructuring. Unless faculty alienation was dealt with, it was going to be impossible to build trust and communication across function groups.

Outcomes

The value the Professional Development Committee placed on the needs assessment and our recommendations was demonstrated by the actions they took after receiving the results. For example, they immediately began planning the recommended high-yield training and scheduled a meeting during which they could learn more about the performance technology model. However, they chose not to directly address the solutions related to resources and incentives for two reasons. First, the original committee was not empowered to authorize the budget expenditures that might be necessary to implement resource and incentive solutions. Second, their mission was to plan professional development activities within the traditional paradigm of professional development.

Once their vision had shifted from *professional development training* to *performance improvement solutions* that included nontraining options, they felt that the most responsible strategy would be to have a committee established that could focus exclusively on nontraining performance improvement solutions. Consequently, they recommended to the president of the college that such a committee be established.

Benefits of the Process

The models and methods used in planning and implementing the needs assessment provided the data that supported the committee's actions. They also facilitated decision-making on the relative worth of the actions for promoting both professional growth and institutional development. The models and methods also addressed the challenges that we identified at the beginning of the project:

- All employees (stakeholders) were involved equally in identifying professional development needs. The support staff indicated in their evaluations that it was the first time they felt anyone had listened to their concerns or ideas.
- The planning committee recognized that certain nontraining actions were required to increase the worth of training.

- The step of the nominal group technique in which ideas were clarified provided an opportunity for group members to question and even challenge what someone else had suggested. While this did not guarantee that the ideas generated in the first nominal group process represented needs instead of wants, it did increase the likelihood that they would. One part of the clarification step requires group members to substantiate their needs. If they'd filled out a questionnaire or participated in a traditional focus group, instead of the nominal group technique, their responses might have been more spontaneous, less thoughtful, and subsequently of less value.
- Decision makers were provided with a systematic process for selecting professional development activities that are likely to yield maximum results for cost and effort. The matrices used to report the data enabled the committee to compare the number of responses in need themes and solution categories. The trends that emerged have become the focal points for future professional development planning. When necessary, the committee can look back at the original data that were keyed by themes.

The project also revealed the benefits of the process related to the practice of performance technology:

- This project illustrates the number and kind of responses generated through the nominal group technique, as well as the range of professional development options that emerge from nominal group technique responses. It also models how to introduce performance technology to decision makers without giving them the theory "up front."
- Professional development for all employees is new to many academic institutions. Performance technology is seldom used to improve professional performance. This project illustrates the application and value of performance technology for addressing the desire of academic institutions for training while simultaneously presenting alternative performance improvement solutions.

- The findings of this project were quite different from those anticipated by the Professional Development Committee. As a result, they became convinced of the value of needs assessment. The project illustrates techniques, references, and examples that can be used in convincing other decision makers of the value of conducting a needs assessment and using performance technology as the decisionmaking model for all HRD functions of the organization.
- Presenting the needs assessment data within the framework of the performance technology model also added validity to the high-yield training. A training course in interpersonal communications and problem solving was offered to administrators. Some had signed up for it because the president of the college encouraged them to, not because they wanted to. During the introduction to the course, the responses the function groups had developed were presented.
- The participants saw that communication was among the highest need theme for all function groups and there were more solution suggestions in the information column than any other. Their perception of the training suddenly changed. Their comments indicated that they no longer saw the training as remedial, an effort to "fix" their poor communication skills. Instead, they saw it as providing them with tools for addressing the communication and information needs of others. Their body language relaxed immediately and they began participating in the group discussion. The communication skills training was an opportunity to teach the performance technology model to the administrators.

Limitations

There were some limitations to the process as well:

- Typing and categorizing the data was time-consuming. It is unlikely that many organizations would commit as much staff support to a needs assessment project.

- Although focus groups were used to gather pre-assessment information, the nominal group technique was the primary source of needs assessment data. This methodology placed great reliance on the perceptions of the community college personnel. Studies have shown that people see or perceive what they are prepared to see or hear (e.g., Dean, 1986). The fact that there was a consistency of responses within function groups, coupled with a large number of responses, increased the likelihood that the responses represented genuine needs, and not just wants. Validity of the data could have been better assured, however, by triangulation of methodologies.[225] Triangulation is the use of two or more different types of measures of the same thing to arrive at one conclusion for the purpose of strengthening the validity of the conclusion. A questionnaire could have been used, or random interviews could have been conducted. In this project, time and money constraints precluded these measures.
- The Professional Development Committee understood the role of nontraining professional development opportunities and was receptive to the recommendation that nontraining solutions should be implemented along with high-yield training. However, they had no experience in determining the worth of development opportunities. As a result, they needed follow-up information about how to select the solutions with greatest potential for performance improvement.

Conclusions

The needs assessment we report in this paper used a combination of models and methods to strengthen the accuracy and usefulness of its conclusions. The evaluation research model provided a guideline for involving stakeholders throughout the needs assessment process. It also demonstrated to the planning committee a new strategy for selecting professional development options. The nominal group technique strengthened the proprietorship and accuracy by involving all employees equally in a process whereby they reflected on all ideas and had their questions and concerns addressed. Perhaps the most powerful aspect of this approach is in the way the data were reported.

Organizing the needs and solutions according to the performance technology model enabled the decision makers to recognize the need to address both training and nontraining professional development options. Finally, we would like to emphasize that the techniques we have described in this chapter-evaluation research, nominal group technique, and data presentation within the framework of the performance technology model can be used to improve almost any system.

CHAPTER 9 REVIEW

Answers to the review questions and self-test questions are found in the back of the textbook.

Review Questions

9-1. Why was the Community College needs assessment conducted?
9-2. What are the four steps when using the nominal group technique?
9-3. How was the Behavior Engineering Model used in the assessment?
9-4. Describe the six steps used in the assessment planning and implementation of the project.
9-5. What similarities and difference were found between function groups in the suggestions made?
9-6 Of the recommendations made, which three to four do you feel would have the greatest impact?
9-7. At the conclusion of the project, what benefits and limitations of the process were uncovered?

Self-Test Questions

T F 9-1. Feasibility in terms of cost, timeliness, and manner of implementation; and utility, accuracy, and proprietorship in terms of outcome, are examples of how feedback from stakeholders can influence a project.

T F 9-2. In the study, linking professional development with performance improvement was unnecessary because all participants at the college were highly incentivized and motivated.

T F 9-3. A key question for all participants in the study was: "What do I need to meet my professional goals and objectives?"

T F 9-4. The purpose of evaluation research is to provide "blue sky" data that allows for computer modeling decision-making based on external predetermined x/y variables.

T F 9-5. The nominal group technique expedites problem assessment and is more productive than other techniques because it helps limit the participation to express ideas to those with decision-making authority.

T F 9-6. A high-yield intervention is one where the benefits of an intervention exceed the costs of intervention.

CHAPTER 10

Fundamental Ten: Leading Whole Systems Change

Learning Objectives

10-1. Have a comprehensive understanding of large group interventions and how they can address organizational elements including strategy, structure, processes, people, and culture
10-2. Recognize the need for everyday leaders to build organizations where people are continually expanding their capabilities in their work
10-3. See what makes up a learning organization and what each element consists of
10-4. Become familiar with Lewin's principles and understand why they are practical and important
10-5. Explain how everyday leaders can become change professionals encouraging development of organizational members and the enterprise
10-6. See how leaders in learning organizations are designers, teachers, and stewards
10-7. Appreciate the skills needed for leading in learning organization
10-8. Have a comprehensive understanding of a sample Future Search conference including the benefits, phases, agenda, conditions for success, and barriers to change
10-9. Recognize the organizational design process and the key design principles
10-10. Be familiar with the benefits of large-scale organizational design conferences

CHAPTER OUTLINE

Introduction

Leadership of an organization emerges when the company is able to compete successfully by continuously aligning strategy, structure, and processes, and learning to deal with the needs of incremental change while simultaneously preparing for radical change caused by the discontinuous pressure of the external market. This requires that the organization be designed to account for competition in a mature market where cost, efficiency, and incremental innovation are vital while developing new products and services where speed, flexibility, and radical change are critically important.[227] Both of these notions are easily understood, yet usurping one to make more sumptuous the other may create short-term success but will eventually lead the organization to long-term failure. Leading organizations proactively align their strategy, structure, processes, people, and culture through incremental evolutionary change. This change is punctuated by radical and discontinuous change that requires simultaneous shifting of the strategy, structure, processes, people, and culture to deal with sudden changes in technology, regulatory events, changes in the political environment, economic conditions, and competitive shifts in the market.[228] It is the knowledge of some kind of organizational design process, maybe even a self-designing process, that is required by management to deal with this phenomenon.[229]

In this chapter we see how large group interventions and the organizational design process can help companies organize themselves and deal with the complexities of organizational life. The chapter includes a through explanation of Future Search and includes a detailed description of a sample future search conference. The phases of the sample conference are explained: planning the conference; the conference itself; and follow-up implementation. The organization, everyday leaders, and stakeholders benefit when strategic direction, work processes, organizational structure, and jobs are aligned through the whole system change.

Large Group Interventions

What Is a Future Search Conference?

Weisbord and Janoff[230] suggest that the Future Search Conference is a constructive action as well as a building block of theory and practice for a house that will never be finished. They view it as a progress report from a learning laboratory that has literally thousands of constructive action projects inputting into the theory and the practice all the time. The learning that results from a Future Search Conference does have three uses:

1. Future Search processes lead stakeholders to create a shared future vision for their organization or community
2. Future Search meetings enable all stakeholders to discover shared intentions and take responsibility for their own plans
3. Future Search can help people implement a shared vision that already exists by building aligned strategies for getting there
4. A brief overview of the Future Search process shows that there are some mutually reinforcing conditions for success which include:
    - Whole system in the room

- Global context, local action
- Common ground and future focus, not problems and conflicts
- Self-managed small groups
- Full attendance
- Healthy meeting conditions
- Three-day event (sleep twice)
- Public responsibility for follow-up

Why Are These Ideas Relevant for Everyday Leaders?

Those who work in the private or public sectors have witnessed the oppression of power by managers. Many are committed to improving that situation, not just the performance of workers and managers, but also the worth and development that can result from work for all in the work environment. These dedicated writers, researchers, and practitioners have contributed to a profession and others who have come later stand on their shoulders to see farther.

Much is owed to these pathfinders of change. The present-day and future workers need to further develop the means through which work can be democratic and have developmental worth to individuals. So much can happen at work more than just higher value of productivity and shareholder value. The value of meaningful work where the above concepts are applied can bring about accomplishments resulting in satisfaction and happier people.

Action Research: From Where Future Search Emerged

Kurt Lewin[231] created a conceptual tool of tension between the person and the environmental constructs. Being a social scientist (phenomenologist), Lewin stressed the psychological ecology, or the factors in the environment, such as behavioral settings surrounding the individual at work. Here Lewin hoped to identify the immediate determinants of action. Lewin's tools were both practical and ethical.

Lewin's Principles

The principles from the Lewin readings[232] that are important and relevant to the practice of organizational change today include the following:

1. Understanding the interplay between the work environment and the individual worker is critical for change in organizations. Any change in personal growth of individuals within a work group due to training, for example, should have a correlate attempt for social and cultural change within the entire organization. If there is no attempt to change both individuals and the environmental culture of an organization, any change is not likely to succeed. That is why one training session is not likely to bring about significant organizational change. This principle is reflected in the formula B = f (p,e), where Behavior (B) change is the function (f) of the person (p) and the environment (e).
2. To understand the system, you must first seek to change it. Lewin called this action research. Accurate measurement of environmental and individual perceptions helps to clarify false perceptions and create correct knowledge about problems blocking performance of individuals. Gathering, measuring, and evaluating this evidence of perceptions must involve all who create the perceptions.
3. Wed scientific thinking (action research) to democratic values for organizational change. Democracy in the practice of change is critical because every work system is a value system as well. It is not possible to have a value-neutral work system. Whereas action research allows for the practice of accurate inquiry and measurement, democracy encourages participants to clarify their own feelings of ambivalence or frustration as well as their own perceptions of what would or wouldn't work. The combination of action research and democracy creates new energy around accepting new values at work as well as the cohesiveness necessary for change in organizations. The more cohesive the group, the greater the readiness for members to influence and be influenced by others.

Lewin[233] contended that it is very difficult to get productivity if you do things *to people*. It is better to do things *with them*. His re-educative approach was sometimes called an action research or action learning approach, which is only a partial use of the principles stated above. As mentioned above, a re-educative approach involves those with a stake in the problem helping to accurately define it and solve it. The more involved those who are affected are in the problem-solving process, the more likely a long-lasting solution will be devised. The author contends that the players involved have to view themselves and act like everyday leaders in order to make this work.

The Re-Educative Approach to Organizational Change

This re-educative approach is based on the idea of systems changing themselves through a communal effort by the people affected by the change acting as everyday leaders.

As mentioned above, Weisbord and Janoffl[234] recalibrated the principles of Lewin and tips of Trist and Emery into the following learning assumptions for leading change:

- Each person has a unique learning style. Some learn best by reading, others by doing, still others by discussing or listening. Hence, we provide in the Future Search a variety of methods not all of which will suit everyone.
- Each person learns at a different rate. Hence some may be confused or lost in early stages. It is okay not to get it the first time you hear it. Try to be patient with yourself and others.
- Each person learns different things from a common experience. Hence, we encourage trading of perceptions and acceptance of different feelings and views.
- Each person learns best from his or her own experience. Hence, we urge testing ideas against your own situation and support a healthy skepticism toward a one best way to process change in organizations.

Rethinking involves cognitive change, which leads to behavioral change, which then leads to performance improvement. This requires a work environment of systems thinking, where there is an integration of technical (control), personal (autonomy), and organizational (cooperation) lenses simultaneously. This is what has come to be called a "learning organization."

Learning Organizations

Leaders in learning organizations are designers, teachers, and stewards. Thus, they are responsible to build organizations where people are continually expanding their capabilities in their work.

Designers - The first task for the everyday leader is putting in place the governing ideas of purpose, vision, and core values. The policies, strategies, and structures translate the ideas of purpose into business decisions. The basic mental model of a learning organization is "planning as learning" where the organization fosters learning.

Teachers - Max dePree says the first responsibility of any leader is to define reality—and not act as an authoritarian expert. In learning organizations, much attention is paid to people's mental models and the influence of the systems perspective. Leaders as teachers help people adjust their views of reality to see beyond superficial conditions and events and thus see new possibilities for shaping the future.

Stewards - Robert Greenleaf's explanation of leader as servant comes closest to what Senge means by "steward." The author contends both are part of the everyday leader's skill set. It is one who serves first. The conscious choice by the everyday leader to serve first brings others to aspire to lead. This is a different source of leadership as it is not the power drive or the need to acquire material possessions. The energy to lead comes from the stewardship for the people they work with and the larger mission that underlies the enterprise.

Skills Needed

The skills required for leading in a learning organization include:

1. Building a shared vision so people's capacity for caring can be engaged
2. Once engaged, communicate and ask for feedback and support
3. Distinguish the vision as one of aspiration and accomplishment, not one of responding in fear
4. Recognize that new ideas often conflict with current mental models, so a leader must use the skills of reflection and inquiry to balance inquiry and advocacy, espoused theory from theory in use, and recognize and defuse defensive reactions
5. Successful leaders often use systems thinking, which help them focus on underlying trends and the forces behind change as well as day-to-day events. This allows them to see interrelationships, not things; processes, not snapshots of behavior; and to separate out complex details from complex dynamics

Takeaways - Learning Organization

A learning organization is important for a number of reasons:

1. Employee development is intrinsically right
2. Strategic advantage depends on capable, committed, empowered employees in all areas, and on all levels
3. Productive employment helps economic health of society—more people working equals more customers

Anxiety of Unlearning

To speed up creation of a learning organization, a parallel system of a psychologically safe environment for learning and a support system for dealing with anxiety of unlearning must be created:

1. Leaders must be able to learn something new to help them overcome their own cultural past learnings.
2. Leaders must create a change management group (steering committee) in which the leader is able to express concerns in a supportive environment and to express his or her own anxiety
3. The old mental model was that "the top thinks and the bottom acts." This is being replaced by thinking and action at all levels of the organization. - Senge

Key Learning Insights

"Learning occurs when we detect and correct error . . . Learning also occurs when we produce a match between intentions and results for the first time."[235]

- "Organizations 'learn' when useable knowledge is created, and improvements occur from it."
- "In general, the more an organization depends for its survival on innovation and adaptation to a changing environment, the more essential its interest in organizational learning."[236]
- "Learning should be in the service of action, not simply discovery or insight"[237]
- "Action learning asks managers to focus primarily on their own live experiences, rather than dissecting dead bodies such as case studies of how other managers have behaved in other situations."[238]

How Does One Conduct a Future Search

Future Search is a process that simultaneously addresses the incremental and whole-system change needs in the vision, mission, goals, objectives, structure, and operations of the organization. The process can unearth internal and external problems, concerns and issues. Thus, the everyday leaders involved in the process should focus on the informal culture of the organization and how that culture may or may not be allowing the development of the members and the development of the enterprise.

Some suggestions for everyday leaders[239] as change professionals are as follows:

- Think in wholes: The effectiveness of the whole is of greater importance than the effectiveness of the parts.
- Create self-regulating teams: This allows the possibilities of coping with problems immediately, seizing opportunities in a timely fashion, providing internal coordination for multiskilled contributors, and enhancing capacity of the work system by enlarging roles and not adding specialists.
- View peers as a resources, not commodities: This provides autonomy, learning, variety, mutual support and respect, and meaningfulness as the big picture is seen along with a mutually desirable future.
- Demonstrate the change members want: everyday leaders: By modeling what they want to see happen at work, get the system to see and adapt itself. Thus, the change is brought about by the people who make the change work in the first place.

Alternate Team Approaches

If management attempts to make the changes, change will be speedy and achieve what management wants, but the change may not be what they need. The disadvantage of this attempt is that it does not include input from knowledgeable sources and lacks support from those most affected by the change.

If one learning team sets out to make the changes, it will provide higher quality as the change will be designed by those who know the work the best. Also, it will gain grass-root support as members are bringing about the change. On the other hand, the disadvantages are that implementation may be slow due to an effort to ensure the team be representative. Widespread support may be lacking with only one learning team, which over time may become isolated from the rest of the organization.

If a critical mass of members, acting as everyday leaders, it will produce a high-quality change, greater ownership and speed in decisionmaking. It does require careful planning as facilitating a critical mass of members is no small accomplishment. Another benefit is that management will see that having change brought about this way is much more a morale boost than a morale bust.

Benefits of Future Search

Large-scale change conferences organized by everyday leaders involve the stakeholders as significant and as a result can redesign work to align strategic direction, work processes, organizational structure, and jobs. They can achieve:

- Better coordination and information flow around goals
- Reduced costs and cycle time by removing or minimizing steps that do not add value
- Improved responsiveness to customers and their needs
- More innovation that shorten the distance between ideas and implementation
- More value added through people where customers receive whole services, not isolated fragments
- A sharper focus for managers integrating their efforts across boundaries
- A workforce that is more flexible and broadly skilled

Phases of a Future Search Process

Summary of Four Phases of a Future Search Process:

1. Planning the Future Search Conference including describing the purpose of the conference and how the results will be carried forward.
2. Future Search Conference (2½ days) - getting started; recalling the past; appreciating the present; living the future; confirming common futures; moving into action
3. Follow-up implementation (3–6 months); make plans more precise; create decision-making process; implement projects; summarize experiences; make new action plans
4. Follow-up implementation (1–3 years); implementation of projects; decision to form a continuous search process

Expanded Four Phases of the Future Search Process

Phase 1: Planning a Future Search Conference

Preliminary planning includes the decision to hold a conference and planning the conference: selecting stakeholders/participants, setting expectations for the Future Search Conference, and deciding on the program, times, and location of the conference(s).

Decision to Hold a Future Search Conference

Consider a Future Search If . . .	**Go Slow When . . .**
• A shared vision is needed	• Leadership is reluctant
• An action plan is needed	• Minimum conditions above are met
• Other efforts have stalled	• Nobody but you sees the need
• New leadership is taking over	• Leadership wants to force it in their plan
• When key transition is at hand	• The agenda is preset

- Opposing parties have no good forum to meet
- They have no planning time
- Time is growing short
- Everybody but you wants it

Choosing Participants:

- Participants should be the stakeholders affected by the planning
- Include stakeholders who have a special interest in probable outcomes
- Participants do not have to be experts in the planning situation
- Prepare people to be comfortable in groups with mixed rank and status

Conditions for Participation:

- All participants must attend all activities
- A Future Search Conference is not a convention for speeches or testimonials
- Participants should not be disturbed in the process by outside activities
- The process is best facilitated from a location away from daily disturbances
- All opinions and perspectives of participants must be respected by all the participants

Expectations of Outcome:

- Consensus generation with creative strategies and collaborative approaches
- Awareness of shared values and commitment to change
- Enjoying the learning from each other
- Integration of cultural, regional, and value differences

<u>Phase 2: Future Search Conference (2 ½ days)</u>

Framework of Principles

The future search conference is unlike a participative meeting. It involves a cross section of the whole system, which allows more diversity and less hierarchy than is typical in participative meetings. It provides an opportunity for each person to be heard and to learn from others. Future scenarios are put into a global perspective before action is taken on a local scene later on in the process. People self-manage themselves and use dialogue as the tool to help each other find common ground where differences are honored but not necessarily reconciled.[240] Thus, the framework of the process includes:

- The whole system, or representation of that system, present in the room at one time
- Global and historical context that allows the work to occur in the context of the larger environment
- Focus on the future and common ground
- Self-management and dialogue rather than problem solving and conflict management

Future Search Working Agreements:

- These agreements should be posted on the wall and visible at all times throughout the two and a half days. They are as follows:
- Conference participants are responsible for:
    - o providing information/meaning
    - o self-managing in small groups
    - o generating future scenarios/actions
- Conference manager is responsible for:
    - o setting times and tasks
    - o managing/facilitating/gatekeeping large group discussions
    - o keeping the purpose "front and center"
- Ground rules to be used in the process (also posted and visible at all times) from beginning to end include:
    - o All ideas are valid
    - o All information is posted on flip charts
    - o Observe time frame
    - o Discover common ground and possibilities for action
    - o Differences will be acknowledged and understood but not worked through
    - o Listen to others—every voice is important

Self-Managing Roles:

- *Discussion leader* assures that everyone is heard who wants to be heard within the time available. It is important that the discussion leader "Accept each other's reality as fact for that person." If this is done well, then there is meaningful dialogue and participants can discover common ground for action. Also, the discussion leader and the timekeeper help each other keep the participants on task to finish on time.
- *Timekeeper keeps* the participants aware of the time left and signals what time there is remaining to the person who is talking. This avoids grandstanding and unequal allocation of time among participants. Timekeepers make sure that group tasks are completed on time and he or she monitors the group reports.
- *Recorder* writes on flip charts the group's work in the participants' own words. Often the recorder needs to ask participants to restate lengthy ideas in a more succinct manner.
- *Reporter(s)* presents group results in the time allotted. This role can be shared among many of the participants.

Awareness of the Future Search Conference as a Change in Paradigm:

The conference manager needs to be mindful of the tacit task of seizing teachable moments to point out that the participants are probably experiencing pulls from two different paradigms of working together. This is one of many ways that the Future Search process itself gives the group the energy it needs to complete the conference. That experience is then hopefully carried over to the workplace and the follow-up meetings. These two paradigms can be explained by the following breakdown.

OLD	**NEW**
• Things break down over time	• Can always self-organize to create anew
• Equilibrium is desired	• Two kinds of change happen all the time

• Structure is made by us	• Structure is always unfolding
• Structure gives order	• Information gives order
• Information is controlled	• Information is freely generated

No one can force change on anyone else. It has to be experienced. Unless we invent ways where paradigm shifts can be experienced by large numbers of people, then change will remain a myth. - Eric Trist[241]

The other essential awareness that the conference manager needs to keep front and center makes up what is called the core values of the process. Each core value is to be treated equally. When this is modeled by the conference manager, the participants begin to model that behavior.

The core values of the Future Search Process[242] include:

- *Epistemology:* The real world is knowable to ordinary people and their knowledge can be collectively and meaningfully organized. Thus, people can create their own future.
- *People:* Employees want to engage their hands, heads, and heart to create the necessary processes for success.
- *Participation:* The best results come from everyone participating like an equal.
- *Process:* The first three values emerge if the process uses cooperation, empowerment, and shared control and appreciates diversity.
- *Prejudice-Free*: Working together with shared tasks across lines of ethnicity, race, gender, class, hierarchy, and special function breaks down negative stereotypes and minimizes bias.

At the actual Future Search Conference, the agenda, as seen below, should be posted on the wall and visible at all times so participants can keep track of the progress of the process. A typical agenda is as follows:

Typical Future Search Conference Agenda

Day 1, Afternoon (Where We Have Been)
GETTING ABOARD 1:00 p.m. to 2:00 p.m.
Welcome and Introductions 2:00 p.m. to 6:00 p.m.
Focus on the Past (world trends: political, economic, sociological, and technological)
Focus on the Present (external trends that affect the organization)

Day 2, Morning (Where We Are)
PLUNGING THE DEPTHS 8:30 a.m. to 12:30 p.m.
External Trends Continued
Focus on Present Trends (external and internal) That Affect the Organization (Group Mind Map)
Owning Our Actions ("prouds" and "sorries")

Day 2, Afternoon (What We Want to Be)
VIEWING THE HEIGHTS 12:30 p.m. to 3:00 p.m. (includes lunch)
Ideal Future Scenarios for the Organization 3:00 p.m. to 4:30 p.m.
Identify Common Ground 4:30 p.m. to end
Present Common Ground on the Future

Day 3, Morning (How to Get There)
DIALOGUING THE REAL CHOICES 8:30 a.m. to 1:00 p.m.
Confirm Common Future (reality dialogue)
Action Planning (strategies, structures, processes, systems, competencies, learning)

Past as a Prelude to Future Outcomes

The focus on the past, going back over the last thirty years, should always be completed as it sets up the dynamics for the group's involvement. What has happened to the organization over the same time should be covered, as well as what has happened to each participant over the same thirty years. Past is a prelude to the future outcomes of the process. It can be completed in many ways, but it should involve all the participants. It is meant to show the common experiences that are shared and open the group up for more rigorous sharing of information.

This part of the program can be missed, but by the same token it is part of the process that should never be missed. It is essential for what follows.

Examination of the Present

The present is then examined. It is at this time that the conference becomes a community in and of itself. The giant Group Mind Map that gets created in this stage of the conference brings about the recognition that with the sheer number of forces that impinge on people in the organization no one can deal with it all alone. This recognition of the complexity and hugeness of it all opens up avenues for working on changing the system.

The Group Mind Map involves the recording of the trends that affect the future of the group and is particularly important to the process. It is a wall map where the entire group will place trends affecting them right now. This is a group brainstorm technique in which there is no evaluation and no censorship. An example given by Weisbord and Janoff[242] is as follows: "More cell phones is an example of a trend toward more frequent communication." The Group Mind Map builds a shared context of concerns and priorities. The ground rules follow.

Ground Rules for Group Mind Map:

- "We all see what we all see"
- Key things impacting culture change in the organization
- Remember: "No evaluation or censorship of any item put on wall map"
- Discover major trends and related trends.

Once the Group Mind Map is complete, then in small groups the participants talk over the trends that are of concern to your stakeholder group. Then make your own map on a flip chart to show how these trends are related and how they affect you. On this new map, note the examples of what you are doing right now in response to these trends and what you want to do that you aren't doing right now. The participants then report back to the larger group in a four-minute report.

This allows the participants to see the most important factors affecting the organization.

Once the reports are completed, the information is used to prepare the "prouds" and "sorries" report on the present. Based on the second set of smaller maps, with new people in the leader roles take the information and do the following:

- List what you are doing right now that you are proud of in your relationship to the task of the Future Search Conference
- List things you are doing right now that you are sorry about

As a group, select the proudest "prouds" and the sorriest "sorries" and prepare another report three minutes in length to be presented to the whole group. This is the last step in looking at the current reality and is a critical time in the process. Bunker and Alban[243] suggest that by this juncture, participants will have a better understanding of the whole system, internal and external, and it becomes clear that to improve the whole the different parts will have to act with the whole in mind. Now, and only now, can the large group begin to think about the future.

Imagining the Future

Imagining ideal future scenarios in heterogeneous groups is next. Ask the participants individually to put themselves thirty years into the future. Ask them to visualize the organization they would really want as if it exists now. Then ask them to list on single sheets of paper the accomplishments that were completed in those ten years that caused the ideal future to happen. Then, on a flip chart, list the major barriers you had to overcome and the opportunities you worked for those accomplishments. Ask each group at this point to choose a creative way to present all of those futures to the larger group, such as in a skit, drama, or TV special. Next, we attempt to discover the common ground across all of these futures.

What Do You Want?

To focus the group to discover their common ground, simply ask about the desired themes in the ideal scenarios, What Do You Want?

Ask them to record these desires. Have the smaller groups report back to the larger groups these themes as well as how they might be achieved. The result is a long list of what is wanted and how it might be achieved. From this collection comes the common future desired by the whole conference. In the large group, prepare a list of themes that make up the common future agenda (what is wanted) and a second list of the ways to work toward it (how it is to be achieved). These are agreed upon by a consensus of the large group. A third list is created of themes that are not agreed upon but are felt to be strong candidates. These lists are then merged into one list.

Joint Action from Consensus

At this time, the conference manager must seek to understand what the group really wants. Also, the point must be made regularly that the participants should move ahead only on what they can agree on and are willing to support. That means that each person must be willing to take action to support the point. All points are accepted and heard, but some may not be reconciled. People can and should work toward their preferred goals, whether or not supported by the whole conference, only not during the conference as democracy dictates. The purpose here is to base the conference on joint action from consensus and then plan common futures.

The next steps are relatively easier. Brainstorm short- and long-term action steps. These include steps you can take right now. Also, list what is needed and the due dates of the series of actions. Then set times for follow-up meetings.

Phases 3 and 4: Follow-up Implementation (3–6 months and 1–3 years)

Conditions for Success Following the Future Search Conference

Organizations that are capable of undergoing significant change must be able to recognize the barriers to change and the ways to encourage support for change. Weisbord and Janoffl[244] suggest that these followups be planned as reunions that include newcomers and newsletters. Follow-ups are a critical component of the process because the power of the bureaucratic system in the organization has a tendency to slow down or stop the momentous effects of the Future Search.

Barriers That Stimulate Resistance to Change

Change-capable organizations must recognize the barriers to change and the ways to encourage support for change. Weisbord[245] identified several barriers that stimulate resistance to change:

- Failing to be specific about a change
- Failing to show why a change is necessary
- Failing to allow those affected by the change to be involved in the planning and process
- Using personal appeal to gain acceptance
- Disregarding a work group's habit patterns
- Failing to keep employees informed
- Failing to allay employees worries about failure
- Creating excessive work pressures during change
- Failing to deal with anxiety over job security

Weisbord[246] provides several ways to encourage support for change. They include involving employees in planning the change, providing accurate and complete information, and giving employees a chance to air their objections. Other ways include always taking group norms, values, beliefs, and habits into account as change moves along, making only essential changes, and learning to use problem-solving techniques.

An Organizational Design Process

Hupp[247] developed a process for designing work to achieve fit among purpose or strategy, processes, and people. The organization by design process,[248] as described below, was created from the following selected sources: Galbraith,[249] Trist,[250] Weisbord,[251] Cummings and Worley,[252] M. Emery,[253] and Bunker and Alban.[254] It is important to remember that the purpose is not to create the perfect design, but to create a design of a self-adaptive system.

The three parts of this overall, self-adaptive system include the following:

Environment

Environment (the external context) interacting with the strategic direction (the organization's response, its corresponding purpose, and strategy). This captures the leaders' need for knowledge of organizational design. The categories of this knowledge are environmental pressures of international business on the organization; flexibility of the organization's structure and its design; knowing the uniqueness of the organization's culture and potential competing values; know-how and learn-how of managing large-scale organizational change supported by appropriate developmental techniques; and understanding group dynamics and group process during change, especially in relationship to conflict and collaboration.

Work Process and Technology

Work process and technology involve the work processes and tools that it takes to produce the organization's products and services, how the information flows, and the measure of the accomplishment of work. This captures the need for alignment in organizational design factors discussed above. The knowledge that enables a leader to bring about this change involves understanding the interactions among power, leadership, and management; understanding the importance of information technology (see chapters by Jackson and Ray in this volume and understanding the importance of comprehensive organizational communication and interpersonal communication).

People

People, their performance, their organizational structures, and HR systems involve how people are organized, how authority and responsibility are distributed, how people are selected, developed, and rewarded. What enables a leader for this part includes the following: understanding how people are different in their work styles; understanding how people perceive differently owing to their positions; understanding how a worker's attitude is actually shaped by his or her style and perception; understanding how the motives of people are impacted by their attitude and by the feedback they receive from the work environment.

Self-Designing System Concept

A self-designing system[255] is designed to do the following:

- Be increasingly self-regulating and more responsive to its business context
- Deploy a work process that is fast, focused, and flexible
- Include members with the collective expertise to plan, coordinate, control, and troubleshoot their own start-to-finish work process
- Construct jobs that build contributors' ownership and commitment

Key design principles for a self-designing system drawn from the literature of organizational design summed up by Hupp[256] include the following:

Think in Wholes

- The best design for a productive system is one in which each part of the system embodies the goals of the overall system. Maintain principles of ethics as standards against which to measure true progress.
- Joint optimization: Effectiveness of the whole is more important than effectiveness of the parts.

Create Self-Regulating Units

- Units should be sufficiently self-regulating so that they can cope with problems and seize opportunities by rearranging their own resources.

- Provide internal coordination and control. Provide information and discretion directly to those who need it, when they need it.
- Provide requisite variety in control systems. Internal flexibility should be appropriate to environmental variability. Feedback systems should be as complex as the variances they need to control.
- Provide for redundancy of functions (multiskilled contributors) rather than redundancy of parts (staffing to support narrowly sliced, specialized functions). Enhance capacity by enlarging roles, not by adding specialists.
- The design process should set "minimal critical specifications." Do not carve in stone what should be left to local discretion.

View People as Resources with Free Speech, Not as a Commodities

(Provide jobs that meet M. Emery's[257] six psychological criteria):

- Elbow room (autonomy)
- Learning (allow individuals to set goals and get direct feedback)
- Variety
- Mutual support and respect
- Meaningfulness (allow doers to "see the big picture" and create something important)
- A desirable future

Walk the Talk - "Be the Change You Want to See"

- Use a change process that demonstrates and reinforces the outcomes you hope to achieve.
- The design process is more about getting the system to see and adapt itself than it is about perfecting workflow and structure. Redesign should be participative, not representative. That is, redesign should be done by people who must make the redesign work, not by a representative design team in isolation.

Realize that it is never finished. You are not making a transition between one stable state and another. You are moving from one period of transition to another.

Benefits of Large-Scale Organizational Design Conferences

There are unique benefits of large-scale organizational design conferences by the stakeholders.[258] When you design work to align strategic direction, work processes, organizational structure, and jobs, you can get the following:

Better coordination and information flow

When you organize work around whole products or services, people who need to cooperate with each other are on the same team, focused on a common goal. (In the past, work has typically been organized around functions, putting people who need to cooperate with each other in different work groups, pursuing function-specific goals.)

Reduced costs and cycle time

When you streamline workflow, you remove or minimize nonvalue-adding steps. This reduces cost, cycle time, and opportunity for error. In addition, when mature work teams plan and monitor their own work, you need fewer managers. The managers who remain can focus on integrating efforts across teams and developing business strategy.

Improved responsiveness to customers

When you organize work around products, services, or customer groups, employees get greater access to customers, become better at anticipating customer needs, and provide better-informed, more responsive customer service.

Innovation

When you provide employees with the opportunity and responsibility to improve their products, services, and processes, you shorten the distance between ideas and their implementation.

More value added through people

When employees produce whole products or services, not isolated fragments, they take more ownership over their jobs. Also, jobs that integrate thinking with doing result in greater job satisfaction. Finally, when managers focus on integrating, instead of supervising, they concentrate on getting people to work together across boundaries, not second-guessing individual efforts. This focuses them on adding value, not reworking their subordinates' work.

Greater flexibility

When the organization deploys a broadly skilled workforce, it gets more flexibility than when it deploys a narrowly skilled one.

Hupp[259] recommended some special precautions for large-scale organizational design:

- Management needs to do the hard work of thinking through what it will and will not accept on the front end.
- Aligning the organization (becoming an open, learning system where the workers who perform the core process are invested with the authority and accountability to plan, make decisions, and seize opportunities that are embedded in their processes) involves a fundamental power shift from the following:
    - Hierarchical to participative power
    - Expert diagnosis and prescription (doing it to the line organization) to line contributors examining and adapting their own system (doing it through the line organization)

Confirm Management Support

Before you begin the process, confirm that management is ready for this shift. Make sure it intends to become strategic rather than tactical, integrative rather than empire-building, resource brokering rather than resource controlling. Members of the planning or steering team need to play the role of advocates, not critics, of the process. Change management means more than good public relations. It means engaging stakeholders in working through the real conflicts and polarities that underlie differences, not smoothing them over with sound bites.

If you use large-scale conferencing methodologies,[260] facilitators need to make sure that the conferences allow enough time and provide forums to engage the real conflict and polarities that exist in the system. Facilitators need to be skilled in building sustainable agreements among diverse stakeholders. Sponsors, advocates, and consultants need to remember that the ultimate answers are not in the methodology—it is simply a tool. The system's stakeholders already have all the wisdom they need to find their answers. It's the job of sponsors, advocates, and consultants to get them to discuss the right questions, so they can collectively uncover the truth that is already there, buried under organizational clutter.

CHAPTER 10 REVIEW

Answers to the review questions and self-test questions are found in the back of the textbook.

Review Questions

10-1. In what ways are leaders in learning organizations designers, teachers, and stewards?

10-2. Describe three to four skills needed for leading in a learning organization. Of the three or four which one would you say is most important and why?

10-3. What is meant by the "anxiety of unlearning"?

10-4. What are the three uses for a Future Search Conference? What are three to four conditions for success?

10-5. What is meant by "To understand the system, you must first seek to change it"? What did Lewin call this?

10-6. When planning a Future Search Conference, name the conditions for choosing participants, conditions for participation, and expectations of outcome.

10-7. What are the roles of the discussion leader, timekeeper, recorder, and reporter during a Future Search conference?

10-8. In what ways are "process" and "prejudice-free" core values of the Future Search process?

10-9. Name four to five barriers that stimulate resistance to change.

10-10. Why is it important to confirm management support before commencing a large-scale organizational design conference?

Self-Test Questions

T F 10-1. The re-educative approach is based on the idea of systems changing themselves through a communal effort by the people affected by the change acting as everyday leaders.

T F 10-2. As a core value of the Future Search process, epistemology means documenting, presenting, and discussing stories that show everyone participating as equals to achieve consensus.

T F 10-3. The disadvantages of a single team attempting to implement change include a potentially slow implementation (due to an attempt to ensure that the team is representative), and a lack of widespread support thus isolating the team from the rest of the organization.

T F 10-4. According to Lewin, the more cohesive the group, the more resistant members are to being influenced by other members of the group.

T F 10-5. The work processes and tools that it takes to produce the organization's products and services, how the information flows, and the measure of the accomplishment of work are one part of an overall self-adaptive system.

T F 10-6. "More value added through people" is a benefit of a large-scale organizational design conference and results in managers focusing on integrating (instead of supervising) and getting people to work together across boundaries (not second-guessing individual efforts).

EPILOGUE

Kristin Lytle, MBA, PCC

I am convinced that the organizations that will be "winners" in the future are the ones that figure out how to stop wasting potential today by usurping the personal power of a person with an overemphasis on position power.

Not wasting potential is a concept that seems incredibly simple, but the reality is that it is not easy to execute. If it was, we wouldn't see things like gender wage gaps or significantly fewer women in senior-level roles across most industries. Perhaps, if we had learned to stop wasting potential, we would be experiencing what used to be called "turnover" instead of "The Great Resignation."

Thankfully, there is good news. There are simple fundamental actions any organization can take that will reduce the quantity of potential wasted in their ranks.

Action 1: Increase Transparency

To be clear, I am not advocating for total transparency (e.g., making potential ratings public for all to see). Transparency for transparency's stake only leads to more "noise" and confusion for employees. Transparency for the purpose of clarity is a necessary action to unlock the full potential of your workforce.

Clarity enables employees to understand the "rules of the game." For example, share the definition of high potential at your organization and share the experiences and capabilities that are required to reach various levels of leadership. Ensure that having this information is not a result of being in the right crowd, in the right room at the right time, or even winning the boss lottery. If all employees know what it means to be considered for leadership investments and roles, they can opt in based on desire and capability.

Think about it, if you are staying true to your own rules and definitions, the worst-case scenario if you share these "rules of the game" is that more people will be striving to meet them.

Factor 2: Support Authenticity

Authenticity is a word that is being used heavily in recent leadership literature and therefore can have a variety of interpretations. However, despite it becoming a buzzword, the case for supporting authenticity is strong. Quite simply, authenticity reduces waste.

We all have a finite number of "mental calories" we can burn each day. In environments where people are not allowed to be their authentic selves, a significant number of mental calories are used for continuous self-monitoring. This leads to fewer mental calories being spent on solving business problems and driving results.

The narrower the norms at your organization, the higher percentage of mental calories are likely being used for self-monitoring and not on business impact items.

As a leader, you have to ask yourself, "Where do you want your employees burning their mental calories?": On continuous self-monitoring to ensure they fit the norms or molds of your corporate environment? Or on producing results?

Factor 3: Leading in an Asynchronous World

Dorie Clark said it beautifully in her book, *The Long Game*: "Do you want the best talent for the job? Or the best talent in your zip code?" It is widely understood that the global pandemic has changed how, when, and where work happens. The full extent of that impact is not yet known. It is probably a "no-fail bet" that we will never work in the same synchronous fashion as we did before the pandemic (i.e., most people working in the office during "business hours," five days a week). Consequently, if you want to ensure you are not wasting potential at your organization, learning to be a great leader in asynchronous environments will be a basic requirement.

A few things to consider when asking how ready you are to lead in this new world:

How clear and consistent are your objectives and priorities?

Do your team members know what is most important when they are being asked to take on new initiatives, even when you are not present?

How often do you put your ideas into writing?

How strong and clear is your writing?

A good rule of thumb is, the more you relied on MBWA (managing by walking around) prior to the pandemic, the more likely it is you need to bolster your skills in asynchronous leadership to include being proficient with virtual tools and resources.

In summary, nothing I have shared is rocket science. If anything, it is quite fundamental and one might argue that these skills have always been important for leadership. As with most principles in business that are not complex, it is the firm, made up of the human beings, that executes the most effectively, that is the one that "wins."

REVIEW

Self-Test Questions and Answers

REVIEW AND SELF-TEST QUESTIONS AND ANSWERS

CHAPTER 1

Review Questions

- *What have studies shown about being able to correlate specific traits (popularity, verbal facility, initiative, etc.) and leadership effectiveness?*

  In general, studies showed that the selection of leaders on the basis of traits was unsuccessful.

- *What do studies of behavioral styles show about their influence on effective leadership? What does the Ohio State model explain? What happens when the Ohio State model is superimposed on the managerial grid?*

  What correlations did Clothier discover?

  In general, studies showed no single style of leadership is the best for all situations. The Ohio State model plots consideration (likelihood of job relationships with subordinates; respect their ideas, etc.) and initiating structure (structure toward goal attainment). According to most experts (e.g., Korman, Sales, etc.) the model has little predictive value. Merging the Ohio State Model and Managerial Grid produces a grid-mapping concern for people and concern for production, even though there is significant differences between the models. Clothier found high correlations between a high "Initiating Structure" style and increased worker productivity and between a high "Consideration" style and increased worker satisfaction.

- *What is meant by leadership functions? Give two or three examples of comparing the scientific management school and human relation school when addressing specific approaches.*

  Leadership functions are what a leader does and should do to become effective. Examples: (1) Nature of Authority. Scientific: Autocratic. Humanistic: Democratic. (2) Communication. Scientific: One way. Humanistic: Flows between Levels. (3) Organizational Structure. Scientific: Rigid. Humanistic: Decentralized.

- *Distinguish McGregor's Theory X and Theory Y. Distinguish between task behavior and relationship behavior.*

  Theory X: Goals of the organization are emphasized. Theory Y: Balanced view of the worker in the organization.

  Task behavior: the extent to which leaders organize and define roles of followers; explain activities; and define ways the job is to be accomplished. Relationship behavior: the extent to which leaders maintain personal relationships between themselves and the group.

- *Fiedler's theory measured leadership effectiveness and aspects of group behavior. What is the principal value of Fiedler's theory?*

  The principal value of this theory is that it lends support to the premise that different leadership styles are appropriate in different situations.

- *List Clothier's four leadership styles to Reddin's eight leader styles.*

  Clothiers four styles of leadership: instrumental; participative; supportive; achievement-oriented. Reddins: autocratic; benevolent autocratic; bureaucratic; compromiser; deserter; developer; executive; missionary.

- *What is meant by style adaptability? How do people with a narrow style range differ from those with a wide range of styles?*

  Style adaptability is the degree to which leaders are able to vary their style appropriately to the demands of a given situation. Narrow range of styles: people can be effective over a long period of time when the style has a high probability of success. Wide range of styles: may be ineffective if the behaviors are not consistent with the demands of the situation.

- *According to Hersey and Blanchard, how should a leader respond (in terms of task behavior and relationship behavior) as the level of maturity of a follower increases in terms of completing a specific task?*

  As the level of maturity of the follower(s) continues to increase in terms of accomplishing a specific task, the leader should begin to reduce task behavior and increase relationship behavior.

- *How does transactional leadership differ from transforming leadership? What is meant by fusion leadership?*

  Transactional: joint effort of follower and leader with a common aim of exchanging one thing for another.

  Transforming: eventually, the leader seeks to satisfy the higher needs of the followers. Fusion leadership creates a robust common vision, reducing obstacles or barriers to change.

- *Name and describe four to five of Kouzes and Posner's commitments and explain how each might operate in a real-life situation.*

  Find challenging opportunities; learn from success and failure; envision an ennobling future; enlist others to a common vision; promote cooperative goals.

Self-Test Questions

T F 1-1. Trait theory of leadership focuses on social skills; popularity; sensitivity, etc.; behavioral theory focuses on style (e.g., democratic, authoritarian, concern for people, concern for production, etc.)
True

T F 1-2. In studies of leadership functions, specifically organizational structure, scientific management would favor decentralization; human relations would favor centralization.
False. Scientific management favors centralization; human relations favor decentralization.

T F 1-3. The Managerial Grid is used in management development and describes five types of leadership behavior including task, team, and middle-of-the-road.
True.

T F 1-4. Situational leadership theory is prescriptive (indicating how a leader should act in various situations) and developmental (with an increase in task-relevant maturity, style should progress).
True.

T F 1-5. According to Reddin, the benevolent autocrat style of leader is perceived as distant and passive (low task, high relationship) but interested in the task and therefore highly effective.
False. Benevolent autocrat is high task/low relationship. Perceived as knowing what he or she wants.

T F 1-6. Transformational leadership is called fusion (as opposed to fission) since it creates the energy needed to overcome obstacles to change.
True

T F 1-7. Kouzes and Posner identified five fundamental practices of exemplary leadership, including encouraging the heart and enabling others to act.
True

CHAPTER 2

Review Questions

- *Outline the intersection of Maslow's hierarchy of needs with the roles people occupy suggested by Oshry.*

  In the context of Oshry's role relationships:
  Bottoms are concerned with safety, job security, and their vulnerability.
  Tops have achieved higher status and already have addressed their safety/belonging needs. They are focused on self-esteem needs.
  Tops are motivated by their need for self-actualization in order to fulfill their potential as human beings.

- *What is system blindness? In what ways does it negatively affect the interpretation and response to events?*

  System blindness is seeing individuals within the system without seeing the whole system—the team, the partnerships, the processes, and the overall environment. In spatial blindness, one sees only that part of the system he or she is involved with. Temporal blindness is seeing only the present and not the past. Relational blindness is not seeing relationships or their impact

- *Define the terms tops, bottoms, and middles as they apply to roles? How does one differ from the others?*

  Tops occupy positions of great power in the system. Middles have neither high or low rank in the system; Bottoms are low-ranking members of the system. Tops are conscious of prestige differentials; middles often judge based on superficial qualities; bottoms share a feeling of vulnerability and tend to band together.

- *Generally, which role (top, bottom or middle) seems to have the best understanding of the system as a whole? Why is that?*

Bottoms have the best grasp of the overall system, probably because they tend to band together and share information.

- *Describe the outcome of a scenario when all three roles are in play.*

  In a business situation, middles may be tom between demands of tops and bottoms. Tops and bottoms become dependent on the middles to solve problems, and the middles accept problem-solving responsibility. Since it is unrealistic to expect middles to resolve their problems, middles blame themselves for failure.

- *What is the name for the situation which occurs when HOW things are done is institutionalized? Does this facilitate change?*

  Cultural inertia results in inertia and complacency and becomes a barrier to change.

- *In what way is structural inertia an obstacle to everyday leadership? Give an example how this might manifest itself in an organization.*

  Structural inertia blocks everyday leadership by presenting obstacles (e.g., processes and procedures) to change or improvement. An airline, for example, that relies on an obsolete ticketing system will have a difficult time introducing change throughout the system

- *What are the "invisible systems" posited by Oshry? Are they constructive or destructive? Why is that?*

  Oshry's invisible systems are systems of hierarchy. They can be destructive if they negatively affect our responses to events and people. But if we recognize these systems at work, we can practice everyday leadership and achieve change.

- *As more responsibility is assumed, how can middles and ends put in practice everyday leadership to solve problems?*

  Assuming the acceptance of more responsibility is a problem, middles and ends need to practice everyday leadership. Middles need to become assertive to induce and support ends to solve their own problems. Ends need to realize they have the strength and the capabilities required to resolve their own problems.

- *In what ways is the Paradox of Culture an obstacle to everyday leadership?*

  The culture associated with an earlier success may not be the same culture needed for future success. If an organization is stuck in a past culture, it makes it difficult for everyday leadership to introduce and manage change.

Self-Test Questions

T F 2-1. Middles occupy positions of great power in an organization, often keep responsibilities to themselves and exclude others.
False. Tops occupy positions of great power.

T F 2-2. Spatial blindness results in a confused perspective since it means a lack of an understanding of how an area of specialization fits in with other areas of specialization.
True

T F 2-3. Having a sense of the power in numbers is a characteristic of tops.
False. Bottoms have a sense of power in numbers.

T F 2-4. Temporal blindness is the ability to forecast the future without seeing the present.
False: Temporal blindness is only seeing the present and not the past.

T F 2-5. Everyday leadership will result in a needed change when one "sees" the systems at work within an organization.
True

T F 2-6. Most people regard themselves as self-governing entities; as such, when we understand the roles we play, we can then become more productive.
True

T F 2-7. Everyday leadership applies to individual behavior and should not be used for analyzing group behavior.
False. Everyday leadership is best practiced in one's sphere of influence and throughout the organization and applies to the entire system.

T F 2-8. Power differentials help to equalize relationships and encourage innovation throughout the system.
False. Power differentials are inequities and can produce destructive behavior.

T F 2-9. "Ends" are the roles occupied by those just entering or just exiting an organization.
False. Ends are a term that refers to tops and bottoms as a unit.

T F 2-10. The very culture that encouraged organizational success in the past can become an obstacle in the future when the organization comes face to face with uncertainties.
True

CHAPTER 3

Review Questions

- *Describe the four stages of multidepartmental teams proposed by Gaucher and Coffey. What kinds of malfunctions arise when teams form?*

Form, storm, norm, and perform. Malfunctions can arise from territoriality (by department or profession), role confusion, or lack of experience/training in-group processes.

- *What are the characteristics of successful teams described by the Harpers?*

  Characteristics: a shared goal, a climate of trust and openness, honest communication, diversity valued as an asset, members who are interdependent, and consensus decision making where no one person dominates the team.

- *According to the University of Tennessee study, what was needed in the earliest stage for the team to gel? What makes that factor so important?*

  A group began to form only when feedback about performance (from one another and from university faculty) was introduced in the process. The feedback is essential for the group to interact.

- *Describe synergistic collaboration. Why is it difficult to assess and evaluate?*

  Synergistic collaboration occurs when the team's overall discipline, determination, and dedication work to make the best decisions that can be made. Difficult to assess because working to maintain it causes it to diminish.

- *What are the three features of the Team Learning System? What makes them mutually reinforcing? Does one carry more weight than the others? Use an example from teams you may have participated on in the past to assess each.*

  Innovation, learning culture, diversity. Depending on the situation, one may carry more weight than the others.

- *How do goal setting, decision making, and leadership/participation manifest themselves in an* effective *team environment? In an* ineffective *team environment? Describe two* new *team attributes, not shown in table 3-1, and describe the outcome for effective and ineffective teams.*

  Goals. Effective: (1) Team generated. Ineffective: Leader generated. (2) Decision making: Effective: based on situation. Ineffective: based on authority. (3) Leadership/participation. Effective: All share to participate and achieve goals. Ineffective: Leadership based on authority.

  New attributes: (1) Atmosphere. Effective: Relaxed. Ineffective: Tense (2) Meeting "mechanics" (e.g., coming on time; being prepared). Effective: Meeting mechanics respected. Ineffective: Members arrive late and unprepared.

- *What is "action learning" and how does this subprocess fit in to the overall team dynamic?*

  Action learning is an ethical addition of the team process because each team member can voice his/her opinion. All members can present and can argue their opinions.

- *Which stage of the University of Tennessee study presents the greatest challenge to the formation of a viable team? In what way do individually based-norms and universally accepted norms influence the outcome?*

  Vying for voice presents the greatest challenge for the team-to-be. Individually based norms of behavior (centered around self-interest) need to be reconciled with the more universally accepted norms (fairness and equal dignity to each human person).

- *Define, compare and contrast team "group think" with "diversity of opinions, ideas and experience." In what situations of team dynamics, will one produce a better outcome than the other?*

In group think differences are viewed as deviance from the norm; with diversity of opinions, ideas and experience, these differences are respected. Generally, group think will produce sterile results; diversity will usually produce fresh ideas and concepts.

Self-Test Questions

T F 3-1. Leader-generated (as opposed to team-generated) goals are generally more realistic and therefore pivotal to the success and effectiveness of teams.
False. Team-generated goals are more clearly understood and effective.

T F 3-2. Form, storm, norm, and perform are the four stages of a multidisciplinary team.
True

T F 3-3. The University of Tennessee study found diversity of talent contributed to better decision making.
True

T F 3-4. Via the Team Learning System, team members "learn to learn" and participate as everyday leaders.
True

T F 3-5. Centralized control and fixed boundaries are counterproductive to effective work teams.
True

T F 3-6. For a team to be successful, it is essential that conflict be addressed outside the normal team working process.
False. Conflict is a normal part of the team process.

T F 3-7. Vying for voice is one of *five* stages of team development and disappears once the team forms constructive communication.
False. Vying for voice never disappears.

T F 3-8. Learning about everyday leadership occurs more quickly in a team environment.
True

T F 3-9. Focusing on the maintenance of team synergy ensures it will flourish.
False. Working to maintain synergy causes it to diminish.

T F 3-10. The University of Tennessee study found that when clear goals are articulated, the group as a whole becomes motivated to succeed.
True

CHAPTER 4

Review Questions

- *Describe the difference between continuous (incremental) change and discontinuous (whole system) change.*

  Continuous or incremental change is marked by cost-containment, efficiency, and incremental innovation. Long-term success is marked by increasing alignment among the strategy, structure, process, people, and culture through incremental or evolutionary change punctuated by discontinuous or whole system change that requires a radical, simultaneous shift in strategy. Discontinuous or whole system change driven by organizational performance problems or technological, competitive shifts in the market, regulatory events, or political conditions. Speed, flexibility, and radical innovations are critical to adapt to crises.

- *In order for a company to respond to change and succeed in the longer term, it needs to align its structure, people, and processes, and what other four factors? Of all seven, which three would you say have the greatest impact and why?*

The other factors are strategy (defines how the organization will respond with products and services to customers and prospects), systems (the procedures that make the organization run), competence (the skills of both employees and managers), and culture (includes the values as revealed in everyday work performance). The three with the greatest impact are for the student/reader to respond to.

- *List the elements of the change matrix. Describe why ones are considered incremental, anticipatory, reactive, or discontinuous?*

  Tuning (incremental/anticipatory): no fundamental change; adaptation (incremental/reactive): adaptation is a result of an imperative to change; reorientation (discontinuous/anticipatory): this consists of visionary insights into environmental shifts and involves a fundamental redefinition of the enterprise; and re-creation (discontinuous/reactive): in this case, there is fast and simultaneous change of all basic elements of the organizational system.

- *What do we mean by "ambidextrous" when describing leaders or organizations? Why is it important in times of change? Why is it important that a board of directors has a majority of outside directors? Why should all outside directors meet alone from time to time, without inside directors? How do inside and outside directors impact organizational change? Do they have different priorities, for example?*

  Ambidextrous in times of change: "Ambidextrous" refers to versatile, skillful companies in times of change constantly innovating and taking steps to ensure long-term survival. Majority of outside directors: When compared to inside directors, outside directors bring other corporate experiences and are usually not as beholden to the chairman and other executives. Meeting alone: Outside directors need to exert independence from other inside directors by convening and sharing opinions absent inside influence. Directors and change: The priorities of inside directors will be to protect power and turf when faced with change decisions. Outside directors are more likely to bring independent and unbiased thinking when addressing corporate change issues.

- *How did the Paradox of Culture impact Apple, Johnson & Johnson, IBM, and Sears?*

  The paradox is often that the culture associated with the earlier success of the company is the same culture that can lead to its downfall. Apple: Over a thirty-year period, Apple instituted radical changes in the design so new strategies would be congruent with structures, competencies, cultures, and leadership skills. Apple was not hindered by sticking blindly to an old culture. Johnson & Johnson: J&J responded radically to a changing market and moved successfully into pharmaceuticals. IBM/Sears: Stuck to the very culture that made them successful, did not change, and, in IBM's case was hindered for years; in Sears' case, the company was absorbed by Kmart.

Self-Test Questions

T F 4-1. Whole system change refers, for example, to the systems that a purchasing manager is using to distinguish the calculation of sales tax for the whole country.
False: Whole system change is radical, discontinuous change.

T F 4-2. In the change matrix, a good example of "tuning" is how other providers of cell phones have to respond/will be responding to Apple's introduction of the iPhone.
False: Cell phone companies who only "tune" may be doomed. Other cell phone companies will need to adapt or even re-create.

T F 4-3. In order to stay agile, and respond to change, units within an organization should be kept small, manageable, and autonomous.
True

T F 4-4. The development of a skilled senior team that stays above the fray of everyday operations is vital for ensuring the organization is not distracted from achieving goals.
False. A skilled senior team does not allow itself to become insulated from the rest of the organization.

T F 4-5. Ambidextrous companies are ones that are versatile and skillful, constantly innovating, and taking steps to ensure long-term survival.
True

T F 4-6. Structural and cultural inertia both are essential elements of an organization's long-term success.
False: These kinds of inertia will hinder long-term success.

T F 4-7. Verbal, vocal, and visual components are essential elements of all interactions, and communicate more than any words on a page. This is part of the "S" element of the L.E.A.D.E.R.S. Method.
False. They are part of the Speak with Specificity element of LEADERS.

T F 4-8. Among other things, the S-curve demonstrates the need to reformulate the strategy, design, people, and culture of an organization on an ongoing basis.
True

T F 4-9. Had they invented the quartz technology, the Swiss watch industry would most likely be the leader in that category today.
False: The Swiss did invent quartz technology but chose to stay with the old technology—the tuning fork.

T F 4-10. The VCR industry is a good demonstration that once a standard emerges, competition shifts from the design of the product to price and features until a major new product or service is created.
True

CHAPTER 5

Review Questions

- *Briefly describe the quadrants of the Johari Window.*

  The Johari Window is made up of 4 quadrants – arena (common knowledge), façade (blocking knowledge), blind spot (unaware of self) and unknown potential (hidden potential for team development).

- *What kind of reaction from the group does the "interviewer" style evoke? Does this style help, hinder, or have no effect on the growth of the group?*

  The "interviewer" overuses feedback and does not self-disclose. This creates distrust amongst the group and hinders its growth.

- *In what ways does disclosure expand a leader's sphere of influence?*

  Self-disclosing to another person has incredible impact because it begins to build trust within that interpersonal relationship.

Self-Test Questions

T F 5-1. Providing and receiving information in a relationship increases trust and helps both sides attain aspirations.
True

T F 5-2. Greater knowledge of oneself in relation to others leads to greater self-esteem and self-acceptance.
True

T F 5-3. The Johari Window is a tool that can be used to improve the way we influence others around us.
True

T F 5-4. According to Lewin, it is more productive to do things *with* others than *to* them.
True

CHAPTER 6

Review Questions

- *According to de Geus and the Royal Dutch/Shell Group Study, what are the most important predictors of corporate health?*

  De Geus suggested that corporate health was rooted in the company's ability to grasp the need for change and adapt to it.

- *What is the attribution error that often causes organizational design to be limited or even fail?*

  The attribution error is (a) an overemphasis on humans as the cause of problems and (b) an underestimation of the role environmental factors play in causing resistance to plans for change.

- *Why are attempts to adapt to change incrementally unlikely to succeed?*

  All decisions to deal with system change depend upon leaders both in the organization and in the process they are allowed to use, enabling them to deal with both kinds of change, incremental and discontinuous. Attempting to adapt to discontinuities through incremental adjustments is not likely to succeed.

- *Describe the different vantage points or contexts when optimizing organizational design.*

  Philosophical: the ideals under which the organization operates.
  Cultural: the larger environment in which the organization exists.
  Policy: the vision and missions that define the purpose of the organization.
  Strategic: the plans designed to carry out the mission.
  Tactical: the specific duties that achieve the strategies.
  Logistical: the support system (resources, information, incentives, etc.) that enables workers to carry out duties.

- *In the health care example of organizational design, what are examples of questions that need to be asked when aligning functional groupings?*

  What departments report to what divisions?
  What is the degree of centralization and decentralization? What are the budget structures and procedures?
  How is decision-making authority set up? How are jobs designed?
  What are the control and coaching mechanisms for performance improvement?
  What is the role of human resource management systems? How does the physical location affect the ergonomics of work?

- *What are examples of factors and behaviors in a changing system? Why is each important?*

  The people performing their jobs; the measurement of the performance; the processes that make up the tasks performed; the systems that comprise the processes; the arrangements of the hierarchy and reporting relationships; the informal structure professionals create for themselves; and how the strategy of the organization aligns itself to all these factors.

Important organizational behaviors of everyday leaders: recognition of individual differences in workers; accurate perception of performance; correct assumptions about the motivation of workers; the information technology of organizational communication; the influence of conflict and collaboration on both group and team dynamics.

- *In the health care example, what information would an excellent leader include in a performance support system?*

  Effectively communicate expectations; continuously feedback on the results of performance; objectively allocate resources for task support; consistently base the rewards, recognition, and incentives on the work performed.

Self-Test Questions

T F 6-1. Organizational design is the field of study that focuses on the viewing of an organization as a system and how the framework of that system interfaces and influences the performance of the individual.
True

T F 6-2. In the health care example, cooperative learning of physician leaders and health care workers requires working together on the integration of items such as goals, policies, and procedures.
True

T F 6-3. An essential tenet of organizational design is to respond to change incrementally and individually.
False. The need is to respond to change incrementally and radically.

T F 6-4. Individuals often overemphasize the role humans play and underestimate the role environmental factors play in causing resistance to plans for change.
True

T F 6-5. Someone viewing an organization from a cultural vantage point will address the support systems that enable workers to carry out duties.
False. The cultural vantage assesses the larger environment in which the organization exists.

T F 6-6. Strategic vision describes how the organization acts to survive in the marketplace.
True

T F 6-7. Singh suggests that managers, incorrectly, often attempt to influence workplace behavior via organizational change rather than through individuals in the workplace.
False. Singh suggests managers attempt to fix the individuals in the workplace when they should be working on organizational change.

CHAPTER 7

Review Questions

- *Why are the PROBE Learning questions important? What do they reveal?*

  The questions focus on expectations, feedback, task support, and performance incentives and are designed to begin to uncover the culture of a system of work.

- *Provide two to three examples of how a "battle strategy" might be designed knowing a competitor's strategic profile.*

Examples to be provided by student or reader. (Planning battle strategies requires profiling the enemy's strongholds before you attacking the most obvious one.)

- *Identify the six factors Gilbert identified that can guarantee competence if delivered with a clear mission.*

  Information, resources, incentives, training, capacity, and motives.

- *What do we mean by "functional flow" in the context of behavior?*

  In order to maintain behavior, we must receive information, act upon it, and be motivated to continue.

- *Why are there no "bad" answers when responding to PROBE questions?*

  PROBE is used to profile the barriers to behavior and to help plot a balanced strategic approach to overcoming the barriers. It's not used to judge correct or incorrect responses.

- *How do the strategic profiling questions (figure 7-1) relate to the original Probe questionnaire?*

  Strategic profiling questions include all items in the original PROBE questionnaire but are revised to address a work environment.

- *Identify components of the behavioral engineering model and describe how it is part of the unitary behavioral transaction.*

  Data, instruments, incentives, knowledge, capacity, and motives are components of the model. The model says that information and data are two different things. To be truly informed, we must have knowledge of precisely what the data say.

- *When reviewing behavior, what is meant by "leverage points"?*

If we train them well and provide an efficient working environment, most employees have adequate motives and capacity to do an excellent job. Great leverage points most frequently lie in the environment and in training.

Self-Test Questions

T F 7-1. The six levels of vantage described by Gilbert include training, capacity, and motives.
False. The six levels are philosophical, cultural, policy, strategy, tactical, and logistical.

T F 7-2. For strategic profiling, it is helpful to reword PROBE questions to match the specific situations being addressed.
True

T F 7-3. Leverage of each aspect of behavior of improving performance varies from one person to another.
True

T F 7-4. In strategic profiling, "no" answers are important because they demonstrate a predilection to organizational change.
False. The "no" answers to relevant questions reveal possible barriers to excellent performance.

T F 7-5. PROBE offers a way to analyze tasks and find ways to improve performance by sorting out the high-leverage points in human behavior.
True

T F 7-6. Instruments are the environmental aspect of a response.
True

T F 7-7. PROBE questions are designed to uncover the logistics and data system support (LDSS) of an organization.

False. The questions are designed to uncover the culture of a system of work.

T F 7-8. Something can be done, with reasonable ease, to improve or downgrade performance by changing the task data, knowledge, instruments, capacity incentives, and motives. **True**

CHAPTER 8

Review Questions

- *What are the six factors influencing performance according to Gilbert's Behavioral Engineering Model?*

  Information, resources, incentives, knowledge, capacity, and motives.

- *What does the Taco Bell example tell us about "quality of source" and how it relates to reengineering strategies?*

  No answer provided here

- *"Behavior plus accomplishment equals performance." What does Gilbert mean by the formula?*

  Gilbert felt that behavior is confused with performance and accomplishment. Accomplishments are the important, positive outputs that a manager wants to happen as a result of the behavior of his or her employees. He felt there was a need to understand performance in detail and create the proper measurement systems.

- *Describe the three criteria of an accomplishment and what is meant by each.*

  Quality (accuracy, class, and novelty); quantity (rate, time, and volume); and cost (labor, materials, and management).

- *In general terms, what does Dean ask participants to identify in the exercise "What's My Biggest Performance Block?"? What does the outcome demonstrate?*

  The exercise asks participants to identify one of Gilbert's six factors as the source of performance limitation. Results from the exercise show that participants are more likely to identify environmental factors (rather than individual factors) as hampering better performance.

- *Compare the outcome of the Performance Block exercise when participants were asked to distinguish their own performance from the performance of others.*

  When participants' responses about the performance of others (rather than themselves) were studied, participants identified individual factors (not environmental factors) as blocking the better performance of others.

- *Describe the three levels of Rummler and Brache's Performance Improvement Process.*

  Organizational level, process level, and performer level.

- *What factors does the Human Performance System Checklist assess?*

  The checklist is used to assess the environmental and individual factors that influence the performer.

Self-Test Questions

T F 8-1. "Quality at the Source" requires employees to strictly evaluate and control the performance of managers.
False. Quality at the Source makes employees responsible for the quality of their accomplishments by providing them with the tools to identify and solve work process problems.

T F 8-2. According to Rummler, accomplishments should be measured at all organizational levels.
True

T F 8-3. The Human Performance System Checklist assesses environmental and individual factors that influence performance.
True

T F 8-4. Establishing the reliability of an accomplishment requires observations from two or more independent observers.
True

T F 8-5. Gilbert suggested six performance engineering guidelines including establishing standards based on the performance of exemplary employees.
True

T F 8-6. Results from the Performance Block exercise show individual factors playing a more important role than environmental factors.
False. Participants are more likely to identify environmental factors (rather than individual factors) as hampering their own better performance. (Although when participants' responses about the performance of others (rather than themselves) were studied, participants identified individual factors (not environmental factors) as blocking the better performance of others.)

CHAPTER 9

Review Questions

- *Why was the Community College needs assessment conducted?*

The assessment was conducted to identify the training needs of each function group (administrators, faculty, and support personnel) at the college.

- *What are the four steps when using the nominal group technique?*

  Generation of ideas, sequential reporting of ideas, clarification of ideas, and ranking of ideas by importance.

- *How was the Behavior Engineering Model used in the assessment?*

  The model was used to identify what could be done to improve and maintain performance.

- *Describe the steps used in the assessment planning and implementation of the project.*

  Establish goals, design needs assessment techniques, conduct focus groups, train facilitators, conduct needs assessment, and analyze data.

- *What similarities and differences were found between function groups in the suggestions made?*

  Similarities: (a) the need for information about policies, department structure, decision making, and "what the other person is doing." (b) The need for resources.

  Differences: (a) The administrators suggested training needs/ solutions with a special interest in communication and interpersonal problemsolving skills. (b) The faculty was interested only in training related to their subject-matter area.

- *Of the recommendations made, which three or four do you feel would have the greatest impact?*

  Student/reader to review recommendations and assess.

- *At the conclusion of the project what benefits and limitations of the process were uncovered?*

  Benefits: participants felt they were (finally) being listened to; recognition that nontraining actions were required to increase value of training; nominal technique produced worthwhile suggestions; results produced a benchmark to be used in future assessments; wide range of options produced; demonstrated the value of performance technology and needs assessment; validated training as an excellent solution.

  Limitations: process was time-consuming; excess reliance may have been placed on perceptions; difficult for the client to calculate the value of some recommendations.

Self-Test Questions

T F 9-1. Feasibility in terms of cost, timeliness, and manner of implementation; and utility, accuracy, and proprietorship in terms of outcome, are examples of how feedback from stakeholders can influence a project.
True

T F 9-2. In the study, linking professional development with performance improvement was unnecessary because all participants at the college were highly incentivized and motivated.
False: As a general statement, it's important and necessary to link professional development and performance improvement.

T F 9-3. A key question for all participants in the study was: "What do I need to meet my professional goals and objectives?"
True

T F 9-4. The purpose of evaluation research is to provide "blue sky" data that allows for computer modeling decision-making based on external predetermined x/y variables.
False. The purpose of evaluation research is to provide data that can enable decision-making, through analysis of pros and cons, through prioritizing, and through the application of decision-making criteria and other means.

T F 9-5. The nominal group technique expedites problem assessment and is more productive than other techniques because it helps limit the participation to express ideas to those with decision making authority.
False. The nominal group technique involves stakeholders, with each person assured that he or she has an equal opportunity to express ideas.

T F 9-6. A high-yield intervention is one where the benefits of intervention exceed the costs of intervention.
True

CHAPTER 10

Review Questions

- *In what ways are leaders in learning organizations designers, teachers, and stewards?*

  Designers: the first task for the everyday leader is putting in place the governing ideas of purpose, vision, and core values; Teachers: leaders as teachers help people adjust their views of reality to see beyond superficial conditions; Stewards: the energy to lead comes from the stewardship for the people they work with and the larger mission that underlies the enterprise.

- *Describe three or four skills needed for leading in a learning organization. Of the three or four, which one would you say is most important and why?*

  Building a shared vision; communicate and ask for feedback and support; distinguish the vision as one of aspiration and accomplishment; recognize that new ideas often conflict with current mental models. Student/reader to identify the most important skill and rationale.

- *What is meant by the "anxiety of unlearning"?*

  Leaders must be able to learn something new to help them overcome their own cultural past learnings. Rigid procedures and group beliefs can inhibit the reception and evaluation of new information.

- *What are the three uses for a Future Search Conference? What are three or four conditions for success?*

  Uses: to create a shared future vision; to enable all stakeholders to discover shared intentions; to help people implement a shared vision.

  Success conditions: self-managed small groups; full attendance; healthy meeting conditions; three-day event.

- *What is meant by "To understand the system, you must first seek to change it"? What did Lewin call this?*

  Measurement of environmental and individual perceptions helps to clarify false perceptions and create correct knowledge about problems blocking the performance of individuals. Gathering, measuring, and evaluating this evidence of perceptions must involve all who create the perceptions. Lewin called this action research.

- *When planning a Future Search Conference, name the conditions for choosing participants, conditions for participation, and expectations of the outcome.*

  Choosing participants: should include stakeholders who have a special interest in probable outcomes; do not have to be experts in the planning situation; should be comfortable in groups with mixed rank and status.

  Conditions for Participation: all participants must attend all activities; should not be considered a convention for speeches or testimonials; participants should not be disturbed in the process by outside activities; location should be away from daily disturbances; all opinions should be respected.

  Expectations for outcome: consensus generation with creative strategies and collaborative approaches; awareness of shared values and commitment to change; enjoy the learning from one another; integration of cultural, regional, and value differences.

- *What are the roles of the discussion leader, timekeeper, recorder and reporter during a Future Search conference?*

  Discussion leader: assures that everyone is heard who wants to be heard within the time available.

  Timekeeper: keeps the participants aware of the time, makes sure that group tasks are completed, and monitors the group reports.

  Recorder: records the group's work in the participants' own words. Reporter: presents group results.

- *In what ways are "process" and "prejudice-free" core values of the Future Search process?*

Process: Other values emerge when the process uses cooperation, empowerment, and shared control and appreciates diversity.

Prejudice-Free: Working together with shared tasks across lines of ethnicity, race, gender, class, hierarchy, and special function breaks down negative stereotypes and minimizes bias.

- *Name four or five barriers that stimulate resistance to change.*

Disregarding a work group's habit patterns; failing to keep employees informed; failing to allay employees worries about failure; creating excessive work pressures during change; failing to deal with anxiety over job security.

- *Why is it important to confirm management support before commencing a large-scale organizational design conference?*

Management needs to be an advocate of the process and work; otherwise, the team's work may be in vain.

Self-Test Questions

T F 10-1. The re-educative approach is based on the idea of systems changing themselves through a communal effort by the people affected by the change acting as everyday leaders. **True**

T F 10-2. As a core value of the Future Search process, epistemology means documenting, presenting, and discussing stories that show everyone participating as equals to achieve consensus. **False. In Future Search, epistemology means ordinary people knowing the real world with their knowledge collectively and meaningfully organized.**

T F 10-3. The disadvantages of a single team attempting to implement change include a potentially slow implementation (due to an attempt to ensure that the team is representative), and a lack of widespread support thus isolating the team from the rest of the organization.
True

T F 10-4. According to Lewin, the more cohesive the group the more resistant members are to being influenced by other members of the group.
False: According to Lewin the more cohesive the group, the more likely members can influence others and be influenced by others.

T F 10-5. The work processes and tools that it takes to produce the organization's products and services, how the information flows, and the measure of the accomplishment of work are one part of an overall self-adaptive system.
True

T F 10-6. "More value added through people" is a benefit of a large-scale organizational design conference and results in managers focusing on integrating (instead of supervising) and getting people to work together across boundaries (not second-guessing individual efforts).
True

APPENDIX

Select Historical "Leaders" and Leadership Theories

Ramesses II (1303 BC to 1213 BC) is one of the most famous and longest-ruling pharaohs of the Egyptian empire. He is known for the Battle of Kadash and the peach treaty with the Hittites. It was the first peace treaty in the world.

Confucius and Lao-Tzu (sixth century BC) were the two most influential Chinese leaders and existed simultaneously in Dynastic China attracting a number of followers even in the past 2,500 years. **Lao-tzu** sees the entire universe flows with a mysterious invisible force called "Tao." **Confucius** believed that learning to be human was the ultimate goal and each person should act with virtue in all social matters, family, and state.

Homer (750 BC) wrote both ***Iliad***, where the hero leader excels in action to satisfy the desire in the heart to achieve greatness as seen through the character of Achilles and the ***Odyssey,*** where the leader faces many obstacles to hold and keep together the power of the family where he fights for others, not personal glory.

Plato (424 BC to 348 BC) had influence with classical education with a premier publication on political theory. In his dialogue ***The Republic***, Plato used inductive reasoning, a process that develops a theory to explain the living of life.

Aristotle (384 BC to 322 BC) was coached by Plato and tutored Alexander the Great. Aristotle is credited for the empirical approach—a scientific method that is based on observation, hypothesis, and direct experience.

Alexander the Great (336 BC to 323 BC) created one of the largest empires in history stretching from Greece to northwestern India by the age of thirty. He was undefeated in battle and became legendary as a military hero. Military academies throughout the world still teach his tactics.

Asoka the Great (269 BC to 232 BC) was the last of the great Indian empires of Maurya. He had great conquests and his empire was almost the entire Indian subcontinent. He was kind and a good-hearted leader. After a bloody war, he was so moved and pained by the suffering that he denounced his throne and adopted Buddhism.

Caesar Augustus (27 BC to AD 14) was the first emperor of the Roman Empire. His status as the founder of the Roman Principate has consolidated a legacy as one of the most effective leaders in human history.

Julius Caesar (100 BC to 44 BC) attempted to seize control of the Roman Republic to change it to a Roman empire and he had enough power to worry the Senate. The public revered Caesar and he basked in the glory of leadership, while the Senate plotted to remove the looming threat of his tyranny. He was assassinated by his friend Brutus.

Cleopatra VII Philopator (69 BC to 30 BC) was queen of Egypt from 51 BC to 30 BC and its last active ruler. Cleopatra ruled Egypt as an absolute monarch, serving as the sole lawgiver of her kingdom. She was the chief religious authority in her realm, oversaw the construction of various temples, and was directly involved in the administrative affairs of her domain, tackling crises such as famine. Cleopatra's gender has perhaps led to her depiction as a minor if not insignificant figure in ancient, medieval, and even modern historiography about ancient Egypt and the Greco-Roman world.

Jesus Christ (4 BC to AD 30/33) was a great Jewish teacher and Christian leader who impacted the world for over 2000 years. His key teaching was captured in a phrase, "The kingdom of heaven is within us." Some say this is mindful of the Vedic knowledge of pure consciousness experienced by enquiring within our awareness as a self-directed leadership practice.

Plutarch (AD 46 to AD 119) compiled leadership lessons from successful Greek and Roman men and women into his series of biographies called ***Parallel Lives***. Arranged in pairs to illuminate their common virtues and vices, *Parallel Lives* had enormous influence on English and literature.

Nerva (reigned from AD 96 to AD 98) is considered to be a wise and moderate emperor by historians. His greatest success was ensuring a peaceful transition of power after his death. He selected Trajan as his heir. This choice was based on a man's ability rather than his nationality.

Trajan (reigned from AD 98 to AD 117) had many accomplishments; maintained respect and affability toward the Senate; was generous to the populace; spent treasury money for the common good; lessened taxes; created programs for children; tried to secure competent and honest officials; kept good records of the Roman province; and built many public works for roads, bridges, and aqueducts.

Hadrian (reigned from AD 117 to AD 138) choose to invest in the development of stable, defensible borders and the unification of the empire's disparate people. He built Harian's Wall, which marked the northern limit of Britannia. In Rome itself, he rebuilt the Pantheon and constructed the vast Temple of Venus and Roma. An admirer of Greece, he sought to make Athens the cultural capital of the empire. His reign was peaceful.

Antoninus Pius (reigned from AD 138 to AD 161) suppressed a rebellion in Roman Britain and put down revolts by Mauretania, Germany, Dacia, and Egypt. The feeling of well-being pervaded the empire under Antoninus Pius. His reign was the most peaceful in the empire's history.

Marcus Aurelius (reigned from AD 161 to AD 180) was a state philosopher and the last of the rulers known as the Five Good Emperors. He studied Greek and Latin and wrote *Meditations*, a significant source of the modern understanding of ancient stoic philosophy and spirituality. Marcus acquired the reputation as a philosopher king within his lifetime. He had a blameless character and a temperate way of life.

Charlemagne (AD 748 to AD 814) was king of the Franks, king of the Lombards, and emperor of the Romans. During the early Middle Ages, Charlemagne united the majority of western and central Europe and earned the nickname "Father of Europe." His rule spurred the Carolingian Renaissance, a period of energetic cultural and intellectual activity within the Western Church. He was later canonized by Antipope Paschal III, and is regarded as beatified by the mainstream Catholic Church.

Cyrus II of Persia (660 to 530 BC) founded the Achaemenid Empire, the first Persian empire that lasted for thirty years. Cyrus is well-known for having respected the customs and religions of the lands he conquered. This became a very successful model for centralized administration and established a government that worked to the advantage and profit of its subjects. Cyrus is also well recognized for his achievements in human rights, politics, and military strategy. Cyrus has played a crucial role in defining the national identity of modern Iran.

Alfred the Great (reigned from 871 to 899) was king of Wessex, a strong-minded but high-strung battle veteran at the head of remaining resistance to the Vikings in southern England. Alfred had a reputation as a learned and merciful man of a gracious and level-headed nature who encouraged education, proposing that primary education be conducted in Old English rather than Latin, and improving the legal system and military structure and his people's quality of life.

Genghis Khan (1158 to 1227) was the founder and first Great Khan (emperor) of the Mongol Empire, which became the largest contiguous empire in history after his death. He came to power by uniting many of the nomadic tribes of Northeast Asia, and, after being proclaimed the universal ruler of the Mongols, or *Genghis Khan*, he launched the Mongol invasions, which ultimately conquered most of Eurasia, reaching as far west as Poland and as far south as Egypt. Many medieval chroniclers and modern historians describe Genghis Khan's conquests as wholesale destruction on an unprecedented scale, causing great demographic changes and a drastic decline of population as a result of mass exterminations and famine. Genghis Khan was portrayed positively by early Renaissance sources out of respect for the great spread of culture, technology, and ideas under the Mongol Empire. By the end of the Great Khan's life, the Mongol Empire occupied a substantial portion of Central Asia and China. Due to his exceptional military successes, Genghis Khan is often considered to be one of the greatest conquerors of all time.

Niccolo Machiavelli wrote ***The Prince*** (1513) as a guide for royals and suggested that it was better to be a feared leader rather than a loved leader. He said that his experience and reading of history showed him that politics have always been played with deception, treachery, and crime. He also notably said that a ruler should be excused when the intention and the result are beneficial. The term *Machiavellian* often connotes political deceit, deviousness, and realpolitik, and some say it paved the way for modern republicanism.

Akbar the Great (1542 to 1605) was the third Mughal emperor who reigned from 1556 to 1605. A strong personality and a successful general, Akbar gradually enlarged the Mughal Empire to include much of the Indian subcontinent. Akbar established a centralized system of administration throughout his empire and adopted a policy of conciliating conquered rulers through marriage and diplomacy. To preserve peace and order in a religiously and culturally diverse empire, he adopted policies that won him the support of his non-Muslim subjects. Akbar himself was a patron of art and culture and was fond of literature. During his rule, the Mughal Empire tripled in size and wealth. He created a powerful military system and instituted effective political and social reforms.

Queen Elizabeth I of England (1522 to 1603) was the last ruler of the Tudor dynasty. Her reign as Queen of England and Ireland was a golden era as arts and culture blossomed. The fall of the Spanish Armada helped mark her ability as a military leader ready to defend her country. She was also known as the virgin queen as she remained unwed to a person but very much wed to England. Seems appropriate to go directly to Queen Elizabeth II.

William Shakespeare (1564 to 1616) was an English playwright, poet, and actor, widely regarded as the greatest writer in the English language and the world's greatest dramatist. His extant works, including collaborations, consist of some 39 plays, 154 sonnets, and three long narrative poems. They also continue to be studied and reinterpreted. He was an observer of leadership and allowed us to observe good and bad leadership.

Oliver Cromwell (1599 to 1658) was an English general and statesman who led the armies of the Parliament of England against King Charles I during the English Civil War. He was an intensely religious man and fervently believed in God guiding him to victory. Cromwell demonstrated his ability as a commander and was quickly promoted from leading a single cavalry troop to being one of the principal commanders. Cromwell is one of the most controversial figures in British and Irish history, considered a military dictator by Winston Churchill, and a hero of liberty by others.

Ivan the Terrible (1530 to 1584) was the first ruler who declared himself tsar of Russia. His reign saw the completion of the construction of a centrally administered Russian state and the creation of an empire that included non-Slav states. Ivan engaged in prolonged and largely unsuccessful wars against Sweden and Poland, and, in seeking to impose military discipline and a centralized administration, he instituted a reign of terror against the hereditary nobility. Contemporary sources present disparate accounts of Ivan's complex personality. He was described as intelligent and devout but also prone to paranoia, rage, and episodic outbreaks of mental instability that increased with age. In one fit of anger, he murdered his eldest son and heir.

Peter the Great (1672 to 1725) ruled the Russian Empire from 1682 until his death in 1725. Through a number of successful wars, he laid the groundwork for the Imperial Russian Navy, ending uncontested Swedish supremacy in the Baltic and beginning the tsardom's expansion into a much larger empire that became a major European power. He led a cultural revolution that replaced some of the traditionalist and medieval social and political systems with ones that were modern, scientific, Westernized, and based on the Enlightenment. Peter's reforms had a lasting impact on Russia, and many institutions of the Russian government trace their origins to his reign. He adopted the title of emperor in place of the old title of tsar in 1721 and founded and developed the city of Saint Petersburg, which remained the capital of Russia until 1917.

Frederick II (1712 to 1786) was king of Prussia from 1740 until 1772. His most significant accomplishments include his military successes in the Silesian wars, his reorganization of the Prussian Army, the First Partition of Poland, and his patronage of the arts and the Enlightenment. Prussia greatly increased its territories and became a major military power in Europe under his rule. Frederick was a supporter of enlightened absolutism, stating that the ruler should be the first servant of the state. He modernized the Prussian bureaucracy and civil service and pursued religious policies throughout his realm that ranged from tolerance to segregation. He reformed the judicial system and made it possible for men of lower status to become judges and senior bureaucrats. Frederick also encouraged immigrants of various nationalities and faiths to come to Prussia. He supported the arts and philosophers he favored, as well as allowed freedom of the press and literature. He became known as Frederick the Great.

Catherine II (1729 to 1796), most commonly known as **Catherine the Great**, was the last reigning Empress Regnant of Russia and the country's longest-ruling female leader. Under her reign, Russia grew larger, its culture was revitalized, and it was recognized as one of the great powers of Europe. The period of Catherine the Great's rule is considered a golden age of Russia. She enthusiastically supported the ideals of the Enlightenment, and as a patron of the arts, she presided over the age of the Russian Enlightenment, including the establishment of the Smolny Institute of Noble Maidens, the first state-financed higher education institution for women in Europe.

Napoleon Bonaparte (1769 to 1821) was a French military and political leader who rose to prominence during the French Revolution and led several successful campaigns during the Revolutionary Wars. He was the *de facto* leader of the French Republic as First Consul from 1799 to 1804. As **Napoleon I**, he was emperor of the French from 1804 until 1814 and again in 1815. Napoleon dominated European and global affairs for more than a decade while leading France against a series of coalitions in the Napoleonic Wars. He won most of these wars and the vast majority of his battles, building a large empire that ruled over continental Europe before its final collapse in 1815. He was one of the greatest commanders in history, and his wars and campaigns are studied in military schools worldwide. Napoleon's political and cultural legacy has endured as one of the most celebrated and controversial leaders in world history.

Joan of Arc (1412 to 1431) is considered a heroine of France for her role during the Lancastrian phase of the Hundred Years' War and was later canonized as a saint. Joan said that she received visions of the archangel Michael, Saint Margaret, and Saint Catherine of Alexandria instructing her to support Charles VII and recover France from English domination. King Charles VII sent Joan to the siege of Orléans as part of a relief army. She gained prominence after the siege was lifted only nine days later. This victory boosted French morale and paved the way for the final French victory at Castillon in 1453. She was captured at Compiègne by the Burgundian faction, a group of French nobles allied with the English, and was burned at the stake on 30 May 1431, dying at about nineteen years of age.

Mary Wollstonecraft (1759 to 1797) was an English writer, philosopher, and advocate of women's rights. Until the late twentieth century, Wollstonecraft's life, which encompassed several unconventional personal relationships at the time, received more attention than her writing. Today Wollstonecraft is regarded as one of the founding feminist philosophers, and feminists often cite both her life and her works as important influences.

Maria Theresa Walburga Amalia Christina (1717 to 1780) was the ruler of the Habsburg dominions from 1740 until her death in 1780, and the only woman to hold the position. Maria Theresa promulgated institutional, financial, medical, and educational reforms. She also promoted commerce and the development of agriculture and reorganized Austria's ramshackle military, all of which strengthened Austria's international standing. However, she despised the Jews and the Protestants, and on certain occasions, she ordered their expulsion to remote parts of the realm. She also advocated for the state church and refused to allow religious pluralism. Consequently, her regime was criticized as intolerant by some contemporaries.

George Washington (1732 to 1799) was an American soldier, statesman, and founding father who served as the first President of the United States from 1789 to 1797. Appointed by the Continental Congress as commander of the Continental Army, Washington led the Patriot forces to victory in the American Revolutionary War and presided at the Constitutional Convention of 1787, which established the Constitution of the United States and a federal government. Washington has been called the "Father of the Nation" for his manifold leadership in the formative days of the country.

Thomas Jefferson (1743 to 1826) was an American statesman, diplomat, lawyer, architect, philosopher, and founding father who served as the third president of the United States from 1801 to 1809. The principal author of the Declaration of Independence, Jefferson was a proponent of democracy, republicanism, and individual rights, motivating American colonists to break from the Kingdom of Great Britain and form a new nation. Jefferson promoted a Western expansionist policy, organizing the Louisiana Purchase, which doubled the nation's land area. To make room for settlement, Jefferson began a controversial process of Indian tribal removal from the newly acquired territory. Among his books is *Notes on the State of Virginia* (1785), considered perhaps the most important American book published before 1800, in which he championed the ideals, values, and teachings of the Enlightenment.

During his lifetime, Jefferson owned over 600 slaves, who were kept in his household and on his plantations. Since Jefferson's time, controversy has revolved around his relationship with Sally Hemings with whom he fathered at least six children. After retiring from public office, Jefferson founded the University of Virginia. Presidential scholars and historians generally praise Jefferson's public achievements, including his advocacy of religious freedom and tolerance in Virginia.

Alexander Hamilton (1755 to 1804) was an American statesman, who was one of the founding fathers of the United States. He was an influential interpreter and promoter of the U.S. Constitution, as well as the founder of the nation's financial system, the Federalist Party, the United States Coast Guard, and the *New York Post* newspaper. As the first secretary of the treasury, Hamilton was the main author of the economic policies of the administration of President George Washington. He took the lead in the federal government's funding of the states' American Revolutionary War debts, as well as establishing the nation's first two *de facto* central banks (i.e., the Bank of North America and the First Bank of the United States), a system of tariffs, and friendly trade relations with Britain. His vision included a strong central government led by a vigorous executive branch, a strong commercial economy, support for manufacturing, and a strong national defense. Hamilton is generally regarded as an astute and intellectually brilliant administrator, politician, and financier, if often impetuous. His ideas are credited with laying the foundation for American government and finance.

Abraham Lincoln (1809 to 1865) was an American lawyer and statesman who served as the sixteenth president of the United States from 1861 until his assassination in 1865. Lincoln led the nation through the American Civil War and succeeded in preserving the Union, abolishing slavery, bolstering the federal government, and modernizing the U.S. economy.

Ulysses S. Grant (1822 to 1885) was an American military officer and politician who served as the eighteenth president of the United States from 1869 to 1877. As president, Grant was an effective civil rights executive who created the Justice Department and worked with the Radical Republicans to protect African Americans during Reconstruction. As commanding general, he led the Union Army to victory in the American Civil War in 1865 and thereafter briefly served as Secretary of War. As president, Grant stabilized the post-war national economy, supported Congressional Reconstruction, ratification of the 15th Amendment, and crushed the Ku Klux Klan. Under Grant, the Union was completely restored. He appointed African Americans and Jewish Americans to prominent federal offices. In 1871, Grant created the first Civil Service Commission, advancing civil service more than any prior president.

Theodore Roosevelt Jr (1858 to 1919) was an American politician, statesman, conservationist, naturalist, historian, and writer who served as the twenty-sixth president of the United States from 1901 to 1909. Having assumed the presidency at age forty-two after McKinley's assassination, Roosevelt emerged as a leader of the Republican Party and became a driving force for antitrust and progressive policies. Roosevelt was a leader of the progressive movement and championed his "Square Deal" domestic policies, promising the average citizen fairness, breaking of trusts, regulation of railroads, and pure food and drugs. He prioritized conservation and established national parks, forests, and monuments intended to preserve the nation's natural resources. In foreign policy, he focused on Central America where he began the construction of the Panama Canal. He expanded the navy and sent the Great White Fleet on a world tour to project American naval power. His successful efforts to broker the end of the Russo-Japanese War won him the 1906 Nobel Peace Prize.

Franklin Delano Roosevelt (1882 to 1945) was an American politician and attorney who served as the thirty-second president of the United States from 1933 until his death in 1945. A member of the Democratic Party, he won a record four presidential elections and became a central figure in world events during the first half of the twentieth century. Roosevelt directed the federal government during most of the Great Depression, implementing his New Deal domestic agenda in response to the worst economic crisis in U.S. history. As a dominant leader of his party, he built the New Deal Coalition, which defined modern liberalism in the United States throughout the middle third of the twentieth century. His third and fourth terms were dominated by World War II, which ended shortly after he died in office.

His administration oversaw the construction of The Pentagon, initiated the development of the world's first atomic bomb, and worked with other Allied leaders to lay the groundwork for the United Nations and other post-war institutions. It was under his wartime leadership that the United States would become a superpower on the world stage. Some of Roosevelt's actions have faced substantial criticism, such as his ordering of the relocation and internment of Japanese Americans, as well as his decision to break tradition by running for a third term. Nevertheless, he is consistently ranked by scholars, political scientists, and historians as being among the nation's three greatest presidents.

Anna Eleanor Roosevelt (1884 to 1962) was an American political figure, diplomat, and activist. She served as the first lady of the United States from 1933 to 1945, during her husband President Franklin D. Roosevelt's four terms in office, making her the longest-serving first lady of the United States. President Harry S. Truman later called her the "First Lady of the World" in tribute to her human rights achievements. She persuaded Franklin to stay in politics after he was stricken with a paralytic illness in 1921, which cost him the normal use of his legs and began giving speeches and appearing at campaign events in his place. Following Franklin's election as governor of New York in 1928, and throughout the remainder of Franklin's public career in government, Roosevelt regularly made public appearances on his behalf. As first lady, while her husband served as president, she significantly reshaped and redefined the role.

Though widely respected in her later years, Roosevelt was a controversial first lady at the time for her outspokenness, particularly on civil rights for African Americans. She was the first presidential spouse to hold regular press conferences, write a daily newspaper column, write a monthly magazine column, host a weekly radio show, and speak at a national party convention. She pressed the United States to join and support the United Nations and became its first delegate. She served as the first chair of the UN Commission on Human Rights and oversaw the drafting of the Universal Declaration of Human Rights. Later, she chaired the John F. Kennedy administration's Presidential Commission on the Status of Women. By the time of her death, Roosevelt was regarded as "one of the most esteemed women in the world." *The New York Times* called her "the object of almost universal respect" in her obituary.

Douglas MacArthur (1880 to 1964) was an American military leader who served as General of the Army for the United States, as well as a field marshal to the Philippine Army. He was chief of staff of the United States Army during the 1930s, and he played a prominent role in the Pacific theater during World War II. MacArthur received the Medal of Honor for his service in the Philippine campaign.

Dwight David "Ike" Eisenhower (1890 to 1969) was an American military officer and statesman who served as the thirty-fourth president of the United States from 1953 to 1961. During World War II, he served as Supreme Commander of the Allied Expeditionary Force in Europe, and achieved the rare five-star rank of General of the Army. He was responsible for planning and supervising the invasion of North Africa in Operation Torch in 1942 to 1943 and the successful invasion of Normandy from 1944 to 1945 from the Western Front. Eisenhower's main goals in office were to contain the spread of communism and reduce federal deficits. He was a moderate conservative who continued New Deal agencies and expanded social security.

Sir Winston Churchill (1874 to 1965) was a British statesman who served as prime minister of the United Kingdom from 1940 to 1945 and again from 1951 to 1955. Best known for his wartime leadership as prime minister, Churchill was also a Sandhurst-educated soldier, a Nobel Prize-winning writer and historian, a prolific painter, and one of the longest-serving politicians in British history.

Widely considered one of the twentieth century's most significant figures, Churchill remains popular in the UK and Western world, where he is seen as a victorious wartime leader who played an important role in defending Europe's liberal democracy against the spread of fascism. He is also praised as a social reformer. However, he has been criticized for some wartime events—notably the area bombing of German cities and his government's response to the Bengal famine—and also for his imperialist views, including comments on race.

Sun Yat-sen (1866 to 1925) was a Chinese statesman, physician, and political philosopher, who served as the provisional first president of the Republic of China and the first leader of the Kuomintang (Nationalist Party of China). He is called the "Father of the Nation" in the Republic of China, and the "Forerunner of the Revolution" in the People's Republic of China for his instrumental role in the overthrow of the Qing dynasty during the Xinhai Revolution. Sun's chief legacy is his political philosophy known as the Three Principles of the People: Mínzú or nationalism (independence from foreign domination), Mínquán or "rights of the people" (sometimes translated as "democracy"), and Mínshēng or people's livelihood (sometimes translated as "communitarianism" or "welfare").

Ronald Wilson Reagan (1911 to 2004) was an American politician who served as the fortieth president of the United States from 1981 to 1989. A member of the Republican Party, he previously served as the thirty-third governor of California from 1967 to 1975 after a career as a Hollywood actor and union leader. Early in his presidency, Reagan began implementing new political and economic initiatives. His supply-side economics policies—dubbed "Reaganomics"—advocated tax reduction, economic deregulation, and reduction in government spending. In his first term, he survived an assassination attempt, spurred the war on drugs, invaded Grenada, and fought public sector labor unions. Foreign affairs dominated his second term, including the bombing of Libya, the Iran-Iraq War, the Iran-Contra affair, and the ongoing cold war. Reagan challenged Soviet General Secretary Mikhail Gorbachev to open the Berlin Wall. With Gorbachev he negotiated the INF Treaty, which shrank both countries' nuclear arsenals.

Margaret Thatcher (1925 to 2013) was prime minister of the United Kingdom from 1979 to 1990 and leader of the Conservative Party from 1975 to 1990. The longest-serving British prime minister of the twentieth century, she was the first woman to hold that office. A Soviet journalist dubbed her the "Iron Lady," a nickname that became associated with her uncompromising politics and leadership style. As prime minister, she implemented policies that became known as "Thatcherism"—a series of economic policies intended to reverse high inflation and Britain's struggles in the wake of the Winter of Discontent and an oncoming recession. Her political philosophy and economic policies emphasized deregulation, the privatization of state-owned companies, and reduction of the power and influence of trade unions. She survived an assassination attempt by the Provisional IRA and achieved a political victory against the National Union of Mineworkers in the 1984–85 miners' strike. Thatcher was re-elected for a third term with another landslide in 1987, but her subsequent support for the Community Charge ("poll tax") was widely unpopular, and her increasingly Eurosceptic views on the European community were not shared by others in her cabinet. She resigned as prime minister and party leader in 1990.

Queen Elizabeth II of England (1926 to 2022) was queen of the United Kingdom, Canada, Australia, and New Zealand. She was the sovereign of the Windsor Family and the first woman in the royal family to join the military. In her reign, she served as the head of state, head of the armed forces, and the supreme governor of the Church of England. She was Britain's longest-serving monarch, having embarked on countless overseas tours, welcomed more than 150 heads of state to Buckingham Palace, undertook hundreds of annual official engagements, and at the same time offered calm and empathy in the face of tragedy and crisis.

Mikhail Gorbachev (born March 2, 1931) is a Russian and former Soviet politician. The eighth and final leader of the Soviet Union, he was the general secretary of the Communist Party of the Soviet Union from 1985 until 1991. Ideologically, Gorbachev initially adhered to Marxism–Leninism, although he had moved toward social democracy by the early 1990s. Although committed to preserving the Soviet state and to its socialist ideals, Gorbachev believed significant reform was necessary, particularly after the 1986 Chornobyl disaster. He withdrew from the Soviet–Afghan War and embarked on summits with United States president Ronald Reagan to limit nuclear weapons and end the cold war. Domestically, his policy of *glasnost* ("openness") allowed for enhanced freedom of speech and press, while his *perestroika* ("restructuring") sought to decentralize economic decision making to improve efficiency.

After leaving office, he launched his Gorbachev Foundation, became a vocal critic of Russian presidents Boris Yeltsin and Vladimir Putin, and campaigned for Russia's social-democratic movement.

Golda Meir (1898 to 1978) was an Israeli politician, teacher, and *kibbutznikit* who served as the fourth prime minister of Israel. Meir was elected prime minister of Israel on March 17, 1969, after serving as labor minister and foreign minister. The world's fourth and Israel's only woman to hold the office of prime minister, and the first in any country in the Middle East, she has been described as the "Iron Lady" of Israeli politics.

Muhammad Ali Jinnah (1876 to 1948) was a barrister, politician, and the founder of Pakistan. Jinnah served as the leader of the All-India Muslim League from 1913 until the inception of Pakistan on August 14, 1947, and then as the Dominion of Pakistan's first governor-general until his death. As the first governor-general of Pakistan, Jinnah worked to establish the new nation's government and policies and to aid the millions of Muslim migrants who had emigrated from neighboring India to Pakistan after the two states' independence, personally supervising the establishment of refugee camps. Jinnah died at age seventy-one in September 1948, just over a year after Pakistan gained independence from the United Kingdom. He left a deep and respected legacy in Pakistan and is revered as the *Quaid-i-Azam* ("Great Leader") and *Baba-i-Qaum* ("Father of the Nation"). His birthday is observed as a national holiday in Pakistan.

Yasser Arafat (1929 to 2004) was chairman of the Palestine Liberation Organization (PLO) from 1969 to 2004 and president of the Palestinian National Authority (PNA) from 1994 to 2004. Ideologically an Arab nationalist, he was a founding member of the Fatah political party, which he led from 1959 until 2004. Opposed to the creation of the State of Israel, he fought alongside the Muslim Brotherhood during the 1948 Arab–Israeli War. In the latter part of the 1950s, he co-founded Fatah, a paramilitary organization seeking the removal of Israel and its replacement with a Palestinian state. Arafat began to shift his approach from open conflict with the Israelis to negotiation, and in 1988 he acknowledged Israel's right to exist and sought a two-state solution to the Israeli–Palestinian conflict. In 1994 he returned to Palestine, settling in Gaza City and promoting self-governance for the Palestinian territories. He engaged in a series of negotiations with the Israeli government to end the conflict between it and the PLO. In 1994, Arafat received the Nobel Peace Prize, together with Yitzhak Rabin and Shimon Peres, for the negotiations in Oslo.

Yitzhak Rabin (1922 to 1995) was an Israeli politician, statesman, and general. He was the fifth prime minister of Israel, serving two terms in office, and was Israel's ambassador to the United States during a period of deepening U.S.–Israel ties. In 1992, Rabin focused on embracing the Israeli–Palestinian peace process and signed several historic agreements with the Palestinian leadership as part of the Oslo Accords. In 1994, Rabin won the Nobel Peace Prize together with long-time political rival Shimon Peres and Palestinian leader Yasser Arafat.

Mohandas Gandhi (1869 to 1948) was an Indian lawyer, anti-colonial nationalist, and political ethicist who employed nonviolent resistance to lead the successful campaign for India's independence from British rule, and later inspired movements for civil rights and freedom across the world. Assuming leadership of the Indian National Congress in 1921, Gandhi led nationwide campaigns for easing poverty, expanding women's rights, building religious and ethnic amity, ending untouchability, and achieving *swaraj* or self-rule. Gandhi's birthday is a national holiday in India and worldwide as the International Day of Nonviolence. Gandhi is commonly considered the Father of the Nation in India.

Nelson Rolihlahla Mandela (1918 to 2013) was a South African anti-apartheid revolutionary, political leader, and philanthropist who served as the first president of South Africa from 1994 to 1999. He was the country's first black head of state and the first elected in a fully representative democratic election. His government focused on dismantling the legacy of apartheid by tackling institutionalized racism and fostering racial reconciliation. In 1962 Mandela was sentenced to twenty-seven years in prison for conspiring to overthrow the state when he attempted to take down the National Party's white-only government who established apartheid, a system of racial segregation that privileged whites. He was released in 1990 and helped lead efforts to negotiate an end to apartheid, which resulted in the 1994 multiracial general election in which Mandela led the ANC to victory and became president. Mandela is globally regarded as an icon of democracy and social justice. He received more than 250 honors, including the Nobel Peace Prize.

Rosa Parks (1913 to 2005) was an African-American activist in the civil rights movement best known for her pivotal role in the Montgomery bus boycott. The United States Congress has honored her as "the first lady of civil rights" and "the mother of the freedom movement." On December 1, 1955, in Montgomery, Alabama, Parks rejected the order to vacate a row of four seats in the "colored" section in favor of a white passenger, once the "white" section was filled. Parks was not the first person to resist bus segregation, but the National Association for the Advancement of Colored People (NAACP) believed that she was the best candidate for seeing through a court challenge after her arrest for civil disobedience in violating Alabama segregation laws, and she helped inspire the black community to boycott the Montgomery buses for over a year. Parks's act of defiance and the Montgomery bus boycott became important symbols of the movement. She became an international icon of resistance to racial segregation and organized and collaborated with civil rights.

Indira Priyadarshini Gandhi (1917 to 1984) was an Indian politician and a central figure of the Indian National Congress. She was the third prime minister of India and has so far been the only female prime minister of India. Gandhi was known for her political intransigency and unprecedented centralization of power. She went to war with Pakistan in support of the independence movement, which resulted in an Indian victory and the creation of Bangladesh. Citing separatist tendencies, and in response to a call for revolution, Gandhi instituted a state of emergency from 1975 to 1977 where basic civil liberties were suspended and the press was censored. Widespread atrocities were carried out during the emergency. In 1980, she returned to power after free and fair elections. After Gandhi ordered military action in the Golden Temple in Operation Blue Star, her own bodyguards and Sikh nationalists assassinated her on October 31, 1984. In 1999, Indira Gandhi was named "Woman of the Millennium" in an online poll organized by the BBC. In 2020, Gandhi was named by *Time* magazine among the world's 100 powerful women who defined the last century.

Jawaharlal Nehru (1889 to 1964) was an Indian anti-colonial nationalist, secular humanist, social democrat, and author who was a central figure in India during the middle third of the twentieth century. Nehru was a principal leader of the Indian nationalist movement in the 1930s and 1940s. Upon India's independence in 1947, he served as the country's prime minister for seventeen years. Nehru promoted parliamentary democracy, secularism, and science and technology during the 1950s, powerfully influencing India's arc as a modern nation. In international affairs, he steered India clear of the two blocs of the cold war. He was a well-regarded author, and his books written in prison, such as *Letters from a Father to His Daughter* (1929), *An Autobiography* (1936), and *The Discovery of India* (1946), were read around the world.

John Fitzgerald Kennedy (1917 to 1963) was an American politician who served as the thirty-fifth president of the United States from 1961 until his assassination near the end of his third year in office. Kennedy served at the height of the cold war, and the majority of his work as president concerned relations with the Soviet Union and Cuba.
Due to the high tensions with communist states, he authorized an attempt to overthrow the Cuban government of Fidel Castro in the failed Bay of Pigs Invasion, resulting in a period of tensions, termed the Cuban Missile Crisis, that nearly resulted in the breakout of a global thermonuclear conflict. He also signed the first nuclear weapons treaty in October 1963. Kennedy presided over the establishment of the Peace Corps, the Alliance for Progress with Latin America, and the continuation of the Apollo program with the goal of landing a man on the moon before 1970. He also supported the civil rights movement

but was only somewhat successful in passing his new frontier domestic policies. On November 22, 1963, he was assassinated in Dallas. Vice President Lyndon B. Johnson assumed the presidency upon Kennedy's death.

Martin Luther King Jr. (1929 to 1968) was an American Baptist minister and activist who became the most visible spokesman and leader in the American civil rights movement from 1955 until his assassination in 1968. King advanced civil rights through nonviolence and civil disobedience, inspired by his Christian beliefs and the nonviolent activism of Mahatma Gandhi. King participated in and led marches for blacks' right to vote, desegregation, labor rights, and other basic civil rights. King led the 1955 Montgomery bus boycott and later became the first president of the Southern Christian Leadership Conference (SCLC). King helped organize the 1963 March on Washington, where he delivered his "I Have a Dream" speech on the steps of the Lincoln Memorial.

In 1968, King was planning a national occupation of Washington, D.C., to be called the Poor People's Campaign, when he was assassinated on April 4 in Memphis. King won the Nobel Peace Prize for combating racial inequality through nonviolent resistance and was posthumously awarded the Presidential Medal of Freedom in 1977 and the Congressional Gold Medal in 2003. Martin Luther King Jr. Day was established as a holiday in cities and states throughout the United States beginning in 1971.

Gamal Abdel Nasser Hussein (1918 to 1970) was an Egyptian politician who served as the second president of Egypt from 1954 until his death in 1970. Nasser led the 1952 overthrow of the monarchy and introduced far-reaching land reforms the following year. Nasser's popularity in Egypt and the Arab world skyrocketed after his nationalization of the Suez Canal Company and his political victory in the subsequent Suez Crisis, known in Egypt as the Tripartite Aggression. Nasser remains an iconic figure in the Arab world, particularly for his strides toward social justice and Arab unity, his modernization policies, and his anti-imperialist efforts. His presidency also encouraged and coincided with an Egyptian cultural boom, and the launching of large industrial projects, including the Aswan Dam and Helwan city. Nasser's detractors criticize his authoritarianism, his human rights violations, and the dominance of the military over civil institutions that characterized his tenure, establishing a pattern of military and dictatorial rule in Egypt.

Vladimir Ilyich Ulyanov (1870 to 1924) better known by his alias, **Lenin**, was a Russian revolutionary, politician, and political theorist. He served as the first and founding head of government of Soviet Russia from 1917 to 1924 and of the Soviet Union from 1922 to 1924. Under his administration, Russia, and later the Soviet Union, became a one-party socialist state governed by the Soviet Communist Party. A Marxist, he developed a variant of communist ideology known as Leninism. Lenin's administration redistributed land among the peasantry and nationalized banks and large-scale industry, withdrew from the First World War by signing a treaty conceding territory to the Central Powers, and promoted world revolution through the Communist International.

Widely considered one of the most significant and influential figures of the twentieth century, Lenin was the posthumous subject of a pervasive personality cult within the Soviet Union until its dissolution in 1991. He became an ideological figurehead behind Marxism–Leninism and a prominent influence over the international communist movement. A controversial and highly divisive historical figure, Lenin is viewed by supporters as a champion of socialism and the working class, while critics have accused him of establishing a totalitarian dictatorship and ordering political repression and mass killings.

Mao Zedong (1893 to 1976), also known as **Chairman Mao**, was a Chinese communist revolutionary who was the founding father of the People's Republic of China, which he ruled as the chairman of the Chinese Communist Party from its establishment in 1949 until his death in 1976. As a Marxist–Leninist, his theories, military strategies, and political policies are collectively known as Maoism. Mao played an important role in enforcing the planned economy in China, constructing the first Constitution of the PRC, launching the industrialization program, and initiating military projects. Under his rule, Mao launched the Great Leap Forward that aimed to rapidly transform China's economy from agrarian to industrial, leading to the deadliest famine in history, launched the Socialist Education Movement, and initiated the Cultural Revolution where tens of millions of people were persecuted. A controversial figure, Mao is regarded as one of the most important individuals in the twentieth century.

Hồ Chí Minh (1890 to 1969) was a Vietnamese revolutionary and politician. He served as prime minister of Democratic Republic of Vietnam from 1945 to 1955 and president from 1945 until his death in 1969. Ideologically a Marxist–Leninist, he served as chairman and first secretary of the Workers' Party of Vietnam. Hồ Chí Minh was a key figure in the People's Army of Vietnam and the Việt Cộng during the Vietnam War, officially unifying the country in 1976. Saigon, the former capital of South Vietnam, was renamed Ho Chi Minh City in his honor.

Ernesto "Che" Guevara (1928 to 1967) was a Cuban-Argentinian Marxist revolutionary, physician, author, guerrilla leader, diplomat, and military theorist. He joined Raúl and Fidel Castro in their 26th of July Movement to overthrow the U.S.-backed Cuban dictator Fulgencio Batista and played a pivotal role in the two-year guerrilla campaign that deposed the Batista regime. Following the Cuban Revolution, Guevara played a central role in training the militia forces who repelled the Bay of Pigs Invasion and bringing Soviet nuclear-armed ballistic missiles to Cuba. He was a prolific writer and diarist, composing a seminal guerrilla warfare manual, along with a best-selling memoir.

Guevara is both a revered and reviled historical figure, polarized in the collective imagination in a multitude of biographies, memoirs, essays, documentaries, songs, and films. As a result of his perceived martyrdom, poetic invocations for class struggle, and desire to create the consciousness of a "new man" driven by moral rather than material incentives, Guevara has evolved into a quintessential icon of various leftist movements. In contrast, his ideological critics on the right accuse him of promoting authoritarianism and endorsing violence against his political opponents.

Fidel Alejandro Castro Ruz (1926 to 2016) was a Cuban revolutionary, lawyer, and politician who was the leader of Cuba from 1959 to 2008, serving as both prime minister of Cuba and president. Ideologically a Marxist–Leninist and Cuban nationalist, he also served as the first secretary of the Communist Party of Cuba from 1961 until 2011. Under his administration, Cuba became a one-party communist state, industry and business were nationalized, and state socialist reforms were implemented throughout society.

Castro overthrew Cuban president Fulgencio Batista in 1959 and assumed military and political power as Cuba's prime minister. In opposition to the United States, Castro aligned with the Soviet Union and allowed the Soviets to place nuclear weapons in Cuba, resulting in the Cuban Missile Crisis. Adopting a Marxist–Leninist model of development, Castro converted Cuba into a one-party, socialist state under Communist Party rule, the first in the Western Hemisphere. Policies introducing central economic planning and expanding healthcare and education were accompanied by state control of the press and the suppression of internal dissent. Castro polarized opinion throughout the world. His supporters view him as a champion of socialism and anti-imperialism whose revolutionary government advanced economic and social justice while securing Cuba's independence from U.S. hegemony. Critics call him a dictator whose administration oversaw human rights abuses, the exodus of many Cubans, and the impoverishment of the country's economy.

Nicolae Ceaușescu (1918 to1989) was a Romanian communist politician and dictator. He was the general secretary of the Romanian Communist Party from 1965 to 1989, and the last communist leader of Romania. During his rise to power, he eased press censorship and openly condemned the Warsaw Pact invasion of Czechoslovakia, which was hugely popular. However, the resulting period of stability was brief as his government soon became totalitarian and repressive. Economic mismanagement due to failed oil ventures during the 1970s led to skyrocketing foreign debts for Romania. Ceaușescu directed the government to export much of the country's agricultural and industrial production in an effort to repay these debts leading to drastically lowered living standards, heavy rationing of food, water, oil, heat, electricity, medicine, and other necessities.

Sayyid Ruhollah Musavi Khomeini (1900 to 1989), also known as **Ayatollah Khomeini**, was an Iranian political and religious leader. He was the founder of the Islamic Republic of Iran and the leader of the 1979 Iranian Revolution, which saw the overthrow of the last shah of Iran and the end of the Persian monarchy. Following the revolution, Khomeini became the country's first supreme leader, a position created in the constitution of the Islamic Republic as the highest-ranking political and religious authority of the nation. Most of his period in power was taken up by the Iran–Iraq War of 1980 to 1988. Khomeini has been described as the "face of Shia Islam in Western popular culture" and has been lauded as a "champion of Islamic revival" by Shia scholars, who attempted to establish good relations between Sunnis and Shias and a major innovator in political theory and religious-oriented populist political strategy.

Angela Merkel (July 1954) is a German politician and scientist who served as the chancellor of Germany from 2005 to 2021 and was the first woman to be elected as chancellor of Germany. During her tenure, Merkel was frequently referred to as the *de facto* leader of the European Union (EU) and the most powerful woman in the world. In foreign policy, Merkel has emphasized international cooperation, both in the context of the EU and NATO, and strengthening transatlantic economic relations. In 2008, Merkel served as president of the European Council and played a central role in the negotiation of the Treaty of Lisbon and the Berlin Declaration and played a crucial role in managing the global financial crisis of 2007–2008 and the European debt crisis. She negotiated the 2008 European Union stimulus plan, focusing on infrastructure spending and public investment to counteract the Great Recession. In domestic policy, Merkel's *Energiewende* program has focused on future energy development, seeking to phase out nuclear power in Germany, reduce greenhouse gas emissions, and increase renewable energy sources.

Frida Kahlo (1907 to 1954) was a Mexican painter known for her many portraits, self-portraits, and works inspired by the nature and artifacts of Mexico. Inspired by the country's popular culture, she employed a native folk art style to explore questions of identity, postcolonialism, gender, class, and race in Mexican society. Her paintings often had strong autobiographical elements and mixed realism with fantasy, and she has been described as a surrealist or magical realist. Kahlo's work as an artist remained relatively unknown until the late 1970s, when her work was rediscovered by art historians and political activists. By the early 1990s, she had become not only a recognized figure in art history but also regarded as an icon for Chicanos, the feminism movement, and the LGBTQ+ movement. Kahlo's work has been celebrated internationally as emblematic of Mexican national and indigenous traditions and by feminists for what is seen as its uncompromising depiction of the female experience and form.

Harriet Tubman (1822 to 1913) was an American abolitionist and political activist. Born into slavery, Tubman escaped and subsequently made some thirteen missions to rescue approximately seventy enslaved people using the network of antislavery activists and safe houses known as the Underground Railroad. During the American Civil War, she served as an armed scout and spy for the Union Army. In her later years, Tubman was an activist in the movement for women's suffrage.

Emmeline Pankhurst (1858 to 1928) was an English political activist and is best remembered for organizing the UK suffragette movement and helping women win the right to vote. In 1999, *Time* named her as one of the 100 Most Important People of the 20th Century. Though she was widely criticized for her militant tactics, and historians disagree about their effectiveness, her work is recognized as a crucial element in achieving women's suffrage in the United Kingdom.

Queen Victoria (1819 to 1901) was queen of the United Kingdom of Great Britain and Ireland from 1837 until her death in 1901. Known as the Victorian era, her reign of sixty-three years and seven months was longer than any previous British monarch. It was a period of industrial, political, scientific, and military change within the United Kingdom, and was marked by a great expansion of the British Empire. Though a constitutional monarch, privately, Victoria attempted to influence government policy and ministerial appointments. Publicly, she became a national icon who was identified with strict standards of personal morality.

Eva Perón (1919 to 1952) was an Argentine actress, politician, activist, and philanthropist who served as the first lady of Argentina from June 1946 until her death in July 1952, as the wife of Argentine president Juan Domingo Perón.

Eva Perón became powerful within the pro-Peronist trade unions, primarily for speaking on behalf of labor rights. She also ran the Ministries of Labor and Health, founded and ran the charitable Eva Perón Foundation, championed women's suffrage in Argentina, and founded and ran the nation's first large-scale female political party, the Female Peronist Party.

Alice Stokes Paul (1885 to 1977) was an American Quaker, suffragist, feminist, and women's rights activist, and one of the main leaders and strategists of the campaign for the Nineteenth Amendment to the U.S. Constitution, which prohibits sex discrimination in the right to vote. Paul initiated, and along with Lucy Burns and others, strategized events such as the Woman Suffrage Procession and the Silent Sentinels, which were part of the successful campaign that resulted in the amendment's passage in 1920.

Empress Dowager Cixi (1835 to 1908) was a Chinese noblewoman, concubine, and later regent who effectively controlled the Chinese government in the late Qing dynasty for forty-seven years from 1861 until her death in 1908. Cixi supervised the Tongzhi Restoration, a series of moderate reforms that helped the regime survive until 1911.

Although Cixi refused to adopt Western models of government, she supported technological and military reforms and the Self-Strengthening Movement. Historians have debated her legacy. She is conventionally denounced as a ruthless despot whose reactionary policies—although successfully self-serving in prolonging the ailing Qing dynasty—led to its humiliation and utter downfall. Revisionists suggest that Nationalist and Communist revolutionaries scapegoated Cixi for deep-rooted problems and lauded her maintenance of political order as well as numerous reforms, including the abolition of slavery, ancient torturous punishments, and the ancient examination system by replacing them with institutions such as the new Peking University.

Joan Ruth Bader Ginsburg (1933 to 2020) was an American lawyer and jurist who served as an associate justice of the Supreme Court of the United States from 1993 until her death in 2020. She was nominated by President Bill Clinton, replacing retiring Justice Byron White, and at the time was generally viewed as a moderate consensus-builder. Ginsburg was the first Jewish woman and the second woman to serve on the court, after Sandra Day O'Connor. Ginsburg spent much of her legal career as an advocate for gender equality and women's rights, winning many arguments before the Supreme Court. Ginsburg received attention in American popular culture for her passionate dissents in numerous cases, widely seen as reflecting paradigmatically liberal views of the law. She was dubbed "The Notorious R.B.G." and she later embraced the moniker.

Oprah Winfrey (born 1954) is an American talk show host, television producer, actress, author, and philanthropist. She is best known for her talk show, *The Oprah Winfrey Show*, which was the highest-rated television program of its kind in history and ran in national syndication for twenty years, from 1986 to 2011. Dubbed the "Queen of All Media," she was the richest African American of the twentieth century and was once the world's only black billionaire and the greatest black philanthropist in U.S. history. By 2007, she was sometimes ranked as the most influential woman in the world. In 2013, Winfrey was awarded the Presidential Medal of Freedom by President Obama and received honorary doctorate degrees from Duke and Harvard. In 2008, she formed her own network, the Oprah Winfrey Network (OWN).

Leadership Theories

500 BC, **The Art of War,** Sun Tzu, Strategies for success when meeting challenges.

1840, **Thomas Carlyle, Great Man Theory.** Theorizes that leaders are born not made, and that the unique characteristics of leadership are in their DNA. Research in the area of leadership began with the Great Man Theory.

1880 to 1920s, **Classical Management Theories**

Frederick Taylor, Scientific Management (Time Studies; Standardization, Best Practice)

Max Weber, Bureaucratic Management (Authority from Nobility, Charisma, Rational-Legal) Transcendence is the quality of the leader that is expected and that sets the leader apart from the ordinary members. Bob House used Weber's work to write about leadership.

Luther Gulick, Administrative Management (Planning, Organizing, Staffing, Directing, Coordinating, Reporting and Budgeting) with Technical, Human and Conceptual skills. Inspired by **Henri Fayol's 14 principles** (Division of Labor, Authority, Discipline, Unity of Command, Unity of Direction, Subordination of Individual Interests, Order, Equity, of Personnel and Initiative).

1928, **William Moulton Marston** publishes ***The Emotions of Normal People*** identifying four temperaments: dominance, influence, steadiness, and conscientiousness. In 1970 University of Minnesota professor John Geier developed the first instrument (DISC) using Marston's work. Don't have to be born a leader; just born with certain traits such as intelligence, self-confidence, determination, integrity, and sociability. These five leader traits show up in research over and over. Criticisms: Lots of traits that are not consistent; and the traits sound like behaviors as acting with a trait is behavior. Also, traits are learnable as are behaviors.

1938, **Kurt Lewin,** "There is nothing so practical as a good theory." Lewin's research follows. **Studies at the University of Iowa,** 1938 to 1940 on three dominant leadership styles. **Kurt Lewin, Ronald Lippitt and Ralph White** showed people respond best to democratic leadership, not autocratic or laissez-faire. Democratic approach is collaborative even with the leader having a position of power.

1940, **Ohio State University Leadership Theories**, found two different leadership dimensions: concern for people and initiating structure. Leader can be high or low in both.

1948 to 1970, **R. M. Stogdill**. Personal factors associated with leadership from twenty-five years of research moving from traits to behavior.

1948, **D. Kretch and R. Crutchfield, Major Functions of Dynamic Interdependent Leadership**

1. Leader develops teamwork
2. Representative of subordinates
3. Uses power properly
4. Manages time well
5. Strive for effectiveness
6. Make the environment conducive to work
7. Integrates the efforts of the followers and the organizational objectives
8. Performs the functions of an intermediary between the top management and the work group
9. Work as an appropriate counselor
10. Taking the initiative
11. Representing the enterprise
12. Guiding and directing the organization

1950, **Michigan Leadership Studies.** Looked at three crucial behaviors that propel leadership: task-oriented regards output; relationship-oriented regards personal needs; and participative leadership to build teams. Results indicated that good leaders could be relationship oriented and task oriented. The leader could be high or low in production and people dimensions.

1957, **R. Tannenbaum and W.H. Schmidt** determine that leadership behavior exists on a continuum that ranges from boss centered to subordinate centered.

1960, **D. McGregor** develops Theory X (emphasis on goals of the organization) and Theory Y (view of worker in context of the organization).

1964, **Robert R. Blake and Jane S. Mouton's Managerial Grid** (1978) proposes the managerial grid with concern for production and concern for people as a communication style using X and Y axis. Similar to other leadership studies in the 1940s, 1950s, and 1960s.

1967, **F. E. Fiedler** identifies two major functions: task orientation and relationship orientation. Fiedler's Contingency Theory suggests that traits and behaviors of leader ignores the followership, i.e., the situation. The leader is appropriate for certain situations but not all (not infallible).

1969, **P. Hersey and K. H. Blanchard's** research defined task and relationship as <u>functions of leaders.</u>

1970, **T. Kuhn** publishes *The Structure of Scientific Revolution* where he identifies paradigm as a reigning or dominant approach to solving problems in a given area of science as paradigms shift.

1971, **Bob House, Path-Goal Theory**. Leader can and should adapt to the situation— a given today.

1976, **Bob House, Charismatic Leadership**. Sometimes is confused with transformational leadership. Whereas, transformational leader does have the best interest of followers in mind, charismatic leadership may not the best interests of followers in mind.

Righteous charismatic leaders have five typical behaviors: strong role models; demonstrate competence; communicate goals; communicate high expectations; and arouse service motives. Dark side is that a charismatic leader may use their influence for their own benefit, to gain more power, not to benefit others. Then it becomes a destructive influence on society. Charisma and ethics must go together.

1977, **R. K. Greenleaf** offers a different way of thinking as a counterpoint to traditional leadership theories. He suggests that that best way to invest in others, to lead them, and have influence with them is to be a servant. That will result in empathy, collaboration, respect, and trust. Members will experience good treatment and the organization will benefit. Greenleaf's Servant Leadership moves from boss-centered leadership to other-centered leadership.

1975, **Vertical Dyad Linkage Theory** deals with relationships between leaders and members. It is also widely known as 1975, **Leadership-Member Exchange Theory LMX**. Individual groups get created in an organization where leaders treat individual members differently and followers have different perceptions of leaders, both positive and negative. IN-Groups advise the leader, enjoy trust allowed for freedom in decision-making, are loyal to the leader, and have more influence than others. OUT-Groups treated in authoritarian way, have mutual low levels of trust, not granted much freedom, and are expected to do their job. LMX supports a relational approach to leadership that moves beyond to a high quality of relationship at work. Results are members are less likely to quit, enjoy better mental health, enjoys honest feedback, and committed to organization through fair exchange. Originally developed by **Fred Dansereau, George Graen, and William J. Haga** in 1975.

1978, **J.M. Burns** suggests that leadership is the process that transforms individuals developmentally by elevating their goals, not just focusing on the tasks they complete. He identified two types of leadership: **Transactional** (joint effort between leaders and followers) and **Transformational** (transforming followers into collaborators). Burns based his focus on Abraham Maslow's hierarchy of needs. Physiological, safety, and love and belonging relate to transaction. Self-esteem and self-actualization are based on transformational. Also Burns talked about moral leadership. Five key variables of transformational leadership: creative, interactive, visionary, empowering, and passionate.

1982, **P. Hersey and K. H. Blanchard** argue that there is no one best size that fits all. Certain traits, skills, styles fit better in one situation more than another, so the leader must be able to adapt their approach. They define four management styles of situational leadership: High Task/Low Relationship (Directing); High Task/High Relationship (Coaching); High Relationship/Low Task (Supporting); and Low Relationship/Low Task (Delegating). This theory still revolved around the idea of the best person as hero leader but defined different behaviors based on situations. Closely related to this are the contingency theories of leadership. The situational theory assumes the situation is static and leaders should adapt to it. The contingency theory assumes the leader will default to his or her fixed style.

1988, **V.H. Vroom and P. Yetton Model** promoted the systematic approach to decision making, which allows the leader to bring consistency and order to a process that might otherwise feel idiosyncratic and instinctive. It can also help you to determine the most effective means of reaching a decision.

1993, **E.M. Bensimon and A. Neumann** reach agreement that there is not one best person as hero leader because of the complexity of leadership. Leadership has to be collaborative.

1996, **Peter Block's** description of servant leaders is representative of stewardship by placing stakeholders above the leader's own needs. Servant leadership can be understood as a blend between transactional and transformational leadership. Basically, if a leader makes a priority of identifying and meeting followers' needs, serving them rather than being served, the leader creates an environment of trust, cooperation, reciprocal service, and ultimately increase higher performance.

1987 to 2017, ***The Leadership Challenge*** is a suite of books written by **James Kouzes and Barry Z Posner**. First published in 1987, the sixth edition was released in 2017. A return to Trait theory.

1998, **Richard L. Daft, Robert H. Lengel, *Fusion Leadership*** Their work on transformational leadership is called Fusion (the opposite of fission) Leadership. It is about joining together for information sharing through mindfulness, vision, caring, communication, courage, and integrity.

2001 to 2011, **Jim Collins, *Good to Great*** and ***Great by Choice***. Level 5 leadership is a concept developed in the book *Good to Great*. Level 5 leaders display a powerful mixture of personal humility and indomitable will. They're incredibly ambitious, but their ambition is first and foremost for the cause, for the organization, and its purpose, not themselves. While Level 5 leaders can come in many personality packages, they are often self-effacing, quiet, or reserved.

1998. **Ronald A. Heifetz, *Leadership Without Easy Answers*** Heifetz adopts a contingency approach to leadership driven by two key variables: (a) whether a person has authority; and (b) whether the leader is dealing with routine problems or those demanding innovation and learning. This adaptive approach, at its core, explores the following principles of leadership (1) identifying the adaptive challenge; (2) keeping distress within a productive range; (3) directing attention to ripening issues and not diversion; (4) giving the work back to the people; and (5) protecting voices of leadership in the community. Heifetz presents clear, concrete prescriptions for anyone who needs to take the lead in almost any situation, under almost any organizational conditions, no matter who is in charge, His strategy applies not only to people at the top but also to those who must lead without authority—activists as well as presidents, managers as well as workers on the frontline. Leadership is an activity, and thus can be performed by anyone, including people without formal authority. It is an important distinction, as it makes everyone in the group accountable. Think who the stakeholders are, how to move them in the direction you need them to go, without overstretching the system. One reviewer used Jeet Kun Do's philosophy. As Bruce Lee famously said: "You must be shapeless, formless, like water. When you pour water in a cup, it becomes the cup. When you pour water in a bottle, it becomes the bottle. When you pour water in a teapot, it becomes the teapot. Water can drip and it can crash. Become like water, my friend."

1990s, **Steven R. Covey, *Seven Habits of Effective People.*** Two of the habits deal with leadership.

2002, **Peter J. Dean, *Leadership for Everyone.*** Every encounter and exchange with someone else is an opportunity for interpersonal and inspirational leadership.

2007, **Marie C. Wilson, *Closing the Leadership Gap.*** Diversity can improve the workforce and the workplace and the bottom line.

2005 to 2016, **Richard E. Boyatzis and Annie McKee, *Resonant Leadership.*** Resonant leaders manage their own and others' emotions in ways that drive success. Drawing from multidisciplinary research, the authors provide a guide to overcoming the vicious cycle of stress, sacrifice, and dissonance that affects many leaders. A path to resonance is through mindfulness, hope, and compassion intentionally applied to situations. In their other book, *Primal Leadership,* they describe four styles of leadership: Visionary (see the big picture), Coaching (interacting with general interest in individuals), Affiliative (build relationships by using listening and empathy), and Democratic (draw on the knowledge of the group by collaboration and influence). Each helps build resonance.

NOTES

1. Stogdill, 1974; Ivancevich, Szilagy, and Wallace, 1997.
2. Stogdill, 1974.
3. Stogdill, 1974, p. 18.
4. Stogdill, 1958.
5. Stogdill, 1958, p. 58.
6. Hemphill, 1949.
7. Jennings, 1961.
8. Ghiselli, 1963.
9. Stogdill, 1974, pp. 64–65.
10. Sleeth, 1977.
11. Bird, 1940.
12. Jenkins, 1974.
13. Stogdill, 1948.
14. Lewin and Lippitt, 1938.
15. Lewin, lppitt, and White, 1939.
16. Lippitt, 1966.
17. Stogdill and Coons, 1957.
18. Fleishman and Peters, 1962.
19. Fleishman and Peters, 1962.
20. Korman, 1966, p. 360.
21. Porter, Lawler, and Hackman, 1975, p. 424.
22. Korman, 1996.
23. Sales, 1966.
24. Ivancevich et. a., 1977, p. 270.
25. Blake, Robert R. and Mouton, Jane S., *The Managerial Grid*, 1978.
26. Beck, 1978.
27. Clothier, 1984.
28. Weinholtz, 1981.
29. Adams, 1954; Anderson, 1959; Berkowitz, 1953; Christner and Hemphill, 1955; Gibb, 1951; Hare, 1953; Horowitz and Perlmutter, 1955; Lewin, Lippitt and White; McCandless, 1942; Torrance, 1953.
30. Kretch and Crutchfield, 1948; Hemphill, 1949; Medalia, 1955; Prentice, 1953; Red, 1942; Roby, 1961; Stogdill and Coons, 1957.
31. Taylor, Frederic R., 1911.
32. Mayo, Elton, 1945.
33. Leavitt, 1962.
34. Hersey and Blanchard, 1982, p. 85.

35. Hemphill, 1949.
36. Kretch and Crutchfield, 1948.
37. Stogdill, 1974.
38. Bales, 1958.
39. Fleishman, Harris and Burtt, 1955.
40. Tannenbaum and Schmidt, 1957.
41. Cartwright and Zander, 1968.
42. McGregor, 1960.
43. Likert, 1961.
44. Katz et al., 1950, 1951.
45. Fiedler, 1967.
46. Blake and Multon, 1964.
47. Vroom and Yetton, 1963.
48. Reddin, 1967, 1970.
49. Reddin, 1970.
50. Hersey and Blanchard, 1969.
51. Reddin, 1970, pp. 103–104.
52. Carter et al., 1968, pp. 381–387.
53. Weinholtz, 1981.
54. Hemphill, 1950.
55. Leavitt, 1951.
56. Ruding, 1964.
57. Katzel et. al, 1970.
58. Torrance, 1961.
59. Korten, 1962.
60. For examples, Greening, 1973; Stinson and Robertson, 1973.
61. Fiedler, 1964.
62. Fiedler, 1971, pp. 128–129.
63. Weinholtz, 1981.
64. Fiedler and Chemers, 1974.
65. Weinholtz, 1981.
66. Weed, Mitchell, and Moffitt, 1976, p. 5.
67. Weed et al., 1976, p. 65.
68. Weinholtz, 1981, p. 42.
69. See Evans and Dermer, 1974; Fishbein et al. 1969; Muller, 1970; Shiflett, 1973, 1974; Stinson, 1972.
70. Fiedler, 1971.
71. House, 1971; House and Mitchell, 1974.
72. Clothier, 1984, p. 31.
73. Beck, 1978.
74. Vroom and Yetton, 1973.

75. Vroom and Yetton, 1973.
76. Reddin, 1967, 1970.
77. Reddin, 1967, p. 13.
78. Reddin, 1967.
79. Hersey and Blanchard, 1982.
80. Hersey and Blanchard, 1969, pp. 234–235.
81. Hersey and Blanchard, 19182, pp. 234–235.
82. Reddin, 1967.
83. Hersey and Blanchard, 1982.
84. Hersey and Blanchard, 1977, p. 263.
85. Hersey and Blanchard, 1982, p. 151.
86. Hersey and Blanchard, 1982.
87. Hersey and Blanchard, 1977, p. 163.
88. Hersey and Blanchard, 1982, pp. 153–154.
89. Clothier, 1984.
90. Burns, James MacGregor, 1978.
91. Burns, 1978.
92. Burns, 1978, p. 5.
93. Burns, 1978, p. 18.
94. Stogdill, 1958, p. 58.
95. Bateman and Snell, 1999; Tichy and Devanna, 1990; Daft and Lengel, 1998; Kouzes and Posner, 1995; Block, 1996; Senge, 1990 and Jim Collins, 2001.
96. Bateman and Snell, 1999, p. 432.
97. Tichy and Devanna, 1990, p. 4.
98. Kouzes and Posner, 1995; Block, 1996; Senge, 1990.
99. Collins, Jim, 2001.
100. Collins, 2001, p. 22.
101. Kouzes, James. M., Posner, Barry Z., *The Leadership Challenge,* 1995.
102. Kouzes and Posner, 1995.
103. Kouzes and Posner, 1995.
104. Kouzes and Posner, 1995.
105. Collins and Porras, 1996.
106. Collins and Porras, 1996, p. 66.
107. Kouzes and Posner, 1996.
108. Kotter, 1995.
109. Collins, James, *Good to Great,* 2001.
110. Kouzes and Posner, 1995.
111. Bennis, Warren and Nanus, Burt, *Leaders: Strategies for Taking Charge,* 1985.
112. Kouzes and Posner, 1995.
113. Kouzes and Posner, 1995.
114. Kouzes and Posner, 1995.

115. Collins, James, *Good to Great,* p. 21.
116. Kouzes and Posner, 1995.
117. Collins, Jim, Porras, Jerry, *Built to Last: Successful Habits of Visionary Companies,* 1994. p. 66.
118. Kouzes and Posner, 1995.
119. Kouzes and Posner, 1995.
120. Cable and Parsons, 2001.
121. Cable and Judge, 1997; Kristof-Brown, 2000.
122. Collins, 2001
123. Collins, 2001.
124. Kouzes and Posner, 1995.
125. Kouzes and Posner, 1995.
126. Kouzes and Posner, 1995.
127. Kouzes and Posner, 1995, p. 270.
128. Kouzes and Posner, 1995.
129. Kouzes and Posner, 1995.
130. Kouzes and Posner, 1995.
131. Kouzes and Posner, 1995.
132. Kouzes and Posner, 1995.
133. Kouzes and Posner, 1995.
134. Kouzes and Posner, 1995, p. 299.
135. Barry Oshry, ***Seeing Systems,*** Berrett-Koehler Publishers; l995; 1999.
136. Oshry, 1995.
137. Oshry, 1995.
138. Oshry, 1995.
139. Oshry, 1995.
140. Oshry, 1995.
141. Maslow, Abraham, 1943.
142. Marquardt and Carter, 1998.
143. Berwick, 1989, p. 55.
144. Dean, 1998.
145. Bettenhausen, 1191, p. 356.
146. Gaucher and Coffey, 1993, pp. 235–240.
147. Kochan and Useem, 1992.
148. Lewin, 1951.
149. Lewin and Grabbe, 1945; Lewin et al. 1945; Lewin, 1947a, 1947b, 1948 and 1951.
150. Lewin, 1948.
151. Weisbord and Janoff, 1995, p. 69.
152. Drucker, Peter, 1988.
153. Lawrence and Lorsch, 1967, 1969; Tushman and O'Reilly, 1996.

154. Tushman, and O'Reilly, 1996.
155. Axelrod, 1992; Beckhard, 1969; Beckhard and Harris, 1987; Bunker and Alban, 1992; Lewin, 1945, 1947a, 1947b, 1948, 1951; Likert, 1961, 1967; Lippitt, 1967, 1980, 1983; Weisbord, 1987, 1992; Weisbord and Janoff, 1995; and McLagan and Christo, 1995.
156. Miles and Snow, 1978; Nadler, Gerstein, 1992.
157. Bowditch and Buono, 1997.
158. Senge, 1990; Drucker, 1993; Garvin, 1993; Watkins and Marsick, 1993; and Dean and Ripley, 1997.
159. Stevens, 1991.
160. de Geus, 1997.
161. de Geus, 1997.
162. de Geus, 1997.
163. Hammer and Champy, 1993.
164. Kochan and Useem, 1992.
165. Galbraith and Lawler, 1993.
166. Kochan and Useem, 1992.
167. Gilbert, 1996.
168. Dean, 1999, in press.
169. Jitendra Vir Singh, 1998, personal communication.
170. Singh, 1998.
171. Dean and Ripley, 1997.
172. Dean and Ripley, 1997.
173. Dean and Ripley, 1997, 1998a, 1998b, 1998c.
174. Argyris, 1993; Bowman and Kogut, 1995; Galbraith, 1977, 1995; Galbraith and Lawler, 1993.
175. Senge, 1990.
176. Dean, 1999.
177. M. Emergy, 1993.
178. Kochan and Useem, 1992.
179. Mohrman and Cummings, 1989.
180. Dean, 1999.
181. Robey and Sales, 1994.
182. Nadler and Tushman, 1997
183. Dean and Ripley 1997, 1998a, 1998b, 1998c.
184. Cummings and Worley, 1993; Gilbert, 1996; Levinson, 1972; Rummler, 1997; Rummler and Brache, 1990.
185. Miles and Snow, 1978; Nadler, Gerstein, and Shaw, 1992; Nadler and Tushman, 1997; Tushman, O'Reilley, and Nadler, 1989.
186. Utterback, 1994; von Bertalanffy, 1950, 1952; Weinberg, 1975. clxxxvii. Dean, Peter, *Performance Engineering at Work,* 1999, 2d ed.

187. Hammer and Champy, 1993.
188. Kochan and Useem, 1992.
189. Galbraith and Lawler, 1993.
190. Kochan and Useem, 1992.
191. Gilbert, 1996.
192. Dean, 1999.
193. De Geus, 1997.
194. Senge, 1994.
195. Dean and Rebalsky, 1995.
196. Human Performance System, 1997.
197. Gilbert, Human Competence, 1978.
198. Hammer and Champy, 1993, p. 176.
199. Rummler, Gary, 1976.
200. Gilbert, Tom, 1991.
201. Gilbert, Tom, 1991.
202. Gilbert, 1978.
203. Dean, 1944.
204. Daniels, 1989, p. 135.
205. Dean, 1994.
206. Dean, 1994, pp. 23–25.
207. Dean, 1994, p. 25
208. Weiner, 1985, p. 294.
209. Geroy and Wright, 1988.
210. Geroy and Wright, 1988.
211. Delbecq and Van de Ven, 19971.
212. Gilbert, 1978; Earle, 1990.
213. Geroy and Wright, 1988, p. 23.
214. Delbecq and Vande Ven, 1971.
215. Scott and Deadrick, 1982.
216. Gilbert, 1978.
217. Gilbert, 1982, a and b.
218. Earle, 1990.
219. Gilbert, 1978, p. 87.
220. Geroy & Wright, 1988; Delbecq & Van de Ven, 1971.
221. Gilbert, 1991.
222. Delbecq and Vande Ven, 1971.
223. Earle, 1990.
224. Gilbert, 1991.
225. Baker, et al., 1990, and Dixon, 1990.
226. Nadler, 1984.
227. Lawrence and Lorsch, 1967, 1969; Tushman and O'Reilly, 1996.

228. Tushman and O'Reilly 1996.

229. Axelrod, 1992; Beckhard, 1969; Beckhard and Harris, 1987; Bunker and Alban, 1997; Lewin, 1945, 1947a, 1947b, 1948, 1951; Likert, 1961, 1967; Lippitt, 1967, 1980, 1983; Weisbord, 1987, 1992; Weisbord and Janoff, 1995; McLagan and Christo, 1995.Weisbord and Janoff, 1995.

230. Weisbord and Janoff, 1995.

231. Lewin, Kurt, 1951.

232. Lewin & Grabbe, 1945; Lewin et al. 1945; Lewin, 1947a, 1947b, 1948 and 1951.

233. Lewin, 1948.

234. Weisbord and Janoff, 1995, p. 69.

235. Argyris, 1993.

236. Schon, Donald, *Reflective Practitioner.*

237. Argyris, Chris, "Education for Leading-Learning," *Organizational Dynamics,* Winter 1993.

238. Mumford, Alan, "Learning in Action," *Personal Management,* 7/91.

239. Hupp, 1998.

240. Weisbord and Janoff, 1995.

241. Quoted in Weisbord and Janof, 1995, p. 25.

242. Weibord and Janoff, 1995.

243. Bunker and Alban, 1997.

244. Weibord and Janoff, 1995.

245. Weisbord, 1987.

246. Weisbord, 1987.

247. Hupp, 1998.

248. Hupp, 1998.

249. Galbraith, 19977, 1995.

250. Trist, 1981.

251. Weisbord, 1987, 1992.

252. Cummings and Worley, 1993.

253. Emery, M., 1993.

254. Bunker and Alban, 1997.

255. Hupp, 1998.

256. Hupp, 1998

257. Emery, M., 1993.

258. Hupp, 1998.

259. Hupp, 1998.

260. Bunker and Alban, 1997; Cabana, 1995; Dean, 1983, 1993; Dean, Dean, and Guman, 1992.

INDEX

D

E

F

G

H

I

J

K

L

M

N

O

P

Q

R

U

V

W

X

Made in the USA
Columbia, SC
02 December 2022

72545490R00193